THE DOG LOVER'S COMPANION TO SEATTLE

By Steve Giordano

AVALON
TRAVEL

THE DOG LOVER'S COMPANION TO SEATTLE

Steve Giordano

Published by
Avalon Travel Publishing
5855 Beaudry Street
Emeryville, CA 94608 USA

ISBN: 1-56691-290-3
ISSN: 1534-6772

Printing History
1st edition—1996
2nd edition—June 2001
5 4 3 2 1

Editor: Angelique S. Clarke
Series Manager: Angelique S. Clarke
Copy Editor: Leslie Miller
Graphics: Erika Howsare
Production: Amber Pirker, Melissa Tandysh
Map Editor: Naomi Dancis
Cartography: Mike Morgenfeld, Brandon Taylor
Index: Lynne Lipkind

Cover and interior illustrations: Phil Frank

Distributed by Publishers Group West

Printed in the United States by R.R. Donnelley

PREFACE

So much has changed in the dog world since this book was first published as *The Seattle Dog Lover's Companion* in 1996. Now, as *The Dog Lover's Companion to Seattle* (and to the Olympic and Kitsap Peninsulas, communities all up and down Puget Sound, the San Juan Islands, Victoria, Vancouver, and Whistler), those changes are reflected in the greatly expanded listings and discussions. Because there are more of us with pet dogs, and because we and our dogs are traveling more, public agencies and businesses have responded with increased opportunities for us to enjoy the out-of-doors together, to dine in proximity together at outdoor restaurants, and to holiday together in hotels, B&Bs, and country inns.

Here are a few of the changes: Seattle's pilot program for off-leash park areas was such a success that it's now permanent; Vancouver added morning and evening leash-free hours in 29 city parks; doggie specialty shops have opened all over; upscale hotels have added doggie amenity packages; and perhaps most important, we dog owners have gotten the message about acceptable public behavior for both ourselves and our dogs. We leash and scoop. Well, most of us do, and we're teaching the others to follow suit.

My fox terriers have taught me a lot about having fun, and their spirit infuses my writing. So by all means, have fun with it.

—Steve Giordano, Seattle

To the owner of California license plate 1DOG LVR,
heading north on Interstate 5 through a rainstorm
on her way to Seattle. May you, your dog, and your
slate blue Honda Accord DX find room to roam
in the Evergreen Triangle.

CONTENTS

SEATTLE

ARROOoooooooooo

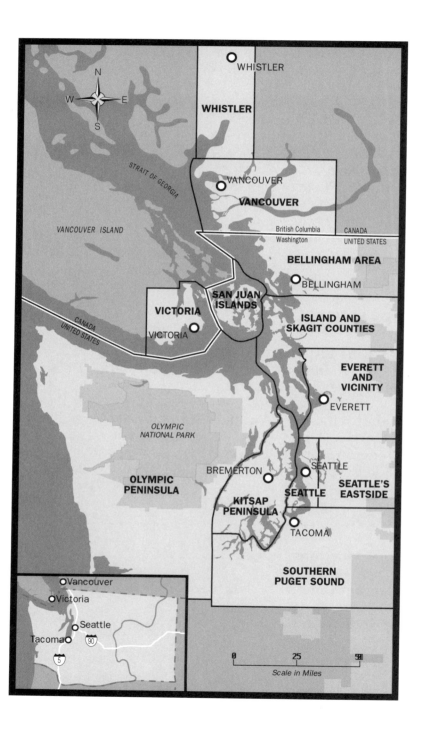

MAPS

INTRODUCTION

"Now, Charley is a mind-reading dog. There have been many trips in his life-time, and often he has to be left at home. He knows we are going long before the suitcases come out, and he paces and worries and whines and goes into a state of mild hysteria, old as he is."

From *Travels with Charley,* by John Steinbeck

There was a time when dogs could go just about anywhere they pleased. Well-dressed dogs with embarrassing names attended afternoon teas, while their less-kempt counterparts sauntered into saloons without anyone blinking a bloodshot eye.

No one thought it strange to see a pug-nosed little snoochum-woochums of a dog snuggled on his mistress's lap on a long train journey. Equally accepted were dogs prancing through fine hotels, dogs at dining establishments, and dogs in almost any park they cared to visit.

But as the world gets more crowded and patience grows thinner, fewer and fewer places permit dogs. As deep as the human-dog bond goes, people seem to feel increasing pressure to leave their dogs behind when they take to the open road.

The guilt that stabs at you as you push your dog's struggling body back inside the house and tug the door shut can be so painful that sometimes you just can't look back. Even a trip to the grocery store can become a heart-wrenching tale of woe.

John Steinbeck's blue poodle, Charley, was a master of powerful pleas that were carefully designed to allow him to accompany his people on trips. Eventually, his hard work paid off and he won himself a seat in Steinbeck's brand-new truck/house on their epic journey across America. They sought and found the heart of this country in their adventures across 34 states.

In my case, I've got a couple of granddogs, Emma and Quinn, and we love to make little journeys throughout Washington, Oregon, and even into British Columbia. Emma and Quinn are distant cousin fox terriers. I carry pictures of them in my wallet, and I bore a lot of polite listeners with tales of their escapades. We've already found hundreds of places that welcome our canine companions, and the best of the lot are described in the following pages. You'll be meeting up with Emma and Quinn throughout this book. I think you'll find them fine representatives of the millions of dogs who live in the Pacific Northwest.

The granddogs' enthusiasm for whatever the next adventure might be is contagious. Whether it's taking an elevator ride in a hotel or coming upon a beaver dam in the woods, the thrills are the same. We don't look for mischief, necessarily, but we're bound to find some in the course of our travels. We head out for a few hours or for up to a week. We never weary of road trips.

Quinn's favorite activity is chasing a ball that's just slightly too big to bite. He noses and snarls the ball over entire parks and fields, looking like a new kind of herding breed of sheep dog being pulled by a self-powered soccer ball. Maybe he thinks the ball is a bald hedgehog. Quinn also likes to take people for walks on his leash, tugging backwards for all he's worth with his end tightly gripped between his teeth, just like he's pulling a fox out of the hole by its tail.

Emma, at age 12, is three years older than Quinn, so she's more mature in her pursuits. She teams up with Quinn for the ball chases and stick fetching, but she keeps tabs on him and nips him back in line when he gets too boisterous.

I've tried to find the very best of everything you can do with your dog in this great big two-nation region, so you'll never again have to face the prospect of shutting the door on your dog's nose. This book is packed with descriptions of dog-friendly parks, restaurants with outdoor tables, and lodgings. There are also dozens of descriptions of unusual adventures you and your furry friend can share. You can ride on ferries or go river rafting. You can march in pet parades, visit an art gallery, browse at bookstores, and shop at high-fashion boutiques. You can even watch Shakespeare under the stars.

After reading even a few pages of this book, I think you'll come to find that the Seattle area is a magical place to be a dog or just to hang out with one. We all hope you have as much fun enjoying the possibilities as we did finding them. Happy road trips and happy trails!

THE PAWS SCALE

At some point, we've got to face the facts: humans and dogs have different tastes. We like eating oranges and smelling lilacs and covering our bodies with soft clothes. They like eating roadkill and smelling each other's unmentionables and covering their bodies with horse manure.

But to the ratings: Emma and Quinn rated the parks, beaches, and recreation areas we visited. They both quite specifically prefer any area where they can run free and pursue their own interests. Those interests include nudging anything that might move, chasing down errant volleyballs and footballs, nabbing sticks in the water, digging up gopher mounds, and sniff-checking everything within a one-mile radius. Dogs' p-mail system is very important to them. If they can do all that, off-leash, then it's bound to be a three or four-paw park, so you'll see three or four paw prints at the head of the listing. If there are only one or two paw prints, they enjoyed it because it was there, but they wouldn't run too many miles to get there. They trust, though, that grandpa won't take them to a dud. They know that if the humans don't have any fun, it's rough on them too. A human footprint ◄● means it's an especially nice park for people.

SNOQUALMIE FALLS

So here's how it breaks down on the four-paw rating scale:

The very lowest rating you'll come across in this book is the fire hydrant symbol ♟ . When you see it, that means the park is merely "worth a squat." Visit one of these parks only if your dog just can't hold it any longer. These parks have virtually no other redeeming qualities for canines.

Beyond that, the paws scale starts at one paw 🐾 and goes up to four paws 🐾🐾🐾🐾. A one-paw park isn't a dog's idea of a great time. Maybe it's a tiny park with few trees and too many kids running around. Or perhaps it's a magnificent-for-people national park that bans dogs from every inch of land except paved roads and a few campsites.

Four-paw parks, on the other hand, are places your dog will drag you to visit again and again. Some of these areas come as close to dog heaven as you can get on this planet. Many have water for swimming or zillions of acres for hiking. Some are small, fenced-in areas where leash-free dogs can tear around without danger of running into the road. Many four-paw parks give you the option of letting your dog off the leash (although most have some restrictions, which I detail in the descriptions).

This book is not a comprehensive guide to all of the parks in the Pacific Northwest. If a book included every park, it would be larger than a multi-volume set of the Encyclopedia Britannica. I tried to find the best, largest, and most convenient parks. Some counties have so many wonderful parks that I had to make some tough choices in deciding which to include and which to leave out. Other counties had such a limited supply of parks that, for the sake of dogs living and visiting there, I ended up listing parks that wouldn't otherwise be worth mentioning.

I've given very specific directions to the major parks and to parks located near highways. Other parks are listed by their cross streets. But I highly recommend picking up detailed street maps before you and your dog set out on your adventures.

TO LEASH OR NOT TO LEASH?

That is not a question that plagues dogs' minds. Ask just about any normal, red-blooded American dog if she'd prefer to visit a park and be on leash or off, and she'll say: "Arf!" No question about it, most dogs would give their canine teeth to be able to frolic about without a cumbersome leash.

When you see the running dog symbol in this book 🐕, you'll know that under certain circumstances your dog can run around in leash-free bliss. The rest of the parks demand leashes. I wish I could write about all of the parks where dogs get away with being scofflaws. Unfortunately, those would be the first parks the animal-control patrols would hit. I don't advocate breaking the law, but if you're going to, please follow your conscience and use common sense.

And just because dogs are permitted off leash in certain areas doesn't necessarily mean you should let your dog run free. In national forests and large tracts of wildland, unless you're sure your dog will come back to you when you call or will never stray more than a few yards from your side, you should probably keep her leashed. An otherwise docile homebody can turn into a savage hunter if the right prey is near. Or your curious dog could perturb a bear or dig up a rodent whose fleas carry bubonic plague. In pursuit of a strange scent, your dog could easily get lost in an unfamiliar area. (Some forest rangers recommend having your dog wear a bright orange collar, vest, or backpack when you're out in the wilderness.) And there are many places where certain animals would love to have your dog for dinner, and not in a way Miss Manners would condone.

Be careful out there. If your dog really needs leash-free exercise but can't be trusted off the leash in remote areas, she'll be happy to know that a growing number of beautiful, fenced-in dog exercise areas permit well-behaved, leashless pooches.

Some dog owners fear the rambunctiousness of free-running dogs and the possibility of fights. They wonder how dog attacks would be stopped. Some reassuring facts might relax their concerns. Dogs in leash-free parks are there because their handlers value socialization, for both themselves and for their dogs. The dogs wouldn't be there if their owners were not confident of their off-leash behavior. Also, park territory is neutral territory. It belongs equally to the whole pack, so there are no claims to either stake or defend. There is, however, the occasional curmudgeon whose hostility and aggression he has projected onto his dog, and the dog can be a bundle of unpredictable snarling. These people and their dogs are a threat to the very existence of leash-free parks, and everybody else there knows it. The perpetrators are made to feel unwelcome, and even asked to leave and not come back until the behaviors are more acceptable. The shunning process is democratic elitism at its best.

THERE'S NO BUSINESS LIKE DOG BUSINESS

There's nothing appealing about bending down with a plastic bag or a piece of newspaper on a chilly morning and grabbing the steaming remnants of what your dog ate for dinner the night before. It's disgusting. Worse yet, you have to hang on to it until you can find a trashcan. And how about when the newspaper doesn't endure before you can dispose of it? Yuck! It's enough to make you wish your dog could wear diapers.

But as gross as it can be to scoop the poop, it's worse to step in it. It's really bad if a child falls in it, or—gasp!—starts eating it. And have you ever walked into a park where few people clean up after their dogs? The stench could make a hog want to hibernate.

Unscooped poop is one of a dog's worst enemies. Public policies banning dogs from parks are enacted because of it. At present, a few good parks that permit dogs are in danger of closing their gates to all canines because of the negligent behavior of a few owners. A worst-case scenario is already in place in several Seattle communities. Dogs are banned from all beaches in parks.

Just be responsible and clean up after your dog everywhere you go. Stuff plastic bags in your jackets, your purse, your car, your pants pockets—anywhere you might be able to pull one out when needed. Or if plastic isn't your bag, newspapers do the trick. If it makes it more palatable, bring along a paper bag, too, and put the used newspaper or plastic bag in it. That way you don't

have to walk around with dripping paper or a plastic bag whose contents are visible to the world.

If you don't enjoy the squishy sensation, try one of those cardboard or plastic bag pooper-scoopers sold at pet stores. If you don't feel like bending down, buy a long-handled scooper. There's a scooper for every taste.

A final note: Do not pretend you don't see your dog while he's doing his bit. And do not pretend to look for it without success. And do not fake scooping it up when you're really just covering it with sand. I know these tricks because I've been guilty of them myself, but no more. I've seen the light. I've been saved. I've been delivered from the depths of dog-doo depravity.

ETIQUETTE REX—
THE WELL-MANNERED MUTT

No matter how you feel about your dog, others will probably not see him in the same way. For a lot of people a dog is a disaster waiting to happen. Leaps, licks, fleas, disastrous wags of the tail, and the various liquid and solid extrusions of dogs are not cute in public.

For non-lovers of dogs, one of the most objectionable things about them is that so few mind their own business. Dogs are gregarious and sociable, nosy and curious, and the only restraint they show is that taught by you, the pack leader. Untrained dogs are as unpredictable as untrained children, but the tide of tolerance these days is swinging in favor of children and away from dogs. So it's up to us to keep our four-legged lovables in line, and yes, lovable.

Start by keeping your dog away from people who haven't sent a clear signal expressing interest in making a canine friend. Remember, dogs are simply repulsive to some people, and we'll never change their minds. They may even be allergic to dogs. It's not enough to say, "Oh just ignore him. He'll go away." Or in the plural, "They won't bite, just go around them." It's already too late in the socialization process if you're saying things like that. What you're doing is further alienating someone who doesn't like your dog in the first place. As I wrote this book I was even told by a non-lover of dogs that she'd buy a copy for sure, just to know what places to avoid that welcomed dogs. She wasn't kidding either, and the fact that she's highly placed in the tourism marketing business told me I'd better watch my step, so to speak, that traveling dogs are an emotional issue on both sides of the fence.

Just remember that our dogs' manners are our manners. Dogs are usually blamed for things that we allow them to do.

Here is some very basic dog etiquette. I'll go through it quickly, but if your dog's a slow reader, he can go over it again: No vicious dogs; no jumping on people; no incessant barking; dogs should come when they're called; dogs should stay on command; no leg lifts on surfboards, backpacks, human legs, or any other personal objects you'll find hanging around parks. Do your best to remedy any problems. It takes patience and it's not always easy.

SAFETY FIRST

A few essentials will keep your traveling dog happy and healthy. When planning a trip with your dog, know his limitations. Some dogs are perfectly fine in a car; others get motion sickness. Some dogs happily hop in their kennel cab for airline flights; others are traumatized for hours. Only you know your dog's temperament. Here are some guidelines to consider before you hit the road:

IN AND OUT OF THE CAR

Road trip! Yay! When the car door opens, Emma and Quinn hop in and they're ready to go to whatever their next success might be. They're spoiled, of course. You wouldn't want your dog to jump in before she's invited. A dog who jumps in, or out, for that matter, before the command to do so, is fair game for dognapping, injury, or general chaos. If a dog is rowdy getting in, he'll be rowdy on the trip, and when you're the driver, you don't need rowdy. You especially don't need rowdy when you stop and open the door. There go the cappuccinos as Thorla leaps between you and the steering wheel to get out the door first. She really only wants to secure the territory for you, but there's usually a cat or something to chase first before you even get the key out of the ignition.

So do some training drills before you tackle the big trip. Be sure your dog is prepped on following your commands to wait, to sit, to remain calm, and in general, to behave himself when he's out in public.

For safety reasons, the dog should ride in the backseat, if your car has one. It's safer if an accident happens, and it leaves you entirely free to concentrate on driving. Front seat dogs have a way of wanting you, the pack leader, to share your window air, to share your lap, and to lend at least one hand for patting, scratching, and rubbing.

The safest thing all around is for the dog to ride in a dog carrier, the mini-den that's a comfort to a dog on the road.

You, of course, would never carry your dog in the back of an open pickup truck, for all the right reasons. It's even against the law in a lot of places.

You would also never leave your dog locked in a car on a warm day. One of the biggest traveling problems is the heat trapped in the car on a sunny day, or even a cloudy day for that matter. You just can't leave a dog in a car, even in the cloudy Pacific Northwest. The temperature goes up quickly, to well over a hundred degrees, and dogs can't sweat to cool down the way we do. They dissipate heat through their tongues, and they can't do that fast enough to do them any good when they're trapped in a hot spot. They simply die. Open windows and a bowl of water just aren't enough for a furry beast. If you can't take the dog with you at your destination, just leave him home. He depends on you, his pack leader, to make the right choices.

HOT DOG

If you must leave your dog alone in the car for a few minutes, do so only if it's cool out and if you can park in the shade. Never, ever, ever leave a dog in a car with the windows rolled up all the way. Even if it seems cool, the sun's heat passing through the window can kill a dog in minutes. Roll down the window just enough for your dog to get air, but so there's no danger of him getting out or someone breaking in. Make sure he has plenty of water.

You also have to watch out for heat exposure when your car is in motion. Certain cars, such as hatchbacks, can make a dog in the backseat extra hot, even while you feel okay in the driver's seat.

Try to take your vacation so you don't visit a place when it's extremely warm. Dogs and heat don't get along, especially if the dog isn't used to heat. The opposite is also true. If a dog lives in a hot climate and you take him to a freezing place, it may not be a healthy shift. Check with your vet if you have any doubts. Spring and fall are usually the best times to travel.

DRINK UP!

Water your dog frequently. Dogs on the road may drink even more than they do at home. Take regular water breaks, or bring a heavy bowl (the thick clay ones do nicely) and set it on the floor so your dog always has access to water. When hiking, be sure to carry enough for yourself and a thirsty dog. When at the beach, remember that if you don't offer your pal fresh water, he may help himself to the salt water. This won't be a pretty picture, we assure you.

Also remember to stop and unwater your dog. There's nothing more miserable than being stuck in a car when you can't find a rest stop. No matter how tightly you cross your legs and try to think of the desert, you're certain you'll burst within the next minute. But think of how a dog feels when the urge strikes and he can't tell you the problem. There are plenty of places listed in our book for you to allow your dog to relieve herself.

How frequently you stop depends on your dog's bladder. If your dog is constantly running out the doggy door at home to relieve himself, you may want to stop every hour. Others can go for significantly longer without being uncomfortable. Watch for any signs of restlessness and gauge it for yourself.

CAR CRUISING

Even the experts differ about how a dog should travel in a car. Some suggest doggy safety belts, available at pet supply stores. Others firmly believe in keeping a dog kenneled. They say it's safer for the dog if there's an accident, and it's safer for the driver because there's no dog underfoot. Still others say you should just let your dog hang out without straps and boxes. They believe that if there's an accident, at least the dog isn't trapped in a cage. They say that dogs enjoy this more anyway.

I tend to agree with the latter school of thought. Emma and Quinn travel very politely in the backseat and occasionally love sticking their snouts out of the windows to smell the world go by. The danger is that if the car kicks up a pebble or annoys a bee, their noses and eyes could be injured. So I usually open the window just enough so the dogs can stick out a little snout.

Whatever way you choose, your pet will be more comfortable if he has his own blanket with him for the journey. A veterinarian acquaintance uses a faux-sheepskin blanket for his dogs. At night in the hotel, the sheepskin doubles as the dog's bed.

FLYING FIDOS

Air travel is even more controversial. Many people feel it's tantamount to cruel and unusual punishment to force a dog to fly in the cargo hold like a piece of luggage. And there are dangers to flying that are somewhat beyond your control, such as runway delays—the cabin is not pressurized when on the ground—and connecting flights that tempt the wrong-way fates.

Personally, unless Emma and Quinn could fly with me in the passenger section (which very tiny dogs are sometimes allowed to do), I'd rather find a way to drive the distance or leave them at home with my daughter or a friend. I've heard too many horror stories of dogs suffocating in what was supposed to be a pressurized cargo section, and of dogs dying of heat exposure, and of dogs going to Miami while their owners end up in Seattle. There's just something unappealing about the idea of a dog flying in the cargo hold, like he's nothing more than a piece of luggage. Of course, many dogs survive just fine, but I'm not willing to take the chance.

But if you need to transport your dog by plane, make sure you schedule takeoff and arrival times when the temperature is below 80 degrees (or not bitterly cold in the winter). You'll want to consult the airline about their regulations and required certificates. And check with your vet to make sure your pooch is healthy enough for the trip. Most airlines will ask you to show a health certificate and possibly proof of a rabies vaccination.

The question of tranquilizing a dog for a plane journey is difficult. Some vets think it's insane to give a dog a sedative before flying. They say a dog will be calmer and less fearful without taking a disorienting drug. Others think it's crazy not to afford your dog the little relaxation he might not otherwise get without a tranquilizer. We suggest discussing the tranquilizer issue with your vet, who will take the trip's length and your dog's personality into account.

THE ULTIMATE DOGGY BAG

Your dog can't pack her own bags, and even if she could, she'd probably fill them with dog biscuits and chew toys. It's important to stash some of those in your dog's vacation kit, but here are some other items to bring along: bowls, bedding, brush, towels (for those muddy days), first-aid kit, pooper-scoopers, water, food, prescription drugs, tags, treats, toys, and, of course, this book.

Be sure your dog wears her license, identification tag, and rabies tag. On a long trip you may even want to bring along your dog's rabies certificate. Some parks and campgrounds require rabies and licensing information. You never know how picky they'll be.

It's a good idea to snap one of those barrel-type IDs on your dog's collar, too, showing the name, address, and phone number of where you'll be vacationing. That way if she should get lost, at least the finder won't be calling your empty house. Carrying a picture of your dog, in case the two of you become separated, is also not a bad idea.

Some people think dogs should drink only water brought from home so their bodies don't have to get used to too many new things. We've never had a problem feeding our dogs tap water from other parts of the state, nor has anyone else we know. Most vets think your dog will be fine drinking tap water in most other U.S. cities.

"Think of it this way," says veterinarian Pete Beeman. "Your dog's probably going to eat poop if he can get some, and even that's probably not going

to harm him. I really don't think that water that's OK for people is going to be bad for dogs."

BONE APPÉTIT

In some European countries, dogs enter restaurants and dine alongside their folks as if they were people, too. (Or at least they sit and watch and drool while their owners dine.) Not so in America and Canada. Rightly or wrongly, dogs are considered a health threat. But health inspectors I've spoken with say they see no reason why clean, well-behaved dogs shouldn't be permitted inside a restaurant. "Aesthetically, it may not appeal to Americans," a government environmental specialist told me, "but the truth is, there's no harm in this practice."

Ernest Hemingway made an expatriate of his dog, Black Dog (a.k.a. Blackie), partly because of America's restrictive views on dogs in dining establishments. In "The Christmas Gift," a story published in *Look* magazine in 1954, he describes how he made the decision to take Black Dog to Cuba, rather than leave him behind in Ketchum, Idaho:

"This was a town where a man was once not regarded as respectable unless he was accompanied by his dog. But a reform movement had set in, led by several local religionists, and gambling had been abolished and there was even a movement on foot to forbid a dog from entering a public eating place with his master. Blackie had always tugged me by the trouser leg as we passed a combination gambling and eating place called the Alpine where they served the finest sizzling steak in the West. Blackie wanted me to order the giant sizzling steak and it was difficult to pass the Alpine. . . . We decided to make a command decision and take Blackie to Cuba."

Fortunately, you don't have to take your dog to a foreign country in order to eat together at a restaurant. More and more restaurants have outdoor tables, and many of them welcome dogs to join their owners for an alfresco experience.

The rules for patio-dining dogs are somewhat vague, and each restaurant enforces them differently. But in general, as long as your dog doesn't go inside a restaurant (even to get to outdoor tables in the back) and isn't near the food preparation areas, it's probably fine. The decision is then up to the restaurant proprietor.

The restaurants listed in this book have given permission to tout them as dog-friendly places. But keep in mind that rules can change and restaurants can close, so I highly recommend phoning before you get your stomach set on a particular kind of cuisine.

Since some of the restaurants close during colder months, calling ahead is a wise thing to do. (Of course, just assume that where there's snow or ultracold temperatures, the outdoor tables are indoors for a part of the year.) If you can't call first, be sure to ask the manager of the restaurant for permission before you sit down with your sidekick. Remember, it's the restaurant owner, not you, who will be in trouble if someone complains.

Some basic restaurant etiquette: Dogs shouldn't beg other diners, no matter how delicious their steak looks. They should not attempt to get their snouts (or their entire bodies) up on the table. They should be clean, quiet, and as unobtrusive as possible. If your dog leaves a good impression with the management and other customers, it will help pave the way for all the other dogs who want to dine alongside their best friends in the future.

Some restaurants, cafés, espresso bars, and pubs consider their courtyards and decks, or even the sidewalk in front, part of their serving area. They say "no" as though wanting to sit a bit with your dog and enjoy a refreshment was a preposterous idea.

Others say, "Sure, no problem," the happiest affirmation in the English language to us who just want to pause a bit mid-mileage on our dog walk of life. The Sheraton Tacoma Hotel even said it was OK to sit with our tired dogs in the lobby and enjoy a brew from the piano lounge. At Portland's Fifth Avenue Suites Hotel we were served dinner at a table in the lobby.

One manager of several northwest resort properties said that a few rooms of each one may be set aside for walk-ins with dogs, but the company didn't want any of its properties mentioned in this book. "We've had some not-so-good experiences," she explained. "We had an awful time with fleas once after a dog left. At another inn a dog chewed up a bed post and then a down comforter."

This caution was taken by the proprietors of a number of northwest places—hotels, restaurants, clothing stores, and an eclectic assortment of retail shops—that welcome dogs on a case-by-case basis. But they in no way want it announced to the public, in this book or otherwise, that they welcome dogs.

A ROOM AT THE INN

Good dogs make great hotel guests. They don't steal towels, and they don't get drunk and keep the neighbors up all night.

The Seattle area is full of lodgings whose owners welcome dogs. This book lists dog-friendly accommodations of all types, from motels to bed-and-breakfast inns to elegant hotels. But the basic dog etiquette rules are the same.

Dogs should never be left alone in your room. Leaving a dog alone in a strange place is inviting serious trouble. Scared, nervous dogs can tear apart drapes, carpeting, and furniture. They can even injure themselves. They can also bark nonstop and scare the daylights out of the housekeeper. Just don't do it.

Only bring a house-trained dog to a lodging. How would you like to have a houseguest go to the bathroom right in the middle of your bedroom?

It helps if you bring your dog's bed or his blanket. Your dog will feel more at home and won't be tempted to jump on the bed. If your dog sleeps on the bed with you at home, bring a sheet and put it on top of the bed so the hotel's bedspread won't get furry or dirty.

After a few days in a hotel, some dogs come to think of it as home. They get territorial. When another hotel guest walks by, it's "Bark! Bark!" When the housekeeper knocks, it's "Bark! Snarl! Bark! Gnash!" Keep your dog quiet or you'll both find yourselves looking for a new home away from home.

For some strange reason, many lodgings prefer small dogs as guests. All I can say is, "Yip! Yap!" It's really ridiculous. Large dogs are often much calmer and quieter than their tiny, high-energy cousins.

If you're in a location where you can't find a hotel that will accept you and your big brute, it's time to try a sell job. Let the manager know how good and quiet your dog is (if he is). Promise he won't eat the bathtub or run around and shake the hotel. Offer a deposit or sign a waiver, even if they're not required for small dogs. It helps if your sweet, soppy-eyed dog is at your side to convince the decision-maker.

I've sneaked dogs into hotels, but I don't recommend doing it. The lodging might have a good reason for its rules. Besides, you always feel as if you're going to get caught and thrown out. You race in and out of your room with your dog as if ducking sniper fire. It's better to avoid feeling like a criminal and move on to a more dog-friendly location. For a sure bet, try a Motel 6. Every single Motel 6 in the nation permits one small pooch per room. Some have more lenient rules than others. Their nationwide reservation and information line is (800) 466-8356.

One friend of ours with a certified AKC Canine Good Citizen dog, Sadie, always takes the dog on trips. Sadie's bed at home is one of those "approved" carriers. In the car or on public transportation Sadie travels in her own bed. At hotels and resorts, the few times Sadie must be left behind, she's snugged into her own bed, with the door to it closed. That way there are no surprises for any staff who enter the room and no chance for gnawed furniture or shredded bed spreads.

Just like confident people, happy dogs will adjust to most experiences that come their way.

The lodgings described in this book are for dogs who obey all the rules. Rates listed are for double rooms, unless otherwise noted.

RUFFING IT TOGETHER

Most park officials recommend that you keep your dog in your tent or vehicle at night. They say it's dangerous to leave even a tethered dog outside your tent at night because the dog can escape or can become bait for some creature hungry for a late-night snack. Use good judgment.

If you're camping with your dog, chances are that you're also hiking with him. Even if you're not hiking for long, you have to watch out for your dog's paws, especially the paws of those who are fair of foot. Rough terrain can cause a dog's pads to become raw and painful, making it almost impossible to walk. Several types of dog boots are now available for such feet. It's easier to carry the booties than to carry your dog home.

Your dog should always be collared away from home, even in the leash-free woods. Not a choke chain either. They're named that for a reason, and it's too easy to snag one on a fence wire or in a thicket, or even on a door handle. Buckle collars are better, or you could use a stretch collar, or even a breakaway collar, when you know the dog will be alone for awhile. Your dog's ID ought to be on the collar somewhere, and possibly your location when traveling. There is always the odd chance you two will be separated, and the phone number of home won't help anybody find you when you're on the road. So a daily piece of tape on the collar, with the phone number of the day, might prove helpful.

And don't forget the baggies. Cleaning up after your dog is the best thing you can do for public relations that will benefit the dogs to visit after you. Just turn the baggie inside out, put your hand inside, scoop the pile, turn the baggie right side out, seal or tie it, and toss it in the next trash can you see. In a pinch, hotel shower caps work just fine.

Always carry a leash, even in leash-free areas. You never know when a tussle might arise and more than verbal control might be required. Use the extra control around bikers, on heavily trafficked trails, and for when the odd horse might be looming ahead. We were in a leash-free park in the Seattle area, when my sister showed us a short cut right up the side of a ravine. It was no problem for Emma and Quinn, of course, but I needed a tow from my brother-in-law, and the leash was perfect for the job.

Here's a trail tip courtesy of Robert Walter, Director of Education, The Humane Society for Tacoma and Pierce County: When you and your leashed dog pass another pair on the trail, don't try to restrain your dog by pulling back on the leash. That just sends your tension through the leash, which increases the dog's tension. Either walk far enough to the side to avoid contact, or stop and let the dogs greet each other in the usual way.

In a picnic area, or when people are around with food, Hungry should be restrained with a leash if verbal commands don't do the job. Anytime someone gives your dog a treat, your training against begging is being sabotaged. Dogs especially shouldn't be allowed on picnic tables. A lot of dog owners think it's cute to be at mouth level with their dogs, and actually invite their dogs to hop on the table. Be aware, though, that this behavior really crosses some bounds of other civilized people. Please, save the tricks for your own yard and insist that your dog act like he's out in public, which he is.

Beaches are generally not a good place for dogs if people are around. It's too easy to kick sand over the evidence and too easy to earn

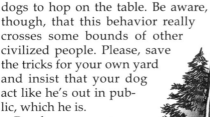

the ire of someone who steps in it, or worse. And for sure don't let your dog into public wading pools.

Be sure to bring plenty of water for you and your pooch. Stop frequently to wet your whistles. Some veterinarians recommend against letting your dog drink out of a stream, because of the chance of ingesting *giardia* and other internal parasites, but it's not always easy to stop a thirsty dog from dipping her muzzle into the water.

PEST CONTROL

Chances are that your adventuring will go without a hitch, but you should always be prepared to deal with trouble. Make sure you know the basics of animal first aid before you embark on a long journey with your dog. The more common woes—ticks, foxtails, and skunks—can make life with a traveling dog a somewhat trying experience.

Ticks can carry Lyme disease, so you should always check yourself and your dog all over after a day in tick country. Don't forget to check ears and between the toes. If you see a tick, just pull it straight out with tweezers, not your bare hands.

The tiny deer ticks that carry Lyme disease are difficult to find. Consult your veterinarian if your dog is lethargic for a few days, has a fever, loses her appetite, or becomes lame. These symptoms could indicate Lyme disease. Some vets recommend a vaccine that is supposed to prevent the onset of the disease.

Foxtails—those arrow-shaped pieces of dry grass (pictured at right) that attach to your socks, your sweater, and your dog—are an everyday annoyance. But in certain cases, they can be lethal. They can stick in your dog's eyes, nose, ears, or mouth and work their way in. Check every nook and cranny of your dog after a walk if you've been anywhere near dry grass. Be vigilant.

If your dog loses a contest with a skunk (and she always will), rinse her eyes first with plain warm water, and then bathe her with dog shampoo. Towel her off, then apply tomato juice—you might need to use as much as four gallons of the stuff before your dog will start smelling less offensive. If you can't get tomato juice, use a solution of one pint of vinegar per gallon of water to decrease the stink.

MEDICAL EMERGENCIES

Your own vet is your best source of information regarding your pet's needs, and she may have suggestions about what to include in a canine first aid kit.

One suggestion is a roll of gauze to make an emergency muzzle. I once attended a dog hit by a car. He had dragged himself to a ditch and turned vicious when anyone got close enough to touch him. He was normally a gentle household pet, but in medical shock, he was in denial as much as most humans are. The helper has to take over in a case like that, and a quick gauze or cloth loop over and under the snout, tied both below the snout and behind the ears, will make help possible. Any important information on the collar can then be deciphered too.

If your dog suffers a trauma or illness and you've been trained in first aid, you know what to do before calling a vet. If you haven't been trained, just remember the A-B-Cs: Airway open; Breathing normal; Circulation, or heart-beat. "He's gotta be getting some air in and he's gotta have a pulse," says a veteran ski patrol mountaineering instructor.

In a medical emergency, take off the dog's collar and make sure the airway is open by pulling the tongue forward and clearing any obstructions at the back of the mouth. Then begin CPR, cardio-pulmonary resuscitation, with a few quick downward thrusts with the palms of your hands placed just behind the dog's shoulder blade. Do this about 12 times per minute. Every five times, pause and force air into the lungs by holding the dog's mouth closed and with your own breath, put your mouth over his nose and blow.

In general, keep your dog warm, stop any bleeding, and tell someone to call for help. Don't move him without instruction from a vet, or until you're sure any breaks have been splinted and bleeding stopped.

We delight in our dogs' swimming abilities, but keep in mind that they're not trained aerobically to swim long distances, or to dog paddle indefinitely in a pool that has no way to climb out.

HE, SHE, IT

In this book, whether neutered, spayed, or *au naturel,* dogs are never referred to as "it." They are given a name, or referred to as "he" or "she." I alternate pronouns so no dog reading this book will feel left out.

BEYOND THE BORDERS

There may be times when you and your dog leave the Seattle area to visit other parts of the United States. Due to the success of *The California Dog Lover's Companion,* the Dog Lover's Companion series has expanded to cover differ-ent parts of the country, including Atlanta, Boston, Chicago, Florida, New England, Texas, and Washington, D.C. All of the authors are experts in their areas and have adventurous dogs who help them explore and rate various attractions. Keep your eyes peeled for upcoming books.

Another fun way to keep up with dog travel news around the country is through a subscription to a doggone fine newsletter called *"DogGone."* As its masthead states, "DogGone" is about "fun places to go and cool stuff to do with your dog." A subscription to this attractive, informative 16-page publi-cation is $24 per year (for six issues). For more information, or to subscribe, contact: "DogGone," (888) DOG-TRAVEL (364-8728).

A DOG IN NEED

If you don't currently have a dog but could provide a good home for one (or another one!), I'd like to make a plea on behalf of all the unwanted dogs who will be euthanized tomorrow and the day after that and the day after that. Animal shelters and humane organizations are overflowing with dogs who would devote their lives to being your best buddy, your faithful traveling companion, and a dedicated listener to all your tales of bliss and woe.

Need a nudge? Remember the oft-quoted words of Samuel Butler: "The great pleasure of a dog is that you may make a fool of yourself with him and not only will he not scold you, but he will make a fool of himself, too."

SEATTLE

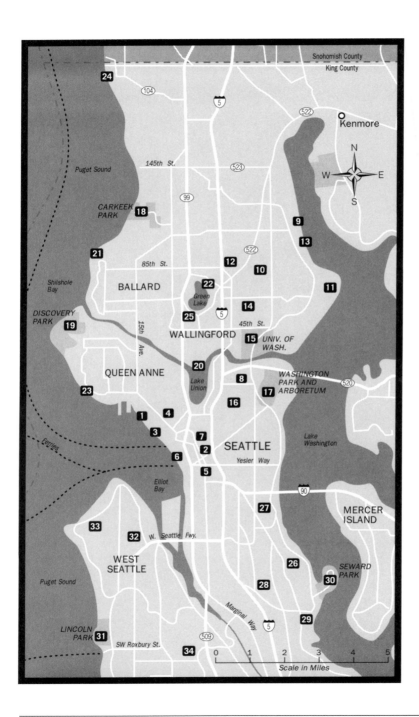

1
SEATTLE

One-third of all Washingtonians reside in 2,126-square-mile King County, mostly in and around Seattle. Subsequently, the shores of Puget Sound, Lake Washington, Lake Union, and Lake Sammamish are lined with housing, parks, commerce, and industry. Interstate 5 may slice Seattle in half from north to south, but citizens countered the traffic chaos by building a popular city park on top of it. Logically, it's called Freeway Park, and it's frequented by dog-walking bellhops from downtown Seattle hotels. Downtown is the geographical center of the city, anchoring the four city quadrants that this book uses to locate parks, lodgings, and restaurants. This Seattle chapter uses Interstate 5 to divide east and west. West of the freeway, the downtown itself separates north from south. East of the freeway, Yesler Way divides north from south.

SEATTLE

Seattle's park system is anchored at its four corners by Lincoln, Discovery, Magnuson, and Seward Parks. Most Seattle parks close at 11:30 P.M. and open again at 4 A.M. daily. The 24-hour parks are Green Lake Park, Myrtle Edwards Park, and the path along Lake Washington Boulevard, together with all city boat ramps and the Kerry and Hamilton viewpoints.

You can be fined $50 for not carrying scooper equipment in Seattle parks or on other public property, or even on private property (not your own).

As for downtown Seattle parks, Myrtle Edwards Park, with seven acres, abuts an additional 4,000 feet of northernmost waterfront owned by the Port of Seattle. Seattle Center has 74 acres. Including the Center, Denny Park and all of Myrtle Edwards Park, downtown Seattle can be considered to have 120 acres of park out of the city's 6,000 acres.

Seattle is estimated to have 150,000 dogs, and only 26,000 of them are licensed. Seattle's 1870 law requires that dogs be restrained at all times or their owners will be subjected to fines.

As part of a pilot project, the Seattle City Council chose—from the city's 6,000 acres of parkland and 400 parks—seven leash-free sites for dogs. And in 1996, these sites became leash-free for a trial period of one year. The program was considered a success and has been continued indefinitely. You'll find the off-leash exercise areas in the following city parks: Blue Dog Pond near the I-90 Lid Park, Golden Gardens Park, Genesee Park, Magnuson Park, Volunteer Park, Westcrest Park, and Woodland Park.

The rules for the leash-free zones are:
1) Aggressive dog behavior is not allowed.
2) Scooping and disposing are required.
3) Dogs must be properly licensed and vaccinated for rabies.
4) Dogs in heat are not allowed.

5) You must attend your dog at all times.
6) You must carry a visible leash at all times.
7) You must leash your dog while entering and exiting all leash-free areas.

DOWNTOWN

BELLTOWN, ELLIOTT BAY, AND SEATTLE CENTER

Downtown Seattle has maintained its vibrancy, even in the face of suburban shopping-mall excess. Westlake Park, at Westlake Center, is a hub of social, political, and party activity (particularly when the SuperSonics win a Western Championship). Westlake is a few blocks from the ever-bustling Pike Place Market.

Seattle's waterfront, below the noisy Alaskan Way Viaduct, is home to three ferry terminals, Piers 48 and 52, Waterfront Park (Pier 57), the Seattle Aquarium (Pier 59), the Hotel Edgewater (Seattle's only waterfront hotel, on Pier 67), and many restaurants and shops. Parks, large and small, dot the downtown area. There's even an area called Freeway Park, on top of Interstate 5.

PARKS, BEACHES, AND RECREATION AREAS

• Elliott Bay Park and Fishing Pier 🐾🐾 See ❶ on page 20.
Elliott Bay Park's shoreline is a seamless, northward extension of Myrtle Edwards Park from Pier 70. You can take a pleasant walk down the L-shaped, 400-foot-long fishing pier and determine how much of a fish maven your pup is—assuming the fish are biting. The pier has tables, benches, shelters, and fish-cleaning stations. Numerous bikers pass by on their way to the next 4,000-foot extension, the Terminal 91 Bike Path to Fisherman's Terminal. Leashes, and respect for anglers' catches, are required.

The north end of the park and pier is accessible from Elliott Avenue via West Galer. (206) 684-8021.

• Freeway Park 🐾 ◀● See ❷ on page 20.
A unique, over-the-freeway retreat, Freeway Park boasts fountains, ivy, a few trees, and some grass. Rest rooms are available. Leashed canines are welcome. The park is located at 6th Avenue and Seneca Street. (206) 684-8021.

• Myrtle Edwards Park 🐾🐾🐾 See ❸ on page 20.
Composed of 3.7 acres, Myrtle Edwards abuts an additional 4,100 feet of waterfront owned by the Port of Seattle. Many downtown dogs visit this park regularly—it's the only grassy area on the Elliott Bay waterfront, and the only place dogs can reach the water in downtown Seattle. Watch out for speeding in-line skaters and bicycles without warning bells. Your pooch must be leashed. Myrtle Edwards is open 24 hours.

The park is located at the north end of Alaskan Way at West Bay Street, just north of Pier 70. (206) 684-8021.

• Seattle Center 🐾 See 4 on page 20.

Dogs are allowed on the Seattle Center grounds, but they must be on a leash and you must scoop. Seattle maintained these grounds and buildings after the 1962 World's Fair; they've been a focal point of the city's cultural and sporting life ever since. People (but not their dogs) are drawn to the Space Needle, Pacific Science Center, International Fountain, Key Arena, Seattle Opera House, Seattle Repertory Theater, Pacific Arts Center, and the inspired homage to Jimi Hendrix and the world of rock music draped over the Monorail — the Experience Music Project.

From downtown Seattle, proceed northwest on 3rd or 4th Avenue to West Denny Way. Continue on West Denny Way to the Seattle Center. (206) 684-7200.

• Waterfall Garden 🐾 See 5 on page 20.

Located in the Pioneer Square district, this park has a 22-foot waterfall, recirculating 5,000 gallons per minute. The park was funded and created by the Annie E. Casey Foundation to honor the people of United Parcel Service. There must be more to it than that, you'd think, and you're right. Annie's son Jim, on this very spot, began a messenger service that later became UPS. The design of the 4,800-square-foot park makes it seem very remote from the streets around it. It uses a lot of granite, which contrasts nicely with all the green and blossoming flowers. It's even heated from the trellises above in cool weather. The garden is open from 8 A.M. to 4 P.M. in winter, and from 8 A.M. to 6 P.M. in the summer. Dogs must be leashed and you must scoop.

The garden is located at 2nd Avenue and South Main Street. (206) 624-6096.

• Waterfront Park 🐾 See 6 on page 20.

This isn't much of a place for a dog, but your leashed, four-legged friend will encounter some strong sea smells and lots of people who'll give him a pat. You can fish at Waterfront, too. The park includes Piers 57–61 on Alaskan Way, south of the aquarium.

From the Seattle Center, drive southwest on Bend Street to the waterfront. Turn left (southeast) on Alaskan Way at Pier 70. Continue past the Hotel Edgewater Inn to the park. (206) 684-8021.

• Westlake Park 🐾 See 7 on page 20.

Although largely devoid of doggy delights, Westlake Park is a decent place for people to sit and relax. It's a stone and marble triangle incorporating a block of Pine Street, in front of Westlake Mall. A path runs through the middle of the park's sculpture fountain; when the fountain is running, it's fun to walk through and try to dodge the water. Watch out for skateboarders. Leashes are required.

Westlake is located at 4th Avenue and Pine Street. (206) 684-8021.

RESTAURANTS

The Bookstore: A delightful combination of restaurant and bookshop, The Bookstore serves a fine Café Fonté espresso, in addition to full lunches and dinners. During the summer, you and your dog Maravella are invited to dine on the patio, a fenced-off section of 1st Avenue's sidewalk. Choice menu items include steamed Penn Cove mussels with basil and roasted tomatoes, salmon cakes, Caesar salads, vegetable risotto, and pan-seared salmon. Its bookshelves are stocked with cookbooks and travel books, sold for 15 percent off the cover price. 1007 1st Avenue; (206) 382-1506.

Crepe de France: Nearly all imaginable crepes are made here, in Pike Place Market next to the Read All About It newsstand, across from DeLaurenti's. It's under a roof here, but it's still open-air service at the counter's four stools. 93 Pike Street; (206) 624-2196.

Daily Dozen Donut Company: This stand-up donut shop is a great place for dessert, after you've had a slice at the DeLaurenti pizza window across the way. 93 Pike Street; (206) 467-7769.

DeLaurenti pizza window: Expect service in seven seconds, max. One slice will keep you and Mozzarella on your collective feet for another few hours. Both the window and the marvelous old-world DeLaurenti Specialty Food Market are at the entrance to Pike Place Market. 1435 1st Avenue; (206) 622-0141.

Grand Central Bakery: Wonderful rustic breads sought by restaurants as far as 80 miles away can be enjoyed on the premises, or at the outside tables right on the brick plaza in back, where dogs are welcome. The pastries, deli items, focaccia, and espressos are darn good, too. 214 1st Avenue South; (206) 682-0762.

Kosher Delight: Glatt Kosher is all you need to know about the Kosher Delight, which is just around the corner from Pike Place Market. Dogs can sit at the sidewalk tables with their humans, but they can't set even one of their paws inside the door. I'd recommend the sautéed eggplant to go with your soup. The falafel is good and the halvah costs just slightly more than a buck. 1509 1st Avenue; (206) 682-8140.

Macrina Bakery & Cafe: The word on the street is that Belltown's Macrina Bakery & Cafe has the best bread and espresso in the city. The apricot bread sure wowed me, and the organic coffee (from Queen Anne Coffee Roasters) was spot on. Macrina has some of the nicest outdoor seating in town too, and dogs are both frequent and welcome. Weekend brunches are popular with the dog-strolling set, and lunches are served weekdays from 11 A.M. to 3 P.M. The Meze is the most popular and easiest to share. 2408 1st Avenue; (206) 448-4032.

Ragin Cajun: If the Ragin Cajun's red beans and rice with andouille sausage was good enough for President Clinton, it's good enough for us. You and Flambé can enjoy the food at the sidewalk tables. You know what she'd really like, don't you? The catfish étouffée. For humans, I'd suggest the Muffuletta, a big Italian hero made with a chopped olive salad for that Cajun twist. 1523 1st Avenue; (206) 624-2598.

Sisters European Snacks: The waitress with a nose ring and earrings looked horrified when presented with the idea of dogs sitting at the outer tables. But her sister said, "Sure, why not?" The food is great and inexpensive. Try the Mediterranean salads, focaccia sandwiches, and Peruvian pinto-bean soup. Sisters' round tables are hand-painted with bullfight arenas and Spanish cities. The Post Alley scene going on around you has all the ambience of a Tangiers marketplace, except that most everyone speaks English. It's one block up from Pike Place Market, toward 1st Avenue. 1530 Post Alley; (206) 623-6723.

PLACES TO STAY

The Seattle Hotel Hot Line operates throughout the year, during standard business hours. Although the information and reservation service does not keep a formal list of lodgings that allow dogs, they may be able to give you the names of a few dog-friendly establishments if the following places are booked. Call (800) 535-7071 for more information.

The Alexis Hotel: The Alexis is an extremely dog-friendly lodging. The manager stops just shy of recruitment, but dogs under 30 pounds get the royal treatment: gentle pats at the front desk and complimentary room-service dog biscuits. This hotel is the first choice of the Sultan of Brunei and Bob Dylan. Bob, by the way, always travels with his very large dog. Emma and Quinn liked it, too.

In addition to June Pet Therapy Day (in honor of Pet Appreciation Week) and a National Pet Month special in May, the Alexis offers a pet package that includes an overnight stay for guests and their pets. For a $25 upgrade, you get a continental breakfast, a morning newspaper, valet parking, wine-tasting in the early evening, morning and afternoon valet doggy walks, and treats for the pampered pooch. Package prices range from $170 to $340, depending on the room and your dog's size. You can also elect for Cleo to have a session with an animal psychologist or a masseuse, $45 each. The Alexis is located on the corner of 1st Avenue and Madison Street, 1007 1st Avenue; (206) 624-4844 or (800) 426-7033.

Aurora Seafair Inn: Housebroken dogs (no larger than a cocker spaniel) are allowed at the Aurora Seafair, which has seven rooms set aside for our canine companions. Room rates range from $68 to $78, with a $5 per-night pet fee. 9100 Aurora Avenue North; (206) 524-3600.

Four Seasons Olympic Hotel: The Olympic's superlative reputation is earned, in part, by the staff's unfailing attention to detail. Lassie, who arrived in a stretch limo, stayed at the Olympic in the fall of 1995. She was treated very well, thank you, and dog groupies were kept at bay, since the screen star was concerned about communicable runny noses. Lassie does have a traveling companion however, so she's not lonely. Your dog will be served out of the same kind of dish that served Lassie. It's elegant, silver, and inscribed with the slogan, "Four Seasons Olympic Very Important Pet." The concierge will even suggest places to walk a dog downtown, such as Freeway Park (see page 22), just across 6th Street. Did I mention that canines receive a free dog biscuit at check-in? Plus pet amenities. Room rates range from $250 to $395. The hotel prefers dogs under 15 pounds. 11 University Street; (206) 621-1700 or (800) 821-8106 in Washington; (800) 223-8772 outside Washington.

Hawthorne Inn & Suites: This inn welcomes pooches and their owners. Rates range from a winter low of $99 to a summer high of $160 and there is a $50 per-stay dog fee. 2224 8th Avenue; (206) 624-6820 or (800) 437-4867.

Hotel Edgewater: The newly dog-friendly Hotel Edgewater is so on the water that it's on a pier, Pier 67, that juts into Elliott Bay. You used to be able to fish from your room (the Beatles did in 1964), but no more since indoor fishing just gets too messy, and practical jokes played with fish became very impractical to clean up. You just have to settle for watching the tugboat races in summer and the year-round nautical life of Elliott Bay.

The manager tells a good fishing story about a guy who would fish by telephone. He'd throw out his line, secure it around the telephone receiver, and head for the bar. He'd telephone his room from the bar after every drink. If the phone rang, he'd have another. If the phone was busy, he'd know a fish was on the line and rush to his room to haul it in.

Just a few blocks up the street from the Edgewater are a few miles of grassy waterfront park on Elliott Bay. The first mile, Myrtle Edwards Park, is one of the few Seattle parks that is open 24 hours per day.

If the Edgewater knows your dog is coming for a visit, a doggie bed will await her, along with food and water bowls, toys, and a book for bedtime reading. There is also a doggie menu for room service. There is no extra charge for dogs and no deposit required. The hotel asks only that you register your dog and sign a responsibility form. A credit card imprint is required. There is no restriction on canine size. "Not too many people travel with their bull mastiffs, but anyone who does is welcome at the Edgewater," said an administrator. Pier 67, 2411 Alaskan Way; (206) 728-7000 or (800) 624-0670; www.noble househotels.com/edgewater.

Hotel Monaco: Seattle is unique in many ways, driven as it is by its smug sense of panache, binging on flavored coffee concoctions, take-out fish tacos and, oddly, for a place where trees grow like weeds, 400 city parks. Now a new downtown Seattle hotel, the Hotel Monaco, is pushing the locals' favorite adjective, "cool," to new heights.

Even before the pet-friendly 189-room Monaco opened, "Seattle's coolest hotel" saw entire floors booked by local companies for strategic business presentations. No, the guests did not all bring their pets, but they had the option of goldfish in their rooms. The goldfish are kept in a huge tank in housekeeping, and are sort of decanted into one-gallon fishbowls for any guest who wants one. Pretty cool.

The Monaco's catch phrase is, "The hotel with a porpoise." But after the doorwoman takes your pet dog Minos and your luggage to the steamer trunk of a check-in counter, you'll notice the mural of Minoan dolphins in the lobby. No matter. The non sequitur is part of the whimsy.

Each design element in the rooms, like the red and white striped wallpaper, mostly-triangular bedside table, brilliant yellow bedspread, and sunburst above the headboard, would look crazy or absurd on a sketch, but all together they work, just the way you knew yours would have worked if only your parents had let you decorate your own bedroom. "Yummy" comes to mind, and, incongruously, luxuriously residential. Perhaps even Minoan.

The AAA Four-Diamond Hotel Monaco is located in the heart of the Seattle business district, at the corner of 4th Avenue and Spring Street. Dogs 20 pounds and under are preferred. Rates range from $295 to $395, but ask about promotional discounts. 1101 4th Avenue; (206) 621-1770 or (800) 945-2240.

Vagabond Inn: You can't spend the night closer to the Space Needle without sleeping in the park. Bring your pup for an extra $10 per night. Rooms range from $50 to $99. 325 Aurora Avenue North; (206) 441-0400 or (800) 522-1555.

"W" Seattle: Dogs are welcome at W, Seattle's newest "boutique" hotel. With 426 guest rooms, W stretches the marketing concept just a tad, but you and Cleopatra sure can't beat the comfort and luxury of the bed anywhere else. The down comforter and 250 thread count sheets will keep you abed until the last possible moment. All rooms have a 27-inch TV and Internet access. W is located downtown on the corner of 4th and Seneca Avenues. Rates start at $375. 1112 4th Avenue; (206) 264-6000 or (877) 946-8357.

DIVERSIONS

Canine company: If you'd like to add to your family of pooches, there are a number of organizations ready to assist you. The Pet Adoption League of Washington website—www.petshelter.org—includes animals posted by the Progressive Animal Welfare Society, Whidbey Animals' Improvement Foundation, Seattle Animal Control, and the Humane Society for Seattle; (425) 556-0502.

Books and bulldogs: If your dog is well-behaved and leashed, and about as excitable as Seattle people who haven't had their second espresso yet, he can join you at the M. Coy Bookstore & Espresso, which has an espresso bar in back with some fine nibbles (for you, not the dog). The book selection is aimed at the thoughtful cosmopolite. 117 Pine Street; (206) 623-5354.

Go, dog, go: Dogs are allowed on all Metro buses in Seattle and King County, although a one-dog-per-bus limit may be enforced by drivers. If your dog rides in your lap, you won't be charged an additional fare, but if he takes up floor space, he has to pay an adult fare. 821 2nd Avenue; (206) 553-3000 (rider information system) or (425) 451-2404 (Metro information system).

I'd Rather be Shopping at Nordstrom: That's what my wife's license plate frame says, and it's true. The grandpups are welcome to join her in any Nordstrom or Nordstrom Rack store, but the problem is they have to be carried. There is not much shopping to be done with two armloads of dog, which is OK by me. Nordstrom, 500 Pine Street; (206) 628-2111.

To market, to market: Pike Place Market, where both Seattleites and tourists do their grocery shopping, is a bizarre scene for a country dog, but our salmon terriers smelled the fresh fish from afar. The salmon-throwing wowed 'em. "Now that's a game worth playing," barked Quinn. "Toss me that salmon and I'll show you a 50-yard run." The human salmon-heavers put on a great show for the tourists, and the receiver never missed. Emma caught sight of Rachael, the life-size bronze boar that guards an entrance to Pike Place Market. The boar's snout is rubbed shiny by the hundreds of people a day who want some good luck, but Emma went bonkers over this intruder. She yapped up a storm from a safe perimeter while Quinn went in close to sniff the teats. No succor there, so he retreated and joined the yapping. Dogs are not allowed in the market's arcades or inside the walkways, but they are allowed on Pike Place's sidewalks and the adjoining street. 85 Pike Street; (206) 682-7453.

NORTHEAST

CAPITOL HILL, RAVENNA, UNIVERSITY, AND VIEW RIDGE

PARKS, BEACHES, AND RECREATION AREAS

• **Boren Park/Interlaken Boulevard** 🐾🐾🐾🐾 ◀ See **8** on page 20.
This is another Seattle City Park that you wouldn't stumble across unless you lived in the neighborhood. And people in the neighborhood like that fact just

fine. Directions could include various combinations of Interlaken Place East, Interlaken Drive East, and East Interlaken Boulevard. And those are just the roads. You should see the trails. The park runs southeast from East Roanoke Street all the way to the Arboretum. The trails are great for dogs, ambitious joggers, maybe even marathoners in training, and mountain bikers. The park is composed of steep hillsides, wooded ravines, woods galore, and awesome trails. You'd have to call this a place of excellence. One road meanders down past the Seattle Hebrew Academy on the left, down deeper into the side of the ravine. An easy driving entrance is from the corner of 19th Avenue East and Interlaken Drive East.

A Seattle buddy runs in the park all the time, especially on the lower road where it's closed off for about a mile. The road used to be open, but it had problems with flooding and drainage and the city didn't have the money to fix it. So the neighborhood petitioned the city to close it off, and it did. There are lots more trails in the park too. The park would make a wonderful campground. On one of the trails there is a newish stone sculpture in the shape of a bench. It's the greatest place to sit for awhile if your dogs are tired.

We also made an attempt from the upper end of Interlaken, parking at the corner of 15th Avenue and East Garfield Street. There is a huge steel sculpture and concrete circular path around it, and just to the right starts the long narrow path that weaves its way down the ravine. On this jaunt, my sister was the alpha human, leading Quinn and me, and niece Jessica and dad Bill. Quinn won't be led, however. As we wound around and down the trail, we watched Quinn the squirrel terrier do his job. This part of Interlaken is overgrowth city, with long, long Tarzan vines hanging from the trees, and ivy doing its best to choke the trees. Even after a big rain, the trail is in good shape. Near the bottom it can get a bit mushy, especially with all the fallen leaves. We heard Quinn boring through the underbrush at top speed. He came back to us looking happy, but with no squirrel. He did have a centipede on his back, which I dispatched. This is for sure Quinn's favorite park all week.

The park entrance is at 19th Avenue East and Interlaken Drive East. (206) 684-8021.

• Burke-Gilman Trail 🐾🐾🐾 See 9 on page 20.

Burke-Gilman, a 16.6-mile hiking and biking trail, starts in Fremont, two miles west of Gas Works Park on Lake Union. It continues eastward and north past Kenmore's Logboom Park and connects with the Sammamish River Trail, which leads to Redmond's Marymoor Park. This well-signed trail also passes through the University of Washington and along the northwest side of Lake Washington. The distance from the trail's origin to Marymoor Park is about 29 miles. The route incorporates many streets and passes through intersections, so it can be accessed at several points. For a dog's purposes, I recommend driving to Matthews Beach Park (see page 29), parking the car, and heading north through some woody areas or south along the shore of Lake Washington. Your pup must be leashed.

To reach the trail, take I-5 to exit 169. After driving slightly more than 1.5 miles east on 45th Street, bear northeast on Sand Point Way Northeast. Continue on Sand Point Way Northeast for 3.2 miles to Northeast 93rd Street. Parking is available about one block up, on your left. (206) 684-8021.

• Dahl Playfield 🐾 🐾 See **10** on page 20.

Dahl was one of the original 38 parks to be considered for a leash-free section, but it didn't make the cut. It's primarily for team sports, but dogs have enjoyed the park for years, leashed, of course. It is located at 25th Avenue Northwest and Northeast 77th Street (206) 684-8021.

• Magnuson Park 🐾 🐾 🐾 🐕 See **11** on page 20.

This huge Sand Point park is the big anchor park in the View Ridge neighborhood of northeast Seattle. It has nearly a mile of shoreline, off limits to dogs ($500 fine) except for way down where the leash-free trail ends that runs behind the play fields. The rest of the park, the 200 acres where leashing is required, has plenty of walking and jogging paths. Some are paved and quite wide. The park appears very much the military base it used to be. The buildings are off-limits, behind gates and fences, so there is really just one way to drive through the park. There are plenty of loop-offs to parking lots for your choice of beaches, playing fields, and mowed trails through the au naturel areas.

For the leash-free trail, use the last parking lot before the playing fields. Park in the far left corner for the leash-free trailhead. It's a well-defined trail that runs around the perimeter of the park, around the playing fields and to a popular doggy swimming spot, small but wet.

In summer, May 1 to September 10, Magnuson Park is closed to cars between 9 P.M. and 6 A.M. The rest of the year, September 11 to April 30, it's closed to cars from 6 P.M. to 6 A.M. Those limits effectively close the park, unless you live nearby and know where the holes in the fence are. There are residential neighborhoods on two sides of the park, but the streets are planted with "DEAD END" and "DON'T PICK THE BLACKBERRIES" signs. There are a few accesses through the tall chain-link fence that surrounds the park, but let's just leave the locals their private gates to the park and drive in the main gate.

To reach the park, take Sand Point Way Northeast to 65th Avenue Northeast. Turn right on 65th Avenue Northeast and enter the park. (206) 684-8021.

• Maple Leaf Park 🐾 See **12** on page 20.

Mainly a playground with some ball fields, Maple Leaf Park can be a pleasant stop for you and Rover. Leashes are a must. The park is several blocks long, starting at the intersection of Roosevelt Way Northeast and Northeast 82nd Street. (206) 684-8021.

• Matthews Beach Park 🐾 See **13** on page 20.

This is a very nice small beach park, but no dogs are allowed on the swimming beach itself, and must be leashed in the rest of the park. There is, however, a nice wooded hillside above the parking area on the left.

To reach Matthews Beach Park, take I-5 to exit 169. After driving slightly more than 1.5 miles on 45th Street, bear northeast on Sand Point Way Northeast. Continue on Sand Point Way Northeast for approximately 3.2 miles to Northeast 93rd Street. The parking lot is about one block up, on your left. (206) 684-8021.

•Ravenna Park 🐾🐾 See **14** on page 20.

Ravenna must mean ravine in some other language, because this park, like so many of Seattle's green areas, is a great big ravine. Ravenna is almost totally wooded, a bit of the wild country in this residential neighborhood north of the University of Washington. The park is full of walking paths, play areas, restrooms, and a picnic shelter. Leashed dogs are welcome, and you must scoop.

We've heard tales of Saturday "happenings" in the park, like play readings and games with costumed adults. There are bridges and stairways to get around, but there is not a lot of car access. This is another one of those Seattle neighborhood ravines that seem closely guarded by the people who live near them, so the locals can maintain their own access. Getting there from Green Lake, Northeast Ravenna Boulevard is itself a sort of park, with a wide 50-foot grassy tree strip down the middle, with well-worn paths. You can park on the north side of the park along Northeast 62nd Street, with the park on one side and houses on the other.

To reach the park, drive on I-5 to exit 169. Proceed east on Northeast 45th Street to Brooklyn Avenue Northeast. Turn left (north) on Brooklyn Avenue Northeast and continue for eight blocks to Northeast 62nd Street and the park. (206) 684-8021.

•University of Washington 🐾🐾 See **15** on page 20.

Dogs are welcome on the U Dub campus, but they must be leashed at all times and you must scoop. The University has nearly 700 acres of lovely landscaped grounds. It includes playing fields, semi-forested woods, and brick squares. The Burke-Gilman Trail crosses the campus beyond the Montlake Bridge, at the corner of Northeast Pacific Street and University Way Northeast. The entire campus stretches from Northeast 45th Street to the Lake Washington Ship Canal and from 15th Avenue Northeast to Union Bay. There is a self-guided walking tour available, with a map, from the information posts. The visitor center is at University Way Northeast and Northeast Campus Parkway, and is open 8 A.M. to 5 P.M. weekdays. (206) 543-9198.

•Volunteer Park 🐾🐾 🦴 🐕 See **16** on page 20.

This glorious piece of land was originally called Washelli Cemetery, but don't concern yourself about it. The gravestones were removed in 1887. The park was offered to the state for a new capitol and renamed Capitol Hill in antici-pation. It didn't happen, so the park was renamed Volunteer Park to honor veterans of the Spanish-American War, which was still going on at the time. This large, nearly 45-acre, Capitol Hill park has something for everybody. Its four square blocks have big grassy areas and woody trails. There's a big con-servatory, a bandstand for concerts and theater and a water tower to climb, via an outside circular stairway, with a 360-degree view that just doesn't quit. It's almost as high as the Space Needle.

The park is very busy. It's bordered on three sides by residential streets. The fourth side abuts a cemetery, which itself has an incredible view of the surroundings. Volunteer Park is largely front yard-type landscaping under a huge canopy of tall trees. You can drive into the park from the northeast corner off 15th East or from 14th East on the south.

It has the sort of nighttime reputation that suggests it would be wise to not linger after dark. Indeed, nearly all parks are supposed to be people-free by 11:30 P.M. and stay that way until 4 A.M. Trespassers will be prosecuted. No vehicles are allowed on the park drives from 11 P.M. to 6 A.M.

In fall, the grass is entirely covered with leaves, just like most of the rest of Capitol Hill. So it's not true that Seattle has no change of seasons. But the colors of fall are mostly visible in urban parks and high mountain passes.

The leash-free area is below the Seattle Asian Art Museum. It's a temporary site while the parks department finds a more suitable spot on Capitol Hill.

From downtown Seattle, drive northeast on Madison Street. Cross I-5, proceed to Broadway, and turn left. In one mile, Broadway becomes 10th Avenue East. Follow 10th Avenue East for three blocks, turn right (east) on East Highland Drive, and drive into the park. (206) 684-8021.

•Washington Park and Arboretum 🐾🐾🐾 🐾 See **17** on page 20.

This park stretches from the shore of Union Bay to East Madison Street, shaped like a giant squid. The 200-acre Arboretum, founded in 1934, is seen as a living display of plant possibilities suitable for the Puget Sound region. It has more than 5,500 different kinds of plants, including more than 130 endangered species. It's the largest public garden north of San Francisco. It would take several visits here to feel you know your way around. Just think of all the sniff-check opportunities for Cyrano. Some people think the layout is like a rabbit warren because of all the mysterious trail starts and finishes.

The powers that be expect you to be passive in the Arboretum. They actually say that active recreation is not allowed. Group activities are restricted. Bikes can be only on the paved areas, and jogging is allowed only on the roadways and gravel trails. No jogging is allowed on Azalea Way, a three-quarter-mile promenade lined with flowering trees, azaleas, and dogwoods. Got that guys? No hasty missteps. No hasty steps period. Dogs are not even allowed in such special areas as the Japanese Garden.

The reasoning is that the plant collections, ponds, and paths are especially vulnerable to damage. They say that dogs who chase waterfowl into Duck Pond tend to trample the vegetation. No, not my granddogs. They're so light on their feet. But be extra careful about the traipsing, leashing, and scooping.

So why is this a three paw park for dogs? It's heavily forested in parts and there are lots of grassy areas. A really good dog run in the Arboretum is along Lake Washington Boulevard East, on the west side of the road. It's a long grassy area with a trail that runs from Boyer Avenue East and the play lot before the brick pedestrian bridge that crosses over the boulevard to the rest of the Arboretum.

The rock garden trails, both the upper and lower, are good walking and the meadows are three paws for sure, especially for gopher terriers. And there are a couple of hillsides with ravines in between, just like everywhere else in Seattle.

You can access Washington Park Arboretum from Lake Washington Boulevard East between East Madison and Highway 520. Or if you're approaching on Highway 520 from the east, just follow the signs to the Arboretum. Just before you leave the floating bridge, check out the playful sculptures, called the Nellie Cornish Memorial Sculptures. Foster Island is down there at Duck Bay. The waterfront trail extends to Foster Island, with a wooden walkway from Foster Island to Marsh Island going over Union Bay. Parking areas at the Arboretum are scattered around, since it's so big. Remember that this is a high car prowl area. The grounds are open daily from 7 A.M. until dusk. (206) 684-8021.

RESTAURANTS

Bow Wow Meow: The Bow Wow Meow Treatoria and Sit Stay Deli has plenty of poochie delights, baked right on the premises. It's open Tuesdays through Saturdays. 8801 Roosevelt Way Northeast; (206) 523-0334.

The Coffee Crew: The Crew is a good pit stop if you're on your way to the park—any park. It offers snacks (such as muffins) and (surprise, surprise) a variety of caffeinated beverages. Dogs are allowed to join their owners at the outside tables. 3614 Northeast 45th Street; (206) 525-2883.

DIVERSIONS

Fly me: Have you had it with trying to get you and your dog Exploratorio to the San Juans or Victoria? On the car ferries dogs have to stay on the car deck, and on the foot ferries they're not allowed at all. Bummer. But WOOF! Kenmore Air will float you and yours to your island destination in a timely fashion, and on regularly scheduled flights from Lake Union. It's the only airline I've found that will take pet dogs on a casual basis. "We're sort of like a country bus, where people come on with chickens and everything," says Craig Sternagel, Director of Marketing. Call ahead, of course, as a courtesy. Dogs fly better on the big Otters, but the Beavers can take them in a pinch. 6321 Northeast 175th Street; (425) 486-1257 or (800) 543-9595.

NORTHWEST

FREMONT, GREEN LAKE, QUEEN ANNE, AND WALLINGFORD

PARKS, BEACHES, AND RECREATION AREAS

•**Carkeek Park** 🐾 🐾 See **18** on page 20.

It's tough to find this 216-acre recreation area. Perhaps that's because the neighborhood wants to keep Carkeek Park to itself. Getting to the park, however, is definitely worth the effort. The park road is a beautiful, winding street covered by a dense canopy of trees. A sign at the entrance points out all the recreational possibilities: picnicking, trails, an environmental education center, a beach, and a model-airplane field. "Leash and scoop" is the law in Carkeek Park, and dogs are not allowed on the beach.

Be aware that activities on the model-airplane field generate enough noise to alarm country canines, like Emma. Quinn faired well, but use discretion when taking your canine companion to watch the fun.

This park offers great mountain-bike opportunities, and a lot of people walk their dogs on a gravel path running up the ravine. Carkeek is also the Pipers Creek Watershed, and a number of trails run through it. Access to the Carkeek Trail is provided at the second parking lot.

From north of Seattle, take I-5 exit 173. Proceed west on North Northgate Way to Fremont Avenue North. Turn right on Fremont Avenue North and continue to Northwest 110th Street. Turn left on Northwest 110th Street and continue straight to Northwest Carkeek Road and the park. (206) 684-8021.

• Discovery Park 🐾🐾 See **19** on page 20.

This 534-acre park is Seattle's largest recreation area. It offers more than seven miles of hiking trails. A 2.8-mile loop trail (an easy, two-hour stroll) passes through several habitats, including meadows, forests, and sand dunes; dogs are not allowed on the beach. Several other trails meander through the woods. There are frequent little signposts at the trail intersections, so there's no reason to fear getting lost.

Discovery Park was one of the original 38 parks considered for leash-freeness, but it was decided that the ecology and the habitat were so special and so fragile that dogs should not be allowed to run loose. But they're certainly welcome on a leash.

We were probably the 50th carload to try driving to the West Point Lighthouse, and the 50th to be stopped at the military gate and turned around. In the 19th century, what is now Discovery Park was entirely Fort Lawton. It became a park in 1972, although it was nicely prelandscaped as a park already by the U.S. Army. There are still 11 federal agencies in the park, and they like to keep to themselves. That's why the gate.

The visitor center is in the east parking lot. Just follow the signs to get there. A free guided nature walk takes place on Saturday at 2 P.M. The Discovery Park Visitor Center is open daily from 8:30 A.M. to 5 P.M.

The main park entrance is at the intersection of 36th Avenue West and West Government Way. The visitor center is located at 3801 West Government Way. Discovery Park: (206) 684-8021 or (206) 386-4236 (visitor center).

• Gas Works Park 🐾 See **20** on page 20.

Gas Works is an industrial-site-turned-park on a Lake Union promontory. Bikers, joggers, and in-line skaters pass the park on the Burke-Gilman Trail, just across the street. Gas Works Park, as you may have guessed, still contains a gasworks. This ugly relic could have been a prop from the movie Road Warrior. At least it's behind a fence.

The rest of the park is green, and offers a big knoll from which to survey the universe, including Chandlers Cove, downtown Seattle, and the Space Needle. Look down and you'll see the Gas Works Memorial Sundial embedded in the cement on top of the knoll; it's a brass sundial emblazoned with colored glass, marbles, seashells, tiles, and brass renderings of the 12 signs of the zodiac. Emma and Quinn, dove terriers, were much more interested in a flock of doves pecking at the ground. Humans, however, will find plenty to admire. Leash your pup.

If you're in Gas Works Park after summer, check out the big fish processing boats off to the right. They're back for the winter from Alaskan waters. They return in mid-October because the crews mostly live in the Seattle area. Besides, wintering in freshwater is better than salt, the climate is much more pleasant for repairs and retrofits, and parts are much cheaper than they are in Alaska.

The park is located on North Northlake Way, between Meridian Avenue North and Wallingford Avenue North. (206) 684-8021.

•Golden Gardens Park 🐾🐾🐾 🐟 🐕 See **21** on page 20.

Located at the north end of Shilshole Bay in Ballard, Golden Gardens falls on both sides of north/south-running railroad tracks. You'll find a forested hillside to the east of the tracks, and a long sandy beach to the west. Unfortunately, dogs are not allowed on the park's beach. When you enter Golden Gardens, park your automobile in the space to your immediate right. A small, grassy, leash-free area is located in the upper portion of the park. That's where Emma and Quinn discovered football. What kind of ball was it that didn't roll to be chased, or nudged? It didn't behave like a basketball, so they couldn't quite figure it out. But they cornered it and bagged their limit for the day.

Golden Gardens teems with families, teenagers, bikers, and scuba divers. People swim here, although the water temperature rarely rises above 50 degrees. The trails above the railroad tracks provide strong and wonderful scents, and (on sunny days) views of the Olympic Mountains.

When you and your pooch are ready for a breather, look for the beautiful tiled benches by the Community Center, the 1993 Whittier Elementary Tile Project. They're surrounded by crabs, shells, starfish, fish, and a mermaid, all crafted in cement.

To reach the park, take I-5 to exit 172, and proceed west to Northwest 85th Street. Turn right at the stop sign on 32nd Avenue Northwest, which becomes Golden Gardens Drive Northwest and leads you into the park. (206) 684-8021.

•Green Lake 🐾🐾🐾 See **22** on page 20.

Green Lake is a recreation focus for people all over Seattle, and beyond as well. Through the 1950s and early 1960s, Green Lake was the site of the annual Aqua Theater, a two-week festival of water follies. Including the lake itself, the park is 342 acres, although the expanse of water makes it seem larger. It takes a good half hour for a slow jogger to run the 2.8-mile perimeter. That's only if it's not rush hour on the paved path around the lake. There are people with baby strollers, people with dogs, people with baby strollers and dogs, bicyclists, in-line skaters, and, would you believe it, people simply out for a pleasurable walk. Someone should put in traffic lights. After sniffing a lot of trees, chasing a few ducks, and swimming in an unpopulated part of the lake, Quinn and Emma cooled out on a grassy slope to watch the physically fit canines and sapiens go by. Most relaxing. The park is open 24 hours per day. Green Lake is located at E. Green Lake Drive North and W. Green Lake Drive North. (206) 684-8021.

•Magnolia Boulevard 🐾 🦴 See **23** on page 20.

This bluff park stretches along the northern shore of Elliott Bay, between Discovery Park and Smith Cove, at the northernmost piers of the Port of Seattle. You and your canine companion can enjoy a stroll on a paved path surrounded by madrona trees. Check out the landscaping in people's yards across the street, but don't let your dog check it out. Stay on the west side of the street. It's quite a place to take a drive or a walk, really nice for humans. That's who it was designed for after all. Busloads of people stop at Magnolia, with cameras ready to capture an image of Mount Rainier. The views over Elliott Bay to Alki Point and downtown Seattle to the mountain are inspirational.

All in all, this park is more attractive to humans than to dogs. It is, however, better than a walk to the corner park (from a doggy perspective), and it beats a fire hydrant. Leashes are the law.

From north Seattle, take I-5 to exit 166. Proceed on Denny Way west for 1.2 miles until it joins Western Avenue. Turn right (north) on Western Avenue; it joins Elliott Avenue West, also going north, in a few blocks. Continue north on Elliott Avenue West, then take the Garfield Street West exit. Garfield Street West swoops left (west) across the Magnolia Bridge and becomes Galer Avenue West. Galer becomes Magnolia Boulevard West as you bear right (north). Follow Magnolia until it turns left (west) at Howe Street West and becomes the park road along the bluff. (206) 684-8021.

•Richmond Beach Park 🐾 🐾 🐾 🐕 See **24** on page 20.

This beach park starts south of Edmonds and the beach walk itself continues north four miles to Edmonds Ferry Dock past the old community of Richmond Beach and along bluffs and fenced estates overlooking Puget Sound. It's a good romp for dogs (leashed, of course), and some even enjoy the chilly water.

To get to Richmond Beach Park, take Aurora Avenue to North 185th Street, turn west on Richmond Beach Road and follow it down and turn left into the parking area. (206) 296-4281.

•Woodland Park 🐾 🐾 🐾 🐕 See **25** on page 20.

The 188 acres of Woodland Park include a renowned zoo, picnic areas, lawn bowling greens, horseshoe pits, a nine-hole mini golf course, tennis courts, a track and field area, too many sports fields to mention and, get this, a soap box derby ramp. But you want to know what's in it for dogs. How about rabbits? No no, I didn't say that. But if you happen to go in by the south entrance, Woodland Park Avenue North from North 50th Street, keep a tight rein on Thing there until you're both past the boulders and into the woods. This is where the leash-free area used to be and it's still great for wandering.

Trails go every which way here. This part of the park is hilly and wooded, and, repeat, no longer leash-free, but it's still Emma and Quinn's favorite part of the park. It's hard to say why such a hilly area is called the Eastern Flats. It feels a lot like Volunteer Park, with a canopy of trees overhead and good wild country for leashed dogs to explore. This Woodland Park Avenue North entrance from Northwest 50th Street has bathrooms, picnic shelters, free parking, some homeless people hanging around sometimes, and a lot of picnic tables. We met a man with a gorgeous Springer Spaniel who comes here almost every morning of the year. He's usually alone in this part of the park but for the company of his dog, especially in the winter. This wooded area is perfect. Emma and Quinn could have stayed all day tracing scents up and down the hilly trails. They had a few startles because these trees have personality; many of them are gnarled oaks that grow bulbous faces on their trunks, a few of which gave the pups reason for a second look. There is no water for swimming here, but all the trees, ferns, and squirrels made for a very OK time.

Woodland Park's off-leash area, fun for the dogs but more mundane for humans, is located just west of the tennis courts on West Green Lake Way. Woodland Park is bisected by limited-access Aurora Avenue North, and bordered by Phinney Avenue North on the west, East Green Lake Way North on the east, North 50th Street on the south, and Northwest 60th Street on the north. (206) 684-8021.

RESTAURANTS

Azteca: This Shilshole Mexican restaurant, with a huge menu, says, "Yes, of course, just walk through to the deck." And if it's a rainy day, anything on the menu can be ordered to take out to the comfort of your car or boat. 6017 Seaview Avenue Northwest; (206) 789-7373.

Charlie's at Shilshole: We nearly tripped over a dog's water bowl when we walked into Charlie's. You can dine outside, near your pooch, who must be tethered on the other side of the chain separating the restaurant from the public walkway. The menu favors seafood, including beer-batter fish-and-chips and pan-fried oysters, but Primordio would be happier if you ordered the liver and onions. 7001 Seaview Avenue Northwest; (206) 783-8338.

Gordo's: Step right up to this Shilshole hot doggery. Dogs are allowed at the outside picnic tables, so your dog Frank can sit with you (just don't tell him what you're eating). 6226 Seaview Avenue Northwest; (206) 784-7333.

Hiram's at the Locks: Sunday brunch at Hiram's is a welcome treat, and you're allowed to tie Spaghettinia up out front. The restaurant specializes in steak and seafood. Most popular are the Dungeness crab cakes and fresh salmon. Hiram's is at the Ballard (Chittenden) Locks, 5300 34th Avenue Northwest; (206) 784-1733.

Perché No: One regular customer of this Queen Anne restaurant ties his dog to the parking meter, just like it was a horse in the old west, and sits inside at a window where he can see him. Perché No, or Why Not? is the question you would ask when you wonder how such delicious Italian dishes could be made by a Chinese couple, Lily and David Kong. There are Chinese cooks in most restaurant kitchens all over the world, so why not? The meals are both imaginative and consistently good. Once, in honor of all the puppies eaten by alligators in Florida over the years, I had a wonderful Filet of Tender Alligator, sautéed with garlic, shallots, sweet vermouth, mushrooms, and capers, plus a touch of marinara and demi-glace. It was both wonderful and redemptive.

Once a month the Kongs celebrate with a special presentation of food and wine in honor of a particular region of Italy, with wine experts on hand to help the diners through the five courses and five wines. The Parpadella Con Porcini Funghi married with Corvo Terre D'Agala '88 was brilliant! Even at

$55 a customer, and after doubling the size of the restaurant, the events sell out. 621^1/$_2$ Queen Anne Avenue North; (206) 298-0230.

Ray's Boat House: Ray's on Shilshole Bay is THE Seattle waterfront restaurant for seafood, and the even better news is that Ray's keeps a bowl of water by the railing under the awning for all the dogs that are parked there. 6049 Seaview Avenue Northwest; (206) 789-3770.

Taco del Mar: Most days it's standing-room-only at the Taco del Mar. The food is good and cheap. Quinn and I ordered a fish taco with a slice of lime—it was Quinn's favorite meal of the day. 3526 Fremont Place North; (206) 545-8001.

DIVERSIONS

Bark Natural Pet Care: This Fremont natural foodery comes most highly recommended by the Bow Wow Meow Treatoria, and who could argue with that? 513 North 36th; (206) 633-2275.

Deluxe Junk: A sign in the doorway, with a picture of a black poodle, says, "A friend is not a feller who is taken in by sham. A friend is one who knows our faults and doesn't give a damn. And a dog is a damn good friend." So we took Emma for a look around. The Deluxe welcomes dogs with open arms. Among the too-many-things-to-mention are thigh-high leather boots for the ladies, a zillion ashtrays, chrome dinette sets, and telephones from another era. I liked the black and red rubberized dinette set ($295), but Quinn went for couches like those my great aunt Pinky had back before there was TV and couch potatoes. Quinn could feel all the good vibes in the Deluxe, but we kept him off the furniture. You wouldn't believe the other stuff even if I COULD describe it to you. It's located at the intersection of North 35th Street and Fremont Place North. Dogs must be leashed. 3518 Fremont Place North; (206) 634-2733.

This little doggy went to market: Fremont Sunday Market's eclectic variety of goods should satisfy any shopping need. A partial list would include cashmere scarves, handicrafts, some farmer booths, blankets, jackets, a book booth with 70 percent savings, underwater housing for a camera, and a guy playing a saw. Quinn met Bailey at the fair and they had a good time. There are two Honey Buckets in the corner of the market, but no grass patch for dogs. 600 North 34th Street; (206) 282-5706.

SOUTHEAST

BEACON HILL, HOLLY PARK, AND MOUNT BAKER

PARKS, BEACHES, AND RECREATION AREAS

• **Genesee Park** 🐾 🐾 🐾 🐕 See **26** on page 20.

Grassy meadows make up the largest part of Genesee's 37 acres. Playgrounds are located in the southeast corner, and the leash-free dog area is fenced. At South Charlestown Street, the park connects with Mount Baker Park, located along more than two miles of Lake Washington shoreline. There are lots of options for the committed dog walker here. We even saw a woman walking her cat in the park's grasslands (someone should have told her Genesee is a leash-free area).

Genesee encompasses a great deal of open-field land. Rock and wet ground are being reclaimed as natural meadows and habitats. Emma and Quinn give this park a high rating, particularly for the scents in the meadow. The park is located at 45th Avenue South and South Genesee. (206) 684-8021.

• I-90 Blue Dog Pond 🐾 🐕 See **27** on page 20.

This is also called the I-90 Lid Drainage Area, left as an overflow drainage for heavy storms. Because of a great big blue steel cutout of a dog, it's also called Blue Dog Pond. It's one of the seven leash-free areas approved by the Seattle City Council, but the campaign's early choice was for the lovely park just on the other side of Martin Luther King, Jr. Way. The final choice is really nothing more than an odd sort of drainage ravine, gully actually, with large playful metal sculptures. It's not very big, and not very inviting, with most of the overgrown grasses and weeds about waist high. It could only be considered a destination park by the people who live nearby. Please note: There are no off-leash areas in I-90 Park, located just east of Blue Dog Pond. Owners with off-leash dogs in I-90 Park will be ticketed.

Blue Dog is located at Martin Luther King Jr. Way and South Massachusetts Street. (206) 684-8021.

• Jefferson Park 🐾 See **28** on page 20.

This is a very large park, primarily a public golf course and two lighted tennis courts. Dogs are OK around, but not on, the golf course. They must be leashed and you must scoop. Jefferson is bisected by Beacon Avenue South between South Spokane Street and South Alaska Street. (206) 684-8021.

• Martha Washington Park 🐾 See **29** on page 20.

Just south of the giant Seward Park on Lake Washington, this lovely, little waterfront park sits on the shoreline. Dogs aren't allowed on the beach, but they may frolic in the grassy, tree-filled area. Pups must be leashed.

The park is located at 57th Avenue South and South Holly Street. (206) 684-8021.

• Seward Park 🐾 🐾 🐾 🐾 🐕 See **30** on page 20.

The marvel with Seward Park is that here's a city park, a peninsula into Lake Washington actually, that is still home to some nesting eagles in the old growth trees. Don't tell the folks back home about it, or their dogs, or it will be inundated. It's already pretty busy because the Lake Washington Boulevard that gets you here is a highly favored cruising zone for the city's young people. Anti-cruising laws are strictly enforced supposedly, but there are a lot of people driving Seward Park's perimeter road. There are plenty of trails through the woods that take off from the drive, so it's easy to feel like you're alone with Beauty in the woods. Just park the vehicle, pick a trail, and go for it; there is no way to get lost on a peninsula. Park amenities include a bike path, swimming beach, fish rearing ponds, madrona trees (In the Northwest, madronas are amenities), and lots of nice covered picnic areas with barbecue stands. Seattle Parks packs a lot of park inside this 2.5-mile-circumference zone. This is a very high paw park, with chthonian trails. Chthonian pertains to the underworld, the deities below, and the humus above; dark, primitive, and mysterious. Leashes and scooping are required.

Seward Park is located at Lake Washington Boulevard South and South Orcas Street. (206) 684-8021.

SOUTHWEST

ALKI AND WEST SEATTLE

The neighborhoods of Georgetown, Alki, West Seattle, Delridge, Highland Park, and Fauntleroy are west of Interstate 5. All of these neighborhoods, with the exception of Georgetown, are also west of the Duwamish River.

PARKS, BEACHES, AND RECREATION AREAS

•Lincoln Park 🐾🐾 **See 31 on page 20.**
Located on Williams Point, this large park is just north of the Southworth and Vashon Island Ferry landing. The beach is pleasant, although there are no lifeguards and it's off-limits to dogs; the main canine attraction is Lincoln Park's trail system. Numerous trails head through large wooded areas toward the beach. Leashes are required.

Parking is available on the street adjacent to the wading pool, near the north end of the park. The central parking lot provides access to the woods and meadow, and the south parking lot brings you close to the shoreline.

From downtown Seattle, drive south on 1st Avenue past Safeco Field, home of the Seattle Mariners. Enter the West Seattle Freeway and proceed west. Follow signs to the Fauntleroy Way Southwest exit. Stay on Fauntleroy Way Southwest and proceed to the park, on your right. (206) 684-8021.

•Riverview Playfield 🐾🐾 **See 32 on page 20.**
Just south of South Seattle Community College and uphill from the Duwamish River, Riverview Playfield contains four softball fields, a football field, a soccer field, and a couple of tennis courts.

It serves as a neighborhood gathering area and a popular destination for runners. Riverview gives a great run for leashed beasts and their humans.

It's at the intersection of Southwest Myrtle Street and 12th Avenue Southwest. (206) 684-8021.

•Schmitz Preserve 🐾🐾🐾🐾 **See 33 on page 20.**
No human amenities are available at this 50-acre preserve, but dogs will love smelling the scent of 800-year-old trees. Emma and Quinn were on total sniff patrol around the western red cedars and hemlocks. A dog could almost forget there's a leashed collar around her neck. If you and your pooch go anywhere in West Seattle, visit Schmitz Preserve. Emma and Quinn's tails wagged wildly, letting us know that Schmitz is their favorite park.

Schmitz also includes a paved area along a big ravine, with a little stream down the middle. Leash and scoop is the law.

The park is accessible from Southwest Admiral Way at Southwest Stevens Street. (206) 684-8021.

•Westcrest Park 🐾🐾🐾 🐕 See **34** on page 20.

At Westcrest, you and your four-legged pal can picnic, walk the nature trails, and (on a clear day) look 80 miles north to Mount Baker, near the Canadian border. The dogs had lots of fun frolicking about on a clearing about the size of two football fields, all open grass, and gopher mounds. The park is pretty peaceful, except for the occasional airplane drone and a bit of traffic noise. Westcrest's leash-free area is located along the southern and western borders of the reservoir. The park entrance is on the corner of Henderson and Barton. (206) 684-8021.

RESTAURANTS

Cats Eye Café: Pups can dine with you at the outside tables, as long as they're not irritated by all of the café's cat memorabilia, cat photos, and cat books. The grilled focaccia sandwiches are yummy, but you and Fortuna may want to avoid the Cat in Heat Sandwich (grilled tuna with cheddar). The café, open from 6:30 A.M. to 7 P.M. daily, is near Lincoln Park. 7301 Bainbridge Place Southwest; (206) 935-2229.

Salty's on Alki: Dogs can enjoy the view from the deck of Salty's, a venerable Alki seafood institution. The deck normally closes in early October, so call ahead. Salty's keeps up with northwest food trends and tries to start a few of its own, like the Tuna Soft Taco, Caesar salad with crumbled salmon flakes, and honey-smoked halibut. Tell Phyllo to relax; dogfish is not on the menu. 1936 Harbor Avenue Southwest; (206) 923-0861.

PLACES TO STAY

Doubletree Hotel Seattle Airport: OK gang, this is the place. Dogs are allowed, and there are no restrictions and no limits. As they say at the front desk, common sense dictates that three or four dogs are a bit much. However, they don't bother trying to define what's big and what's little. Just bring the dog. They'll probably put you on a lower floor, for convenience, and there are a lot of convenience spots on their sprawling grounds. The Doubletree is big, with 850 rooms, and it's close to the airport. A free airport shuttle runs about every 15 minutes. Rates range from $109 to $159. (206) 246-8600.

Doubletree Inn Southcenter: Dogs are welcome at this Doubletree Inn, although you must pay a $50 deposit for your dog, refundable if your room checks out OK. You'll find some trails and a lake behind the buildings across the street. Rooms rates range from $109 to $159. The hotel is located just south of the Southcenter shopping mall. 205 Strander Boulevard; (206) 246-8220 or (800) 222-8733.

La Quinta Motor Inn Sea-Tac International: Dogs may stay at this La Quinta, and a room with a king-size bed may range in price from $94 to $114. 2824 South 188th Street; (206) 241-5211 or (800) 531-5900.

WHO IS A GOOD HOTEL GUEST?

A good guest makes a happy guest, but one is never sure just how to behave in the elegant surroundings of a four-star hotel. Fashions being what they are these days, as long as clothing covers the basic parts of your body, you're probably OK. Wear a coat to dinner though. As for behavior, one hotel offers some ideas:

- A good guest is interested in seeing everything.
- A good guest enjoys using the whole hotel, including tours, tea, dinner, and sitting rooms.
- A good guest treats the staff well.
- A good guest's hotel stay is but part of an extended holiday. The good guest is already relaxed, curious and ready to sightsee.
- A good guest understands, or wants to learn, the heritage of the hotel. The Fairmont Empress, for example, has one hundred different room layouts, and there are good reasons for that. Ask anyone about it—they love to explain.
- A good guest is an experienced and gracious person who knows the art of hotel travel. The good guest feels affiliated with the lifestyle.
- A good guest appreciates that in historic hotels, space is given to the common areas, not to individual bathrooms.
- A good guest finds a comfy chair in one of several sitting rooms, orders a brandy, and reads a book.

Motel 6 Sea-Tac Airport: Located near Seattle's airport, this Motel 6 accepts small dogs. The room rates range from $50 to $65. 16500 Pacific Highway South; (206) 246-4101 or (800) 466-8356.

Motel 6 Sea-Tac Airport South: Twelve miles from downtown Seattle, this Motel 6 says OK to small dogs. Room rates are $40. 18900 47th Avenue South; (206) 241-1648 or (800) 466-8356.

SEATTLE'S EASTSIDE

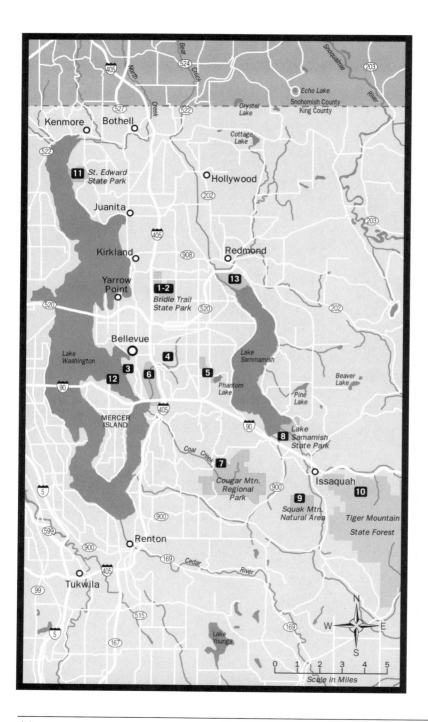

2
BELLEVUE

Known as the Southern California of Puget Sound, Eastside's Bellevue does indeed have a big slice of the lifestyle pie. Seattleites love to joke about people who live anywhere but Seattle, but they view Bellevueites with special alarm. That's because they live so close, and may be thieving in the night some of Seattle's best and brightest. Bellevue has a fine art museum, a symphony orchestra, a primo upscale shopping center, and restaurants that warrant attention in Seattle's newspapers. There's even a neighborhood called Beaux Arts.

Bellevue is bordered on two sides by lakes, Lake Washington to the west and Lake Sammamish to the east. The Eastside is actually Washington's largest concentration of people, but it's hard to see exactly where Bellevue ends and Kirkland and Redmond begin, just like Southern California.

PARKS, BEACHES, AND RECREATION AREAS

• Bridle Crest Trail 🐾 🐾 See ❶ on page 44.

Extending into a lovely corridor between Bridle Trails State Park (see below) and Redmond's Marymoor Park (see Redmond, page 51), Bridle Crest encompasses 13.2 acres. The trail parallels Northeast 60th Street for nearly two miles, and although it was designed for equestrians, it's great for a leisurely stroll with Bowser.

From downtown Bellevue, proceed north on I-405 and take exit 17. Turn right (south) on 116th Avenue Northeast and drive for one-half mile to Northeast 60th Street. Turn left (east) on Northeast 60th Street and continue for three-quarters of a mile to the Bridle Trails State Park entrance on your right. (206) 296-4281.

• Bridle Trails State Park 🐾 🐾 🐾 See ❷ on page 44.

This equestrian park has 28 miles of riding and hiking trails through Douglas fir country, right on the border with the city of Kirkland. You have to bring your own animal though. There are none for rent. But look carefully around the park perimeter. A lot of the residents have their own horses. Very convenient. Remember to keep Zeus on a leash. To get there take I-405 exit 17 (Northeast 70th Street). Go south immediately on the east side of I-405 for 10 blocks to Northeast 60th Street. It's right there on the corner. (800) 233-0321.

• Chism Beach Park 🐾 See ❸ on page 44.

Good swimming in chilly Lake Washington is something you may just want to watch, but there are plenty of trails and picnic areas in this park. Dogs may not be in the park during the summer, but they're welcome the rest of the year on a leash. It's located off 100th Avenue Southeast.

From Bellevue Square in downtown Bellevue, drive south on Bellevue Way Northeast, which becomes Bellevue Way Southeast when it crosses Main Street. Proceed on this street and turn right (west) on Southeast 16th Street. Drive approximately one-half mile on Southeast 16th Street and turn right (north) on 97th Place Southeast. The park entrance is approximately one-quarter mile up on your left. (425) 452-6881.

• Kelsey Creek Community Park 🐾🐾 See **4** on page 44.

With a Japanese garden, one-mile loop trail, children's zoo, and a 1888 pioneer log cabin. Bellevue prides itself on Kelsey Creek Park. Its 150 acres were once a dairy farm, and the two barns remain, along with the Frazer Cabin, the first permanent home in Bellevue, built in 1888. Bellevue Park's offices are in the renovated farmhouse. The park is open dawn to dusk, but the car gates close at 5 P.M. There are no park fees.

From the I-90/I-405 interchange east of Lake Washington, drive north on I-405. Take exit 12 to Southeast 8th Street. At the exit ramp stoplight, turn right (east). Proceed through two stoplights, past the Lake Hills Connector; Southeast 8th Street becomes Southeast 7th Place. Continue to the stop sign at 128th Avenue Southeast. Turn left (north) and then right (east) on Southeast 4th Place. Follow the road into the park. (425) 452-6881.

• Lake Hills Greenbelt 🐾🐾 See **5** on page 44.

This 1.5-mile trail links Larsen and Phantom Lakes. Lake Hills Greenbelt is open to joggers, hikers, cyclists, wheelchair-users, and leashed dogs. The park is located at the intersection of 156th Avenue Southeast and Southeast 16th Street. (425) 452-6881.

• Mercer Slough Nature Park 🐾🐾 See **6** on page 44.

Right in the center of Bellevue, this park has 48 acres of trails and marshlands on the Mercer Slough, and leashed dogs are welcome. The perimeter loop is one mile around. Mercer Slough's boardwalks enable you to get close to the wildlife, but look out for the coyotes—keep a tight hold on the leash. Its location is 118th Street Southeast in Bellevue, with parking on Bellevue Way near I-90. From Bellevue Square in downtown Bellevue, drive south on Bellevue Way Northeast and turn left (east) on Main Street. Just before I-405, turn right (south) on 114th Avenue Southeast, which eventually becomes 118th Avenue Southeast after it crosses Southeast 8th Street. You'll see the sign for Mercer Slough Nature Park on the right. (425) 452-6881.

PLACES TO STAY

Doubletree Hotel—Bellevue Center: There is a $20 doggy fee required at this 208-room Doubletree Hotel, and only small dogs are allowed. It has an outdoor pool and two restaurants. Rates range from $89 to $155. 818 112th Avenue Northeast; (425) 455-1515.

WestCoast Bellevue Hotel: Small, leashed dogs are allowed at this hotel, but they must not be left unattended in the room. There is no pet fee, but WestCoast asks that you pay with a credit card in case pet-related damages need to be added to your bill. Room rates range from $129 to $169. 625 116th Avenue Northeast; (425) 455-9444 or (800) 426-0670.

FESTIVALS

Pacific Northwest Arts and Crafts Fair: Dogs are welcome at this fun fair, held every year on the last weekend of July. The fair is located at Bellevue Square at the corner of Northeast 8th Street and Bellevue Way. (425) 454-3129 (fax only).

ISSAQUAH

Coal mining and logging had Issaquah booming by the turn of the 20th century, but now at the beginning of the 21st, it's noted for being at the foot of "Issaquah Alps." They are within a half-hour drive of Seattle. There are over 200 miles of trails in these alps, a range that's actually older than the Cascades. The three peaks are on Tiger, Cougar, and Squak Mountains. What was once pastoral land below the mountains is now a busy suburban-style metropolis.

PARKS, BEACHES, AND RECREATION AREAS

• King County Cougar Mountain Regional Wildland Park 🐾 🐾 🐾
See **7** on page 44.

The 2,800-acre Cougar Mountain Regional Wildland Park is King County's largest recreation area. Despite its size, the park only offers five picnic tables and one restroom. Cougar Mountain (elevation 1,595 feet) is surrounded by dense forest and 50 miles of crisscrossing trails; it's the westernmost remnant of a mountain range running from Lake Washington to the Cascades. Your dog is welcome in the park, but keep in mind that the park is appropriately named: cougars (in addition to bear, deer, porcupines, bobcats, and weasels) live here. Leashing and scooping are required. Mountain bikes are not allowed.

From Seattle, drive east on I-90 to exit 13. Turn right on Southeast Newport Way. Proceed on Southeast Newport Way to 164th Avenue and turn left (south). Turn right and climb the hill for 1.7 miles to the Lakemont Boulevard junction. At the junction, turn right on Lakemont Boulevard and continue for 1.4 miles. The Red Town trailhead is on the left side of the road. (206) 296-4281.

• Lake Sammamish State Park 🐾 🐾 See **8** on page 44.

This popular day-use area offers access to giant Lake Sammamish, which is about 1.5 miles wide and 10 miles long. Boating and water-skiing are very popular here, and the lake is frequently warm enough for swimming. The well-maintained hiking and jogging trails are heavily used, too. Leashed dogs are allowed in the park, but not on the swimming beach. If you have a salmon terrier who wants to branch out, the lake has plenty of trout, bass, and panfish.

From Seattle, drive east on I-90 and take exit 15. Follow park signs for about one-quarter mile to the park. (425) 455-7010 or (800) 233-0321.

• Squak Mountain State Park 🐾 🐾 🐾 See **9** on page 44.

The top of Squak Mountain belongs to King County, but much of the rest of it belongs to Washington State. Even though it's technically a state park, it has no staff and it's not listed in state park directories. By default, it's considered

---

to be a satellite park of Lake Sammamish State Park, whose staff does the occasional honors. The main recreations on Squak Mountain are hiking and horseback riding. It's the smallest of the three Alps, but it's still about a square mile. There are no restrooms or water, and no trailhead parking to speak of. There are three trailheads and more are in the planning stages. Dogs are welcome, and leashing is required, especially since you may encounter black bears, cougars, and porcupines. Scooping is also mandatory.

From Seattle, drive east on I-90 and take exit 15. Turn right (south) on State Highway 900 (also known as the Renton-Issaquah Road and Southeast 17th Avenue Northwest). Proceed on State Highway 900 to Newport Way and turn left (east). Take Newport Way to Southeast Newport Way and turn right (south). Stay on Southeast Newport Way until you reach Mountain Park Boulevard Southwest and then turn right (southwest). Continue on Mountain Park Boulevard Southwest; then turn left (southwest) on Mountainside Drive Southwest. The trailhead is at the end of the road. (206) 296-4232 or (800) 233-0321.

• **Tiger Mountain State Forest** 🐾🐾🐾 See 🔟 on page 44.
The hundred-odd miles of trails in this 13,000-acre forest that rises to the southeast of Issaquah favor hikers, mountain bikers, and equestrians. You'll want a leash handy, especially since leashing is required here and the park is pretty heavily used. The forest contains three mountains actually, East Tiger, South Tiger, and West Tiger Mountains. The east peak is the highest, at 3,004 feet. The most logical hike is the 6.9-miler up East Side Road to the summit. The views are refreshing, even on cloudy days, because you don't climb into the clouds. The state Department of Natural Resources got this land through a swap with Weyerhauser, and it did some cleaning up of the old railroad rights of way and abandoned logging equipment. It even recreated the view from Poo Poo Point on the south side of the mountain. Did I mention that this is a great place for dogs? Don't neglect to stoop 'n' scoop. Poo Poo Point is one of the best hang gliding spots in western Washington. Park visitors must enter Tiger Mountain State Forest on foot; cars are not allowed within the forest boundaries.

From Seattle, proceed east on I-90 to Issaquah exit 20. Take an immediate right (south) on 270th Avenue Southeast, and take another quick turn right (west) on Southeast 79th Street. Drive on Southeast 79th Street to any of the several parking spots along the road or in the turnaround. (360) 825-1631.

PLACES TO STAY
Motel 6 Seattle/Issaquah: Dogs weighing 20 pounds or less are allowed at this Motel 6, just one mile from Lake Sammamish State Park. One pet per room, please. Rates are about $64 for two. 1885 15th Place Northwest; (425) 392-8405 or (800) 466-8356.

Salish Lodge at Snoqualmie Falls: You won't find many countryside inns more pleasant than the Salish Lodge. In a *Condé Nast Traveler* magazine readers' poll, Salish Lodge was rated as the country's 18th—and the world's 56th—best lodge. Even the ample grounds bespeak leisurely strolls in the more relaxed days of yore. And then there is Snoqualmie Falls, a wonder of

Mother Nature's engineering skills. Some of the Salish rooms have quite a view of the falls. This is the land of "Twin Peaks," the haunting movie and TV series. Dogs, of course, are entirely welcome. They stay on the first floor, very convenient, and there is a $50 nonrefundable fee. There is no size restriction. "But we like to know ahead of time so we can prepare." Room rates range from $259 to $409. Suites cost $899. (425) 888-2556 or (800) 826-6124.

FESTIVALS

Issaquah Salmon Festival: Nearly a quarter million people celebrate the return of the spawning salmon to the lakes, streams, and downtown Issaquah hatchery, at the intersection of Front and Sunset Streets. The annual date to remember is the first full weekend of October. This family-style event has arts and crafts booths, foods from around the world cooked before your very eyes, a children's activity area, live entertainment, pancake breakfast, and a who-would-believe-it salmon bake. It's a great fest for salmon terriers, but there are dogs of all kinds. The nice woman who allows dogs says, "Most dogs are better behaved than my two-year-old grandson, and he gets to come, so why wouldn't dogs?" The pups do need to be socialized to crowds, however, and make sure to bring ample water for Spot. It can get into the 80s and there are not many spigots.

As a matter of curiosity, saber-toothed salmon are known to have lived in the Vancouver Island area 80 million years ago. An amateur digger discovered their fossil remains in 1995. These salmon had twin fangs that were up to two inches long, probably used for defensive protection and biting through shells to nibble the inside delicacies. Were these the first canines? (425) 392-0661.

KIRKLAND

Kirkland appears to be a maze of malls, mallettes, and condo-mania. The old sleepy relaxed atmosphere of entitled Eastside living still exists downtown though, in a business and arts district that feels much like California's Laguna Beach. Some parks along the Kirkland waterfront do not welcome dogs because of the swimming beaches and manicured strips of grass. A sign in Waverley Beach Park announces the bad news: "For the safety of park users, no dogs shall be permitted within any waterfront parks between June 1 and October 1."

PARKS, BEACHES, AND RECREATION AREAS

• **Saint Edward State Park** 🐾🐾 See **11** on page 44.

Located on the grounds of a former seminary, Saint Edward is a large day-use park on northeast Lake Washington. Leashed dogs are permitted, except on designated swimming beaches. Hiking, fitness, and equestrian trails wind throughout the park's generous boundaries. Salmon, trout, and bass fishing are available.

From Seattle, take State Highway 522 (Lake City Way Northeast, which becomes Bothell Way and then Bothell Way Northeast) through the town of Lake Forest Park. About one mile past lake Forest Park, turn right (south) onto

69th Avenue Northeast. Drive for just over 1.5 miles (the road becomes Juanita Drive) to the park entrance on the right, which is Northeast 145th Street. (425) 823-2992 or (800) 233-0321.

PLACES TO STAY

Motel 6 Seattle/Kirkland: Pooches weighing 25 pounds or less are always welcome at this motel, which is about two miles from a 60-acre soccer field. Rooms cost $60 for a single in the high season and $50 in the low season. 12010 120th Place Northeast; (425) 821-5618.

DIVERSIONS

Cow and dog: On a downtown city sidewalk is a bigger than life-size, uh, rendering of a cow with a dog on a its back. The display is at the corner of Lake Street and Central Way. Across the street in front of the Cafe Appassionato are some huge bronze bunnies, much bigger than Emma and Quinn.

    Pedals & Paws Kids Bike & Dog Parade: All participants—costumed bicycle-riding kids, pets, and adults—get treats in this parade. It takes place on a late September afternoon at Peter Kirk Park, 202 3rd Street; (425) 822-7066.

MERCER ISLAND

In an early Olmsted Brothers' proposal (the sons of Frederick Law Olmsted, who designed Central Park in New York), the entirety of Mercer Island was to be the central jewel and anchor of a Seattle-area park system. Voters turned down the grand scheme, but there is one fine park for dogs on the northern tip of this beautiful residential island in the middle of Lake Washington.

PARKS, BEACHES, AND RECREATION AREAS

• Luther Burbank Park 🐾🐾🐾🐾 🐕 See **12** on page 44.

This park provides an off-leash exercise area, although voice control is required at all times. Keep an eye out for the no-pet zones, too.

    The leash-free area is a short stroll past the amphitheater, left of the north parking lot. The boundaries of the free-run area are set by corral-type fencing, and this section of the park is not particularly large. The best part is the swimming access to the lake. It's a low bank that's been muddied away by frisky paws, and below it is a narrow strip of sandy beach. Humans could probably swim here too, but we saw only dogs in the water. And happy dogs they were too.

    Here are the rules governing the leash-free exercise area:

1) Respect other park visitors by keeping your dog from jumping on, or interfering with, other people and their dogs. Off-leash does not mean out of control.

2) You are required by law to pick up your dog's feces and dispose of them in the trashcans located throughout the leash-free area. Bags are provided.

3) Keep your dog on leash in all other areas of the park. By law, dogs must be on leash in King County parks, with the exception of designated dog exercise areas.

At the park's picnic area there was one scene I'll never forget. A woman with two kids set out a picnic lunch on a table near the playground. The two kids, who were not under voice control, tore off toward the lakeshore. Mom went yelling and running after them, but she wasn't more than 20 feet from the table when a murder of crows descended on the table. She stopped at the squawking, looked back, looked at her kids, muttered an oath, and ran for the kids. We, of course, never have such problems with the granddogs, but then lunch for Emma and Quinn doesn't require much preparation.

Great sport for the pups in this park is chasing the squealing orange pumpkin toy, which they seem to think is a rat. They brought snarls and yips and tugs-of-war to the chase. Jaws clamped tightly, Emma and Quinn together race the rat back to my wife Lynn, and it squeals through its whistle with every step they take. Lynn was their best audience of the month; she didn't stop laughing until we got halfway home.

From Seattle, take I-90 east to exit 7A. At the top of the ramp, turn left onto the 77th Avenue Southeast overpass. At the stop sign, turn right on North Mercer Way. Drive one long block to the stoplight. Proceed through the stoplight and turn left on 81st Avenue Southeast. Drive one block to the next stop sign, turn right on Southeast 24th Street, and continue for two long blocks to the intersection of 84th Avenue Southeast. Turn left to reach the park. (206) 296-4232.

RESTAURANTS

Tully's: Tully's is located right next to the Mercer Island I-90 Outdoor Sculpture Gallery, on your way to and from Luther Burbank Park. There are ten fun sculptures, and most of them are for sale. Prices range from $3,200 to $18,000. There's the Wizard, Tuning Fork, and Symphony in Stone. A lot of people stop here in the morning for a fine espresso and maybe a muffin. The counter woman brought out a bowl of water, which Quinn, in his usual leashed anxiety, dumped over. So she brought out another bowl of water, but placed it more strategically. Tully's is a very nice stop, and the espressos were excellent. The freeway noise was a bit much for Emma, so she retreated to the car. But once she saw Quinn and Grandma Lynn enjoying the sculpture garden she joined them lickety split. You and your pooch can munch together at the outside tables. This is another place where Quinn saved us from a dreadful monstrous threat, this time from a chrome-plated trashcan at the front door. He's never barked at mirrors before, but this distorted image of himself, stretched wide and tall, made him realize he needed to protect us from the unlikely looking furry beast barking back at him. He chased it around the side a few times, but it was always there barking back. As you might expect, it was a standoff, as it turned away when Quinn did. So all was well once again. Tully's is open every day. 7810 Southeast 27th Street; (206) 236-2959.

REDMOND

PARKS, BEACHES, AND RECREATION AREAS

• **Marymoor Park** 😊 😊 😊 😊 🐕 See **13** on page 44.

Get ready for bounding dogs. Marymoor Park is over 500 acres of what an ideal world would be like. It has an art museum, an Indian archaeological site, a mansion on the National Register of Historic Places, a windmill, a par course, a model airplane area, the only velodrome in the Northwest, a pea patch, and—are you ready for this?—44 leash-free acres consisting of tufted fields, Sammamish riverfront, and wide trails. Way back in the 1950s, when Marymoor was still private property, dog trials were held here. Today, nearly one-third of the park users come over from Seattle.

The bulletin board at the entrance to the leash-free area is swamped with notices and lost collars, plus a few leashes. "$100 reward for return of class ring; lost on the dog run . . . ." "Lost: brown retriever/husky mix . . . ." "My wife and dog both died, so if you would like a new friend, call Jim at . . . ."

The leash-free riverfront area of King County's Marymoor Park is clearly one of the best playground for dogs in the entire Northwest. A 10-to-20-foot-wide walk/runway parallels nearly a mile of the Sammamish River as it slowly and grudgingly gives up its waters to Lake Sammamish at the end of the trail.

Rules for the Marymoor Park leash-free exercise area are exactly the same as those in Luther Burbank Park on Mercer Island. I especially like the notice that says, "Expect to come upon dogs running free under voice control of their owners. If you are uncomfortable in the presence of unleashed dogs, maybe you could go somewhere else."

There are distinctly different hierarchies of dogs who use Marymoor Park. The fun-loving romping types embrace water sports. They retrieve sticks, logettes, tennis balls, neon orange things, and each other from the placid river waters. The serious working stiffs, the hounds, put in their time in the fields. They're far enough away to be hidden in all the brush, but you can see their handlers gesticulating and running about. I suspect the hounds are in charge of the training that goes on, but it's hard to tell. It's a bit of a surprise that more species of birds have moved into the leash-free area of the park, including an eagle, some owls, and ducks.

I've been told of people who have met through their dogs at parks like this and ended up getting married. I can believe it. Dogs are complete icebreakers at places like Marymoor. Northwest dog behaviorist September Morn says that one-third of dog owners value their dogs for their social lubricant value. They ease the stress of socializing. Another third have dogs to help avoid socializing. They have the type of dog that causes other people to shy away. The rest of dog owners simply like dogs. Any "guard dog" type dogs, and their owners, are politely ostracized and discouraged from coming back to parks like Marymoor.

There's a sort of beach, Beaver Beach, halfway along the river, where most of the stick throwing and socializing goes on. We didn't come well toyed, so Emma and Quinn kept scarfing other dogs' sticks and stuff. But nobody seemed to mind. Everybody throws and every dog chases. To control beach erosion, a wide set of steps was installed to get from the trail to the water. It does the job, but it also creates a problem for some older dogs with arthritis—they can't navigate the steps. If a dog owner can't carry her 130-pounder down the steps, they're both out of luck. Maybe it's time to consider a Dogs with Disabilities Act.

The leash-free stroll is a great opportunity to show off the finer breeds of dogdom. We spoke with a woman who'd been bringing her Afghans to Marymoor for 20 years. She usually raises two at a time, but presently was down to just one. But what a one! It was a beauty of astounding proportions, but Quinn and Emma didn't seem to notice.

The leash-free area is accessible via the main park road, which passes park offices and the museum. Follow the right fork of the road past the picnic area to the leash-free-area parking lot.

Marymoor Park's address is 6046 West Lake Sammamish Parkway Northeast. From Seattle and I-5, drive east on State Highway 520. Take the Lake Sammamish Parkway Northeast exit, and turn right at the first stoplight. Drive one more block and then turn left at the light. (206) 296-2964.

EVERETT AND VICINITY

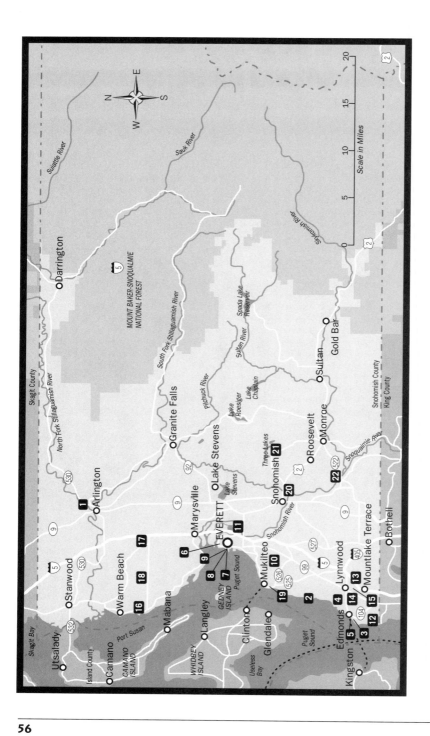

3
EVERETT AND VICINITY

You wouldn't know it from cruising along I-5 in your car, but the countryside north of Seattle is riddled with lakes, rivers, and Puget Sound coastline. In between the shores of Puget Sound and the foothills of the Cascades, you and your dog will find plenty of room to roam. Luckily, especially for residents of the Everett area, many Seattleites consider this too far to venture for a day of fun (the Snohomish County line is but 12 miles north of Seattle). That leaves the locals and a few of the rest of us adventurous types free to enjoy the 6,861 acres of Snohomish County parklands, not to mention the national forests and city parks. The coast is lined with railroad tracks and a parallel (ungroomed) trail from park to park along beaches that vary from sand dunes to rocky beach and craggy bluffs. Dog owners should keep in mind that although leashes and scooping are not necessarily required at all beaches, courtesy to other users should be a rule of thumb.

ARLINGTON

The Wild West isn't so wild around the Cascade foothills town of Arlington these days. Logging has been reined in and property owners can no longer divert the flows of their own streams. But the town, which sits at the confluence of the North and South Forks of the Stillaguamish River, is the economic center of the region's dairy and truck farming industries, even though there are fewer than 5,000 residents.

The town, three miles east of I-5 exit 208, is the westernmost town on the Mountain Loop, an 86-mile round-trip drive around the Boulder River Wilderness within the Mt. Baker-Snoqualmie National Forest. The popular route follows a horseshoe-shaped loop along several rivers and over a mountain pass. The forest is so thick that parts of it feel like you're driving through a green tunnel. These trees are second- and third-growth western hemlock, Douglas fir, western red cedar, black cottonwood, red alder, vine and bigleaf maple, plus some Sitka spruce. The loop is a good three-hour drive. From Arlington itself, fishers and hikers can access a wonder of woodsy opportunities.

PARKS, BEACHES, AND RECREATION AREAS

• Twin Rivers Park 🐾 🐾 🐾 See ➊ on page 56.

Located on a gorgeous section of the South Fork of the Stillaguamish River, 36-acre Twin Rivers Park offers fishing, swimming, and tubing. No one would recommend tubing out loud except the people who do it, and you wouldn't want to tube with a dog anyway. Plenty of trails course through the woods and along the rivers, but keep the pups leashed and please scoop. The North Fork joins the South Fork near the park's western edge.

To get to Twin Rivers Park from I-5, take exit 208 and head east on Highway 530 through Arlington. As you cross the Stillaguamish River, look for the entrance at Park Road on the left (west) side of the highway. (425) 338-6600.

PLACES TO STAY

Smokey Point Motor Inn: Dogs are welcome at the Smokey Point, for an $8 per-night charge. Room rates range from $52 to $57 for two people. Two-story units with kitchens cost $95. It's near I-5 exit 206 at 17329 Smokey Point Drive; (360) 659-8561.

EDMONDS

PARKS, BEACHES, AND RECREATION AREAS

The Edmonds waterfront is host to a fine mix of recreational possibilities. Just get yourself to the vicinity of the ferry terminal, park the rig, leash up, and walk around. There are some cautions, however. Edmonds has struck a compromise between dog walkers and dog avoiders, with the result that on one part of the waterfront dogs may run free, but they are not allowed at all on the rest of the waterfront. Walking your leashed dog on sidewalks is OK, but not in the downtown city and waterfront parks.

•Picnic Point Park 😾😾😾 See ❷ on page 56.

This park is halfway between Edmonds and Mukilteo, and the beach walk extends north five miles to Mukilteo State Park along bluffs, scattered homes, creeks, and gulches. It's the perfect setting for walking Gambolina (on a leash, of course), not to mention picnicking, beachcombing, and viewing the Olympic Mountains. The water is freezing, well, maybe 55°F or so in the summer, but some dogs love to jump in. The park provides excellent disabled access to the beach and picnic area.

To get to Picnic Point, take I-5 exit 182 west onto I-405/Highway 525. Continue for three miles to Highway 99 and turn left (south). In a quarter mile turn right (west) onto Shelby Road. Go for a bit over a mile and then turn right (northwest) onto Picnic Point Road and go downhill to the beach parking area. (425) 388-6600.

•South Marina Park 😾😾😾 🐕 See ❸ on page 56.

If you're looking for a great place to let your dog romp and fetch sticks from the water without getting in the way of other waterfront users, try this beachfront south of the Edmonds Marina. Leashes are not required.

From downtown Edmonds, take Dayton Street to the pier and turn left (south) onto Admiral Way South. The park is located at the southernmost end of Admiral Way South. (425) 771-0230.

•Southwest County Park 😾😾 See ❹ on page 56.

Olympic View Drive runs through this park west of Lynnwood. It's actually more of a pre-park, since it's mostly undeveloped. But there are some terrific hilly trails through the dense woods. One is a nice loop trail, and the other one parallels Olympic View Drive. Southwest Park is open dawn to dusk; leashes are mandatory.

To get there from I-5, take exit 179 and drive west on 220th Street Southwest. Continue past Pacific Highway (Highway 99) for one block and turn right (north) onto 76th Avenue West. In two miles, 76th Avenue intersects with Olympic View Drive. Turn left (west) and very shortly you will be in the park. (425) 388-6600.

•Sunset Beach Park 🐾🐾🐾 🐕 See **5** on page 56.

This park is adjacent to the Edmonds Ferry Dock to the north and the beach walk extends north six miles to Picnic Point Park, past a fishing pier, Meadowdale Beach Park, and Norma Beach. Don't forget to bring fresh water for your buddy, who must be leashed. (Parking at Sunset Beach Park is restricted to four hours, but park south of the ferry dock for longer walks.) Take Highway 104 west from I-5 to the Edmonds Ferry Dock. (425) 388-6600.

PLACES TO STAY

Edmonds Harbor Inn: Small dogs are allowed here near the waterfront for $10/night on top of the room rate that ranges from $79 to $169. 130 West Dayton; (425) 771-5021 or (800) 441-8033.

K & E Motor Inn: One small dog (20 pounds or less) per room is OK at the K & E, and if the owner's in a good mood, you might be able to get the nod for allowing two dogs in a room. The cost for two people, one bed, is $58, and one pup will run you another $5 per night. 23921 Highway 99; (425) 778-2181.

FESTIVALS

Edmonds Summer Market: Market day is Saturday in downtown Edmonds during July, August, and September. Well-behaved dogs on leashes are welcome. (425) 775-5650.

EVERETT

On a peninsula between Port Gardner Bay and the Snohomish River, Everett is home to 70,000 people as well as seven ships (it's a U.S. Navy home port), including the *USS Abraham Lincoln.* It's another in a long list of northwest cities and towns that was promoted back east as an important industry and railroad town. For Everett, the publicity worked. It's now also home to Boeing and the second-largest marina on the West Coast. There's an Amtrak station here, too. Dogs are permitted in all parks, but they must be on a leash and their companions are asked to scoop.

PARKS, BEACHES, AND RECREATION AREAS

•American Legion Memorial Park 🐾 See **6** on page 56.

The Everett Area Arboretum within this park houses a collection of native and exotic trees and plants. Leashed dogs are welcome.

From downtown Everett, drive north on Broadway and turn left (west) onto East Marine View Drive. The park is located where East Marine View Drive becomes West Marine View Drive, near the mouth of the Snohomish River. (425) 259-0300.

• Forest Park 🐾🐾 See **7** on page 56.

This 111-acre park is the city of Everett's largest and perhaps most beautiful. During the Depression, WPA workers created a tree and shrub garden reminiscent of what you'd see in merry ol' England. They neglected to include a maze of shrubs, however, so you can't really perform a serious check of Bowser's tracking skills. The workers also cleared some of the land and created several trails (keep your dog leashed, please).

Head south on Broadway in downtown Everett and then right (west) onto 41st Street, which becomes East Mukilteo Boulevard. The park is at 802 East Mukilteo Boulevard. (425) 259-0300.

• Grand Avenue Park 🐾 See **8** on page 56.

Boasting a sweeping view of Everett's waterfront, 3.5-acre Grand Avenue Park was originally designed to overlook the industrial "smokestack city" at the turn of the 20th century. Most of the smokestacks are gone, but you will get a great view of Puget Sound, Jetty Island, and the Everett Marina. Be sure to keep the leash on while enjoying the scenery.

From downtown Everett, go north on Rucker Avenue to 23rd Street. Turn left (west), then, after one block, right (north) onto West Marine View Drive. The park is at the intersection of West Marine View Drive and Grand Avenue. (425) 259-0300.

• Howarth Park 🐾🐾🐾 See **9** on page 56.

The lower part of this 28-acre park is a natural marsh and wetland habitat, while the upper portion has fine trails and picnic areas. Keep in mind that these woods hid moonshine stills until at least Prohibition. Don't forget to leash and scoop.

Take Rucker Avenue in downtown Everett south to 41st Street. Turn right (west) and after three blocks turn left (south) onto West Mukilteo Boulevard. Turn right (north) onto Olympic Boulevard and drive to the park, at 1127 Olympic Boulevard. (425) 259-0300.

• Interurban Trail 🐾 See **10** on page 56.

Like the Interurban Trail in Whatcom County, this paved path was part of the trolley route that ran between Ballard and Everett for a good part of the 20th century. Everett's eight miles of trail has power lines overhead, but it's paved for walkers, bikers, and joggers, and, of course, leashed dogs. The trail runs pretty much beside I-5 and crosses several intersections, but a good point to access it is where it intersects a bike trail at East Casino Road and 84th Street Southeast.

From I-5, take exit 189 and head east on Highway 526. Take the Evergreen Way exit and turn left (south) onto Evergreen Way. Shortly after making that exit, turn a sharp left (northeast) onto Holly Drive. Just before it passes under Highway 526, turn right (south) at 7th Avenue Southeast. Park at either the Cascade High School parking lot, one block north of the trailhead, or at the Emerson Elementary School lot, one block south. (425) 259-0300.

• Lowell Riverfront Trail 🐾🐾 See **11** on page 56.

This 1.6-mile section of riverfront trail is part of the effort to connect Seattle,

Everett, King County, and Snohomish County by a trail system for hikers, bikers, and joggers. Canine friends are welcome, of course, but they must be leashed. Industries that have traditionally controlled waterfront property throughout Puget Sound are releasing their grasp and joining civic and government groups to enable everybody to enjoy the waterfront, in many cases for the first time in more than 100 years. The Lowell Riverfront section is a 10-foot-wide paved path that begins near Rotary Park in the south and runs to the northern end at the edge of a protected wetlands area near the Burlington Northern Railroad crossing. To start at the southern end, go south on Broadway from downtown Everett and turn east (left) onto 52nd Street. After you cross under I-5, it becomes Lowell Road, which in turn becomes Lowell River Road at Rotary Park, the start point. (425) 259-0300.

PLACES TO STAY

Holiday Inn Everett: Another hound-hospitable inn. This one sits right alongside the freeway. Rates for two people start at $89, with a $50 nonrefundable pet fee per stay. The neighboring Snohomish County Visitor Information Center has a knowledgeable staff and one of the best selections of travel brochures on Puget Sound. 101 128th Street Southeast; (425) 337-2900.

Motel 6 Everett North: Motel 6 doesn't mind if guests show up at the front desk with a small dog (less than 30 pounds) and a pile of luggage. This particular establishment is 25 minutes north of Seattle. Two people cost about $52; the pup stays for free. 10006 Evergreen Way; (425) 347-2060 or (800) 466-8356.

Motel 6 Everett South: Small dogs (again, those weighing in at less than 30 pounds) are welcome here, too. The cost for two people is $57, and there's no extra charge for the pet. 224 128th Street Southwest; (425) 353-8120 or (800) 466-8356.

LYNNWOOD

Lynnwood, with myriad strip malls, shopping centers, apartment complexes, and auto rows, looks a lot like Southern California 20 years ago. Everyone's on the move in Lynnwood, and nearly all of them get around by car. This would be OK except for the fact that I-5 did for Lynnwood just what it did for every other Puget Sound city it went through: bisected it with too few ways over or under the freeway. Happily though, away from the hustle and bustle of the freeway and Highway 99 corridors, Lynnwood is delightful, relaxed, hilly, and green. Forget shortcuts, though, since most streets don't go through.

PARKS, BEACHES, AND RECREATION AREAS

• **Lynndale Park** 🐾 🐾 See **12** on page 56.

This 37-acre park features an amphitheater and some pleasant trails that zigzag through the woods. Dogs must be leashed, and scooping is required. The park closes at dusk.

To get there from I-5, take exit 179 and drive west on 220th Street Southwest. Continue past Pacific Highway (Highway 99) for one block and turn right (north) onto 76th Avenue West. In two miles, 76th Avenue West intersects with

Olympic View Drive, where you will turn right (east). The park entrance is at the intersection of Olympic View Drive and 72nd Avenue West. (425) 771-4030.

•Lynnwood Interurban Trail 🐾 See **13** on page 56.

Another section of the route originally traversed by train until 1939, the Lynnwood Interurban Trail begins just north of Alderwood Mall in Lynnwood and continues south to the intersection of 196th Street Southwest and 37th Avenue West, basically along the western side of I-5. Dogs must be leashed and scooping is required.

The I-5/196th Street Southwest interchange is a good access point. The trail begins one block west of the freeway at 37th Avenue West. (425) 771-4030.

•Lynnwood Municipal Golf Course 🐾🐾🐾 See **14** on page 56.

No, no. Don't go here to play golf. What you and Mercuria want is the trail that goes around the 75-acre course. It's a soft chip trail replete with forest scents to last a daytime. The path is not exactly a loop, unless you go through the college campus or around it on the sidewalk. Most people do an out-and-back, making it about a mile's excursion. Dogs must stay leashed and you are required to scoop. The golf course itself is very much off-limits. The trail closes at dusk.

To reach Lynnwood Municipal Golf Course from I-5, take the 196th Street Southwest exit and head west. Turn left (south) onto 68th Avenue West until you reach Edmonds Community College's Lynnwood Campus. The course is behind the campus, at 20200 68th Avenue West. (425) 771-4030.

•Scriber Lake Park 🐾🐾 See **15** on page 56.

There's nothing like a lake with a park around it within a stone's throw of a shopping center, and Scriber is a very nice one. It's 20 acres, with plenty of trails to amuse Olfactoria. The half-mile raised walkway around the lake turns into a floating boardwalk (keep leashed, especially if you have a duck terrier) that takes you out onto the lake. The park closes at dusk.

To get to Scriber Lake Park from I-5, exit at 196th Street Southwest and head west. Just before Highway 99, turn left (south) onto Scriber Lake Road, which runs behind the Lynnwood Shopping Center. After one block, turn left (west) onto Scriber Lake Street Southwest, and you've reached the park, at 5322 198th Street Southwest. (425) 771-4030.

PLACES TO STAY

Best Western Lynnwood North Seattle: Small dogs can spend the night here for an extra charge of $10 per day. A room for two people in the peak summer season costs about $75. 4300 200th Street Southwest; (425) 775-7447.

Homestead Village Guest Studios North Seattle: Homestead Village is actually in Mountlake Terrace (I-5 exit 177), just north of the county line from Seattle. Dogs are welcome (no size restrictions) for $75 per stay. All units are efficiencies, designed for extended stays. Nightly costs are $57 for a single and $62 for two. Weekly stays are $325 (single) and $340 (double). 6017 244th Street Southwest; (425) 771-3139.

The Residence Inn by Marriott: Centrally located to as much shopping as you could ever hope for, this Residence Inn welcomes you and Rover to its all-suite lodgings. Breakfast and evening snacks are complimentary, and there's a Keg restaurant next door. The Residence has three spas and an outdoor pool. Suite rates range between $155 and $205, plus $10 per night for each dog (there is a two-pet maximum). 18200 Alderwood Mall Parkway; (425) 771-1100.

MARYSVILLE

Named by two settlers from Marysville, California, this town started as a trading post to serve the Tulalip Indian Reservation. It sits on a fertile floodplain, so farmers prospered once they drained and diked the fields.

PARKS, BEACHES, AND RECREATION AREAS

•Kayak Point Park 🐾🐾🐾 See **16** on page 56.

This 428-acre Snohomish County park gets pretty close to being dog heaven. It's mostly wooded and it has a beach, so there is plenty of (leashed) roaming to be done. It's on the southern end of Susan Bay, which is one of the most productive estuaries on Puget Sound, lush in its mix of organic matter on which intertidal animals thrive. The park has a 300-foot fishing pier. Keep an eye out for gray whales, which sometimes come within 100 feet of the pier. Don't forget your kayak, and you can try your hand at clam digging, or if you've got clam terriers, let them give it a try. For camping, there are nine tent sites and 23 RV sites, open year-round; rates are $14.

From I-5, take the Marysville exit 199 and proceed west on Tulalip-Marine Drive. Continue for 14 miles through the Tulalip Indian Reservation. The entrance to Kayak Point Park is on your left. (425) 388-6600.

•Twin Lakes Park 🐾 See **17** on page 56.

The two lakes in this 44-acre park beside I-5 fill up with swimmers in summer. There are some good meandering trails in the adjacent woods, but dogs must be leashed.

From I-5 north of Marysville, take exit 206 and turn west onto 172nd Street Northeast. Continue for one-quarter of a mile to 27th Avenue Northeast. Bear left (south) on 27th Avenue Northeast. Turn left again (east) onto 169th Street Northeast, then bear right (south) and drive one mile to the park entrance on the right. (425) 388-6600.

•Wenberg State Park 🐾🐾 See **18** on page 56.

On Lake Goodwin, 18 miles north of Everett, Wenberg State Park has 65 standard tent sites ($11 a night) and 10 utility sites with water and electricity ($16 a night). The park has a boat launch (power boats are OK), and decent bass and trout fishing. Dogs are allowed anywhere in the park, but they must be leashed. Hiking trails are located near the park and within the park is a gentle half-mile trail in the woods.

To get there from I-5, take exit 206 and follow the signs west for five miles. (425) 652-7417 or (800) 233-0321.

PLACES TO STAY

Kayak Point Park camping: See above.
Wenberg State Park camping: See above.

MUKILTEO

In 1877, Mukilteo became home to the first salmon cannery on Puget Sound. Washington State Ferries sail frequently from here to Clinton on Whidbey Island; the three-mile crossing takes about 20 minutes.

PARKS, BEACHES, AND RECREATION AREAS

•Mukilteo State Park 🐾🐾 See **19** on page 56.

This day-use-only park on Elliott Point and Desolation Sound is a fine spot for a morning beach romp or an afternoon picnic. Salmon, rockfish, and sea perch have been known to nibble after bait, and the park has a boat launch. The Mukilteo Lighthouse is here, along with picnic grounds and plenty of room for kite fliers. Dogs must be leashed. There are no day-use fees.

The park has great views of the ferry crossing to Whidbey Island. The beach walk extends five miles north and east to Harborview Park and another half mile to Howarth Park. Much of the beach is bluff, but several creeks break up the beach and a trail staircase leads to a spectacular viewpoint. Then bluffs give way to shallower beach and waterfront homes. Howarth Park has its own maze of two miles of trail to walk.

Mukilteo State Park is on the waterfront west of I-5 between Lynnwood and Everett. To reach the state park from I-5, take exit 189 and drive west on Highway 526. In Mukilteo, Highway 526 intersects with Highway 525. Turn right (north) on Highway 525 and proceed five miles to the park, which is just south of the ferry dock. You'll find the lighthouse at 600 Front Street. (425) 353-2923 or (800) 233-0321.

SNOHOMISH

The quaint town of Snohomish is listed on both the State and National Register of Historic Places. It's a haven for antique buffs, as evidenced by the 350 antique dealers. Snohomish is 10 miles east of Everett on U.S. 2.

When you've filled the minivan with antiques, leaving room for Bounder of course, head on out to a fine dog-friendly local park. These are all Snohomish County parks.

PARKS, BEACHES, AND RECREATION AREAS

•Centennial Trail 🐾🐾 See **20** on page 56.

This 12-foot-wide paved trail runs between Snohomish and Lake Stevens, an out-and-back 13-mile trek. Horses have their own six-foot-wide trail running alongside. Leashes are required for dogs. Benches, picnic tables, and trees line the trail.

The southern end of the trail begins in Snohomish at the intersection of Maple Street and Pine Avenue. To get there from eastbound U.S. 2, exit and turn right (west) at the 88th Street interchange. Continue on 88th Street to Maple Avenue, then turn right (north) and drive until you reach Pine Avenue. (425) 388-6600.

•Flowing Lake Park 🐾🐾🐾 See **21** on page 56.

This 38-acre Snohomish County park is great for the whole family, including the dog (who must be leashed). Campers can choose from eight tent sites ($14 a night) and 29 RV utility sites ($10 a night). The park also gets a lot of use from daytimers who come to fish, picnic, and hike the trails. There is even occasional live entertainment in the amphitheater.

To get there from I-5, turn east at Everett exit 194 onto U.S. 2 and follow it for 10 miles. Turn left (east) onto 100th Street Southeast (Westwick Road). Just after the French Creek Grange, bear left (north) as it becomes 171st Avenue Southeast. Continue to 48th Street Southeast and turn right (east). The park entrance is at the end of the road. (425) 388-6600.

• Lord Hill Park 🐾 🐾 🐾 See 22 on page 56.

The biggest and newest park in the Snohomish County Park system covers 1,308 acres of back-to-nature woods and trails, along with a picnic area. Leashed dogs are entirely welcome here. This is not an old-growth forest, but it's been many decades since it was logged. The trails are not difficult, so don't plan on a serious hike. Dogs who lead with their noses (I can't think of any who don't) will thrill to the forest scents.

To get there from I-5, take exit 194 in Everett and drive east on U.S. 2. Take the second exit (east) to the town of Snohomish, turning right (west) onto 88th Street (2nd Street). Turn left (south) onto Lincoln Avenue South, which becomes the Old Snohomish-Monroe Highway. Turn right (south) onto 127th Avenue Southeast. Drive south for 2.25 miles and turn left (east) onto 150th Street Southeast. The park entrance will be on your left. (425) 388-6600.

PLACES TO STAY

Inn at Snohomish: Pups are welcome to stay with you at this Snohomish inn. There is no size restriction, but a credit card imprint is required. Rates range from $69 for a normal room to $105 for a suite. 323 2nd Street; (360) 568-2208 or (800) 548-9993.

DIVERSIONS

Follow your nose: At the intersection of Washington Highways 522 and 524, about 20 miles northeast of downtown Seattle, is a collection of yellow buildings that look like several schoolhouses and a garage. This is downtown Maltby, and only one of the buildings was ever actually the Old Maltby School.

Downstairs in the schoolhouse, let your buddy Sherlock's nose guide you to Stillwater Reflections. Owners Kimberley and Patrick Washburn know their scents, and while primarily in business to serve humans, there is a section set aside for canines. Who are, of course, welcome to browse too. There is a good selection of herbal pet care products, our favorite being those herbal Companion Cookies from Big Paws Pantry in Okanogan. 8731 Maltby Road; (360) 668-2024.

ISLAND AND SKAGIT COUNTIES

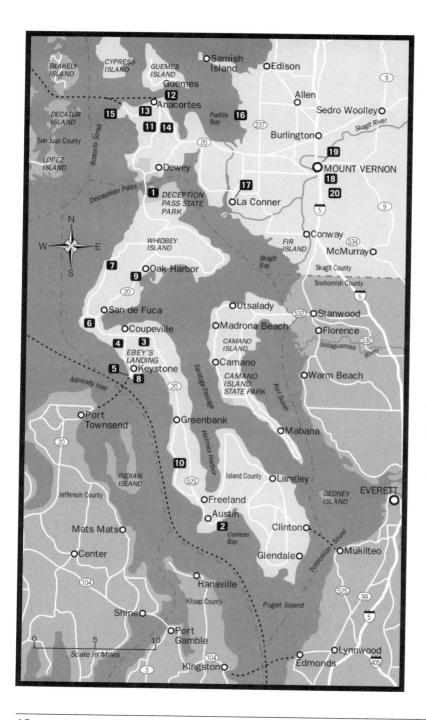

4
ISLAND AND
SKAGIT COUNTIES

ISLAND COUNTY

The watery world of Island County is composed almost entirely of Whidbey Island. There are seven other islands that make up Island County, two of them are inhabited by people, but Camano Island is the only other one that you hear about. People surf Whidbey's beach on the western shore, under the flight path of jets from the Whidbey Island Naval Air Station.

CAMANO ISLAND

No ferries are needed here. From I-5, Highway 532 crosses Davis Slough onto Camano Island. The island lies west of the town of Stanwood and stretches south along Saratoga Passage almost as far as Langley on Whidbey Island, just across the way. Camano Island has 52 miles of shoreline and has long been a favorite of the summer home crowd. But now, the great big park-and-ride by the freeway suggests that a lot of island residents are commuting to Seattle.

WHIDBEY ISLAND

One of the island's main features, the Whidbey Island Naval Air Station, is a few miles north of Oak Harbor, and has long been an important ingredient in Whidbey Island's culture and economy. The airborne Navy is here because of the good flying weather. Whidbey's delightful string of tiny towns just charm the dollars off visitors. Quaint, crafty (in both senses of the word) shops and towns dot the island's narrow roads and thrive on tourists driving through. Driving is the main thing to do on Whidbey, but bicycling is catching on too, since the terrain is mostly flat. The island is home to about 60,000 people, and spans 50 miles in length and one to eight miles in width. The southern tip of the island is a 20-minute ferry ride from Mukilteo, and ferries leave every half-hour until midnight.

PARKS, BEACHES, AND RECREATION AREAS

• **Deception Pass State Park** 🐾 🐾 🐾 See **1** on page 68.
This park, the busiest state park in Washington (six million visitors per year), straddles the land on both sides of Deception Pass, at the north of Whidbey Island (Island County) and the south of Fidalgo Island (Skagit County). The pass between the two islands, rushes both the incoming and outgoing tides through at a pace too swift for paddled boats, although I know a scuba diver

who claims to bodysurf the currents 80 feet down. But that's a story for another time. The rushing waters are quite a sight from the bridge 182 feet up. The state park has 3,700 acres, which contain a few lakes, some old-growth Douglas-fir forests, marshland, sand dunes, and a few smaller islands. Black-tail deer are common in the park and bald eagles nest in the treetops. It has 15 miles of saltwater shoreline, composed of all manner of rocky bluffs, coves, tide flats, and sandy beaches. Dogs are welcome, but must be leashed. The park has 241 standard campsites ($11 per night), 10 primitive campsites ($5 to $7 per night), and 304 picnic areas.

From Oak Harbor, drive 10 miles north on State Highway 20 to the park. (800) 233-0321.

• Double Bluff Off-Leash Park 🐾🐾🐾🐾 🐕 See **2** on page 68.

On the sunset side of southern Whidbey Island, two miles of tideland beach will give good vent to your roaming instincts. The park is on Useless Bay, a misnomer for sure, and it's entirely leash-free. From the parking area there is 900 feet of on-leash walking access to the beach, but once there, fuhgedda-boudit. Don't forget to scoop, and mind the posted behavior rules. The park is open during daylight hours only. From one mile west of Freeland on State Highway 525, turn south onto Double Bluff Road and continue for nearly two miles to the park. (360) 678-5816.

• Ebey's Landing National Historical Reserve 🐾 See **3** on page 68.

The National Park Service established this historical reserve in 1978. Its 22 square miles include farmlands, beaches, parks, trails, 91 nationally registered historic buildings, and the town of Coupeville. Private owners still work the historic farms, but they're under an agreement with the feds to preserve the prairies. At Ebey's Landing proper there's a good bluff trail and plenty of beach to explore. Please leash your pooch.

From Clinton's ferry landing, drive north on State Highway 525. Proceed on State Highway 525 until it connects 22 miles later with State Highway 20. Highway 20 heads straight (north) to Coupeville. You'll find the historical reserve about two miles ahead on Highway 20. (360) 678-6084.

• Ebey's Landing State Park 🐾 See **4** on page 68.

Rumors of good surfing here presume the waves make it all the way in through the Strait of Juan de Fuca from the Pacific. It could happen. Two-hundred-foot sandstone bluffs back the sandy beach here. Look closely for cactus. It's not planted as a joke; it actually grows here in the rain shadow of the Olympic Peninsula. Washington State Parks maintains a day-use parking lot, plus owns and manages a nearly one-mile strip of coastal bluffs between the sea and the farmland, directly north of Ebey's Landing. The beach trail goes all the way from Ebey's Landing to Fort Ebey State Park, a distance of nearly three miles. Leashed dogs are welcome.

From the intersection of Coupeville's Main Street and State Highway 20, drive south on Main Street (which becomes Engle Road) for 1.7 miles. Turn right (west) on Hill Road and continue for about a mile to Ebey's Landing. (800) 233-0321.

• Fort Casey State Park 🐾🐾🐾 See **5** on page 68.

Old gunnery fortifications are still in place at Fort Casey. The westside beach is fine for walks and exploring. Both from Fort Casey and Ebey's Landing you can see whales on occasion. Orca pods that stray from their usual waters around the San Juan Islands are the most fun, but there are plenty of river otters, harbor seals, and California sea lions. More rare are sightings of dolphins, minke whales, and humpback whales. In late spring and early summer you can see gray whales migrating from California to the Arctic. You can walk north along the beach for four miles to Fort Ebey. The park has 35 campsites ($11 per night for standard sites and $5 per night for primitive sites), some of which are located along the beach, but there are no RV hookups. Good-sized grass fields are available for roaming with Rover, too, but leashes are required.

From Coupeville, drive three miles south on State Highway 20 to the park. (360) 678-4519 or (800) 233-0321.

• Fort Ebey State Park 🐾🐾 See **6** on page 68.

You'll find Fort Ebey on the bluffs high above the Strait of Juan de Fuca, where the strait is joined by Admiralty Inlet. There are 24 picnic sites in the day-use area. The park offers three miles of bluff trails and 1.5 miles of beach trails. Follow the curving, plank boardwalk to the beach, which is difficult to navigate because of monster driftwood logs, and look for Japanese glass fishing floats. Gun batteries and bunkers remain from the old fort days, and they're fun to explore. The park has 50 campsites ($11 for standard sites and $5 for primitive sites), but no RV hookups. Leash your pooch.

From Oak Harbor, drive eight miles south on State Highway 20 to its intersection with Libbey Road. Turn right (west) on Libbey Road, then turn left (south) on Fort Ebey Road, after 1.2 miles. Proceed for one-quarter mile on Fort Ebey Road to the park. (360) 678-4636 or (800) 233-0321.

• Joseph Whidbey State Park 🐾🐾🐾 See **7** on page 68.

Offering more than a half-mile of beachfront on the Strait of Juan de Fuca, this area was called Civil Service Beach when the Navy used it for a rifle range. Log steps lead down to the beach, an ideal spot for bird-watching. You and your leashed pooch can explore a half-mile trail through a freshwater wetland and, during the summer, look for orcas swimming offshore (bring binoculars).

From Oak Harbor, drive approximately three miles west on Swantown Road to reach Joseph Whidbey State Park. (360) 678-4636 or (800) 233-0321.

• Keystone Spit State Park 🐾🐾 See **8** on page 68.

Excellent picnicking and scuba-diving opportunities are provided at this day-use park, although its steep, gravel beach is tough to navigate with a hundred pounds of scuba gear on your back. Nothing compares, though, with coming face-to-face with a wolf's head eel 30 feet down. Leashed dogs are welcome in the park. Washington State Ferries cross Admiralty Inlet from Keystone to Port Townsend; your dog must remain inside your auto while on the ferry.

From Coupeville, take Eagle Road three miles south to the park. (800) 233-0321.

• Smith Park ❧ See 🔟 on page 68.

This Oak Harbor park is a preserve for hundreds of Garry oak trees. Oak Harbor was named for these white oaks, and the city preserves a stand of 500-year-old Garry trees. This park provides shady picnic areas, benches, and a playground, too. Your leashed pup is welcome.

The park is located at 300 Avenue West and Midway Boulevard. (360) 679-5551.

• South Whidbey State Park ❧❧ See 🔟 on page 68.

You'll find 54 campsites (for a fee of $10 per night) and two miles of beach within this state park. The 3.5-mile Wilbert Trail provides a great sniffing loop through an old-growth cluster of western red cedar and Douglas fir. Some of these trees are more than 250 years old. Dogs are welcome, but they must be leashed.

The park is located four miles north of Freeland and three miles south of Greenbank on Smugglers Cove Road. (360) 331-4559 or (800) 233-0321.

RESTAURANTS

Knead & Feed: The fresh cinnamon rolls at the Knead & Feed will keep you and yours going for the rest of the day. This is a lunchtime restaurant with a lot of baked goods plus soups and salads. I hope you're there during marionberry season, because the pies are wonderful. The building was first built as a store in 1871, but about a hundred years later it turned into a bakery and restaurant, with a great view of Penn Cove. The restaurant is on the second level as you walk down toward the beach, but there is a bench to hitch-up Euphonia to, visible from inside. It's located on the Coupeville waterfront. 4 Front Street; (360) 678-5431.

Star Bistro: This Langley restaurant, tending strongly toward Middle Eastern foods, has no room for dogs on the deck, but people park them within sight across the street or arrange dog sitters. The meals are so good that they postpone the needs of Charlie to satisfy their own. Just don't forget who the doggie bag is for. 201¹/₂ 1st Street; (360) 221-2627.

Teddy's on Whidbey: Weekend breakfasts at Teddy's are something to phone home about. This is a classy classic Victorian restaurant that has good pastas, prime rib, and seafood. The best thing is that you can eat outside and tend your nearby Garbanzo. There are woods on both sides of the driveway, so most people tether their dog while they eat and then take him for a run before returning to their car. 1804 East Scott Road; (360) 331-2882.

PLACES TO STAY

Acorn Motor Inn: Oak Harbor's Acorn welcomes dogs for a fee of $10 per day for the first seven days only. Room rates range from $44 to $85, and should you and your pooch get hungry, you'll only be a stroll away from Godfather's Pizza and the pet-food aisle at the local Safeway. 31530 State Highway 20; (360) 675-6646 or (800) 280-6646.

City Beach RV Park: Dogs are permitted at this year-round Oak Harbor RV park; the usual rules (leash and scoop) apply. City Beach offers 56 sites with regular hookups ($17 per night) and 26 overflow sites, without water, electricity, or sewer ($10 nightly). As the name suggests, it's on the beach, which is a swimming beach, and there's even a boat launch.

From Oak Harbor (at the intersection of State Highway 20 and West Pioneer Way), turn left (east) on West Pioneer Way, proceed for one block, turn right (south) on 70th Southwest Street, and continue to the RV park. 865 Southeast Berrington Drive; (360) 679-5551.

Deception Pass State Park camping: See page 69.

Drake's Landing Bed & Breakfast: Drake's is actually more like a pensione, and it's right on the Langley beach. It offers one room with an outside entrance to travelers with dogs (one dog per room, please). Canines are not allowed in the rest of the house. The room rate is $65, plus a $5 fee for the dog. 203 Wharf Street, Langley; (360) 221-3999.

Fort Casey State Park camping: See page 70.

Fort Ebey State Park camping: See page 71.

The Harbor Plaza: This four-star Oak Harbor hotel fronted by a Dutch windmill welcomes dogs for a $10 per-night dog fee and a $50 refundable deposit. The Harbor Plaza is a good location for exploring the island's central and northern regions, and it offers a heated pool, spa, fitness center, lounge, and a restaurant with its own bakery. Room rates range from $78 to $119, which include breakfast. 33175 State Route 20; (360) 679-4567 or (800) 528-1234.

Island County Fairgrounds: This Langley RV and camping facility allows dogs, but they must be kept on a leash at all times. RV sites with hookups cost $15 per night and campsites cost $10. 819 Camano Avenue; (360) 221-4677.

Island Tyme Bed & Breakfast: As long as your dog isn't a goat terrier, he's welcome at Island Tyme, which has a 10-acre pasture full of pygmy goats. The good news: dogs under firm voice control don't need to be leashed. The doggy-accessible room costs $95 per night. It's on the ground level with a queen bed, a gas fireplace, and a deck, located within four miles of the Double Bluff Off-Leash Park. 4940 South Bayview Road; (800) 898-8963.

South Whidbey State Park camping: See page 72.

FESTIVALS

Greenbank Farm Loganberry Festival: Whidbey's Greenbank Farm, just north of Greenbank, is one of the world's largest (125 acres) loganberry vineyards. To my taste, Whidbey's Port is one of the wonders of the world. The festival, held for two weekend days in mid-July, is free, and of course, leashed dogs are welcome. There are always display booths of some very talented artists and craftspeople. A number of them give demonstrations, and you can pick your own loganberries.

The farm and tasting room are located at the intersection of Wonn Road and Highway 525, just south of the detour route on Smuggler's Cove Road. (360) 678-7700.

DIVERSIONS

A boy and his dog: Check out the sculpture on 1st Street in Langley: a life-size bronze of a boy and his dog. The same artist made Rachael, the famed bronze pig that guards Seattle's Pike Place Market. The boy looks out over the railing to the Saratoga Passage and the dog, which bears a resemblance to a golden retriever, holds a ball in his mouth. The duo is standing on 1st Street, between Wayward Son and Village Pizzeria. (360) 221-6765.

SKAGIT COUNTY

The verdant Skagit County is known for its brilliant fields of tulips and farms laced with berries and peas. The rich farming river delta attracts numerous bicyclists and in the spring a Seattle bicycle club hosts a huge-turnout 50-miler. The flat delta is a haven for bird-watchers who scan the skies for the majestic eagle, migrating snow geese, and both whistler and trumpeter swans.

While the popular *Twin Peaks* television series inspired locals to nickname the Cascade region near Seattle the "Land of Bob," Skagit County residents have tipped their hats to author Tom Robbins, who wrote *Another Roadside Attraction* when he lived in the town of La Conner. In deference to Robbins, they commonly call the Skagit Flats area the "Land of Tom" (you might even see a fruit stand bearing the moniker "Another Roadside Attraction").

ANACORTES

PARKS, BEACHES, AND RECREATION AREAS

• Anacortes Community Forest Land 🐾🐾🐾 See **11** on page 68.

Just south of Anacortes, this forest land surrounds Cranberry Lake, Heart Lake, Whistle Lake, and Mount Erie, elevation 1,270 feet. Leashes are required. Including the lakes, this is 2,200 acres of forest, wetlands, and mini-mountains, most of it undeveloped except for the trails. From Mount Erie, you can see in all directions to Vancouver Island, the San Juans, Olympics, Cascades, and Mount Rainier. A narrow road takes you to the summit, via Heart Lake Road, but most people hike up on the trails. Hang gliders dive off the south face. Maps of the many hiking trails are available for $3 at the Anacortes City Hall downtown at 6th Street and Q Avenue. The forest, insofar as it can, closes at 10 P.M.

From downtown Anacortes, drive south on State Highway 20/Commercial Avenue to 34th Street. Turn right (west) on 34th Street and proceed for half a mile. Turn left (south) on H Avenue, which becomes Heart Lake Road. Drive one-third mile on Heart Lake Road, then turn left (east) on an unnamed dirt track leading to the summit. (360) 293-1918.

• Cap Sante Park 🐾 See **12** on page 68.

Set on a rugged headland with picnic sites and great views of the Anacortes waterfront and Fidalgo Bay, Cap Sante Park is located at the east end of Anacortes' business district. Scruffy must be leashed and is not allowed in the woods, which is OK since the few trails resemble steep porcupine paths through thickets in the madrona forest. This is a good spot to water the pups and enjoy the view from one of the few hills in the vicinity.

From downtown Anacortes, proceed north on State Highway 20/Commercial Avenue. Turn right (east) on 4th Street, which ends at V Avenue. At the intersection of 4th Street and V Avenue, turn right (south) onto V Avenue (which later becomes W Avenue) and continue one-half mile to the parking lot. (360) 293-1918.

• **Causland Memorial Park** 🐾 🐾 See **13** on page 68.
This downtown city park, built to honor local men who died in World War I, is a study of interesting trees and shrubs. Have a look at the stone wall too, which completely surrounds the square-block park. The monument and its amphitheater is a mosaic of native colored stones, and it's on the National Register of Historic Places. Half the park is grass, ringed with picnic tables. Leashes are required and the park closes at 10 P.M.

Causland Park is located on 8th Street between M and N Avenues. (360) 293-1918.

• **Storvik Park** 🐾 🐾 See **14** on page 68.
Storvik Park is just plain fun. It's a big park, surrounded by a residential neighborhood, and full of, shall we say, *unusual* play equipment, sculptures, and a bunch of ball fields. Keep the dog leashed, and if you forgot a baggy, there's a dispenser in the park. Leashes are required, and the park closes at 10 P.M.

Storvik Park is on Commercial Avenue between 32nd and 29th Streets. (360) 293-1918.

• **Washington Park** 🐾 🐾 🐾 See **15** on page 68.
Uh oh. Rabbits. Billions and billions of rabbits. Leash up. Washington Park is at the far west end of Anacortes on a promontory that includes Green Point and Fidalgo Head. The park has sandy coves, wooded hillsides, campsites, and miles of hiking trails. Camping for visitors costs $15 for hookups and $12 for tent sites. It's a dollar cheaper between October 1 and March 31.

To reach the park, follow the Highway 20 Spur to the ferry terminal. Drive on Sunset Avenue past the terminal and continue to the park. (360) 293-1918.

PLACES TO STAY

Anacortes Inn: Dogs are more than welcome at the Anacortes Inn, which maintains three rooms just for pets and their owners. The winter room rate is $47, the summer rate is $70, and the year-round dog fee is $10 per stay. 3006 Commercial Avenue; (360) 293-3153.

Islands Inn: Small dogs are quite welcome at the Islands Inn. And there's a bonus: the adjacent La Petite Restaurant, with the same owners as the Inn, is renowned region-wide for its Euro-Dutch cuisine. Better yet, breakfast is included in the cost of the room. Rates range from $48 to $80 for a room with a fireplace and you'll pay up to $75 for a standard room; there's a $5 per-night pet fee. Breakfast is included. La Petite (dogs are not allowed inside) is open for lunch Monday through Friday, and dinner Tuesday through Sunday. 3401 Commercial Avenue; (360) 293-4644.

Pioneer Trails: If you're ready to pull the Conestoga wagon into the circle for the night, Pioneer Trails is where they gather. There are 24 Conestogas on the premises for overnight rentals. Trouble is, pardner, dogs are restricted to the camping and RV areas. So you've got to bring your own lodgings if your side-kick Festus is along. RV sites rent for $25 per night for full hookup, or $22 for just water and electricity, or pitch a tent for $18 per night. If your dog gets a row going, you will be requested to be considerate of the neighbors in camp. From camp, it's a three-hour walk through the woods to Mount Erie, the highest point on Fidalgo Island. Pioneer Trails is located midway between Deception Pass and Anacortes on Highway 20 one-half mile south of the Highway 20 Spur turnoff to Anacortes, on Miller Road. (360) 293-5355 or (888) 777-5355 (U.S. only).

San Juan Motel: Small dogs are welcome at the downtown San Juan, at $15 per stay, but people must pay about $50 per night single or $60 double. 1103 6th Street; (360) 293-5105.

Washington Park camping: See page 75.

ANIMAL MEDICAL CLINICS IN ANACORTES

Anacortes is a jumping-off point to a number of destinations and vets here are used to the needs of traveling dogs, especially on the way to Canada where a health certificate is required. The same is true of some Bellingham vets near Fairhaven.

Anacortes Animal Hospital: The doctor works on a walk-in basis, and sees lots of dogs going to and from the islands. 2504 Commercial; (360) 293-3431.

Fidalgo Animal Medical Center: The three doctors see a lot of traveling pets, and pets from the San Juan Islands. It's open every day but Sunday, and there is always a vet on call, reached by calling the regular phone number below.

A lot of traveling dogs in the Northwest are on their way to Canada, and even in boats, they are required to show proof of rabies vaccinations. Some owners want to board their dogs (what a drag) while they do more traveling, and most boarding facilities require that the dogs have rabies, distemper, parvo, and Bordetella vaccinations. To get to the Fidalgo center, from Washington Highway 20, turn north (right) toward downtown Anacortes and the the ferry. The center is one block ahead on your right. 3303 Commercial; (360) 293-2186.

Fleas: The Northwest has a HUGE flea problem, and many dogs come here unprepared. They pick up fleas in fields and even on beaches, and the result is often a skin allergy and a visit to the vet. Vets urge a bit of preventive care-taking for visiting dogs. There is no heartworm to speak of yet, and not much of a parasite problem in the Northwest.

BURLINGTON

PARKS, BEACHES, AND RECREATION AREAS

• Bay View State Park 🐾 🐾 See 🖪 on page 68.

Located on the shore of Padilla Bay, just north of State Highway 20, Bay View is a 25-acre park and campground. The park's camping area is nestled on a hill above the road. The gravel beach is accessed via a pedestrian tunnel. The park has 78 tent sites ($11 per night) and nine utility sites ($16 per night). Bird-watchers have counted 250 species of birds within the park's boundaries. One mile north of the park is the Padilla Bay National Estuarine Sanctuary. There are some interpretive trails, but they're probably not appropriate for dogs. The state park itself has its own woody trails, big grassy areas, and lots of beach for leashed dogs to enjoy. You can reach the Padilla Bay Shore Trail by walking either north or south along the beach.

From Mount Vernon, take State Highway 20 west. Turn right (north) on La Conner–Whitney Road, which becomes Bayview–Skagit River Road and eventually Bayview-Edison Road. The park entrance is on the right, just after the community of Bayview. (800) 233-0321.

PLACES TO STAY
Bay View State Park camping: See above.

DIVERSIONS
Check the Fit: Big Dog Sportswear in the Burlington Outlets next to I-5 welcomes all well-behaved leashed dogs. The store has a full range of doggy-motif clothing, plus lots of stuff for dogs too. 240 Fashion Way; (360) 757-7331.

FIR ISLAND

Fir Island is delta land. It extends from the origin of Skagit River's North and South Forks to Skagit Bay. The island contains the unique Skagit Wildlife Area, which encompasses wetland and delta farms. This island protects the wintering grounds of more than 35,000 Siberian snow geese. They summer on Wrangel Island in the East Siberian Sea. The best viewing (remember the leash, but it's even better to stay in the car) is between mid-January and late April. Sometimes high tides drive the geese from the Skagit shore mudflats back into the fields. They all head north over a 24-hour period sometime between April 17 and May 5.

While the snow geese are quite something to watch, there are also flocks of trumpeter swans on approximately the same schedule. Cover your dog's ears when they take off. We stopped to watch a flock in the wet fields next to the Skagit River. There were about 10 of them, including some dust-colored babies, about 30 feet from the road and they didn't even budge. Mercifully, the dogs behaved themselves inside the car. Over the years, the swans have gotten used to gawkers in passing cars.

Two bridges (one over the South Fork Skagit River and one over the North Fork Skagit River) provide access to Fir Island. From State Highway 20, between Mount Vernon and Anacortes, turn left (south) on Best Road. From I-5, take exit 221, turn west on Conway Road to the town of Conway, and follow the signs to the island.

PLACES TO STAY
South Fork Moorage: There is nothing more peaceful than sitting in a houseboat on the Skagit River watching the water and its detritus flow toward the sea. South Fork Moorage, on the Skagit River's South Fork, rents two small, homemade houseboats. The houseboat called *Karma* is a 60s-style nautical nest. Innkeeper Jessy Demick, a contractor and builder, lived aboard the boat for several years while perfecting its design. It includes a double bed in the loft and a double futon in the living room, but your dog must bring his own bed. A marine head, shower, and hot and cold running water are included. The galley is fully

supplied (except for food), and there's a barbecue on the foredeck. The owner insists that dogs must be leashed when off the boat. The *Karma* is $120 per night for two people. Additional guests are $10 extra per night. For the recreationally ambitious, Demick will drive kayakers or canoeists up river as far as they wish to go, for a float or paddle back to the *Karma* at South Fork Moorage.

The best part of an overnight on the *Karma:* The owner won't bust in to serve you breakfast. You can make your own or go out. Part of the *Karma's* appeal is its privacy, and Demick knows his customers don't want to be bothered with a wake-up call. City dwellers in need of the sleep cure can bunk in as late as they like. 2187 Mann Road; (360) 445-4803.

LA CONNER

Over the past 20 years, La Conner has substantially developed its tourist trade. I remember when the town's only notable curiosity was a set of neon-green curtains hanging outside of a junk shop window. La Conner's backside hangs over the Swinomish Slough, a nautical shortcut for boats from Seattle. The Swinomish Indian Reservation is located on the other side of the slough. Summer traffic chokes the town's main street, so park the car and enjoy the short walk. First Street is lined with restaurants, boutiques, antique stores, bookshops, and museums.

PARKS, BEACHES, AND RECREATION AREAS

• **Pioneer Park** 🐾 🐾 See **17** on page 68.
This picnic area in the hilly woods of southern La Conner offers a large shelter and walkways to the channel below. Your pooch is welcome, but she must be leashed.

From downtown La Conner, drive south on South 1st Street and turn left (east) on Commercial. Proceed on Commercial for one block and then turn right (south) on South 2nd Street, which eventually becomes Moore Street. Turn left (east) on Caledonia Street and continue to the stop sign at Maple Avenue. Turn right (south) on Maple Avenue, which swings right (north) and becomes Pioneer Parkway. The park entrance is on the left, before the Rainbow Bridge. (360) 466-3125.

PLACES TO STAY

La Conner Country Inn: The inn is just off the main walking/shopping street, and its ambience and decor are comfortable, relaxed, and sort of like a very large ship cabin inside. The inn reserves two rooms for people with dogs, and charges a $25 per-stay fee for the canine privilege. Guests are required to sign a copy of the inn's pet policy, which states that dogs must be leashed in all public areas and handlers are responsible for their pet's behavior. Before you check out, your room will be inspected for any possible pet damage. The room rate is $88 to $98. 107 South 2nd Street; (360) 466-3101.

DIVERSIONS

Doggieware: While admitting to cat paraphernalia, the emphasis here is on gift items for people who have dogs. There is a good line of festive flags, featuring the breed of your persuasion, dog beds, and even a pet carrier for the back of your bicycle. 602 South 1st; (360) 466-1048.

MOUNT VERNON

PARKS, BEACHES, AND RECREATION AREAS

• Hillcrest Park 🐾 🐾 See **18** on page 68.

Thirty-acre Hillcrest is Mount Vernon's oldest park. It offers hiking trails, picnic areas, a baseball field, and courts for basketball, tennis, and volleyball. It's a nice family park with a good view of the Skagit Valley. Don't forget to leash your dog and scoop the poop. The restrooms close at dusk, but the park is always open.

From I-5, take exit 226 and turn right (east) on Broad Street. Continue on Broad Street to South 11th Street and turn right (south). The park is a couple of blocks ahead. (360) 336-6213.

• Lions Club Park 🐾 🐾 See **19** on page 68.

The Lions' park borders a beautiful section of the Skagit River just west of I-5 on Freeway Drive. It's a nice place to take a picnic lunch and still be in town while you try to comprehend the mysteries of the never-ending river. Leashing and scooping are required. The park is always open.

Take I-5 exit 227 and drive west for one block to Freeway Drive. Turn left (south) on Freeway Drive; the park is one-half mile ahead on the right. (360) 336-6213.

• Little Mountain 🐾 🐾 🐾 See **20** on page 68.

With an elevation of 934 feet, Little Mountain is little, but offers a fabulous view of the entire Skagit Valley, the Olympics, and the San Juan Islands. The peak is surrounded by 480 acres of forest and trails, and it's a great place to do some tracking training, or just cut loose and have a good romp. The park also has a picnic area and restrooms. Leashed dogs are welcome.

From I-5 just south of Mount Vernon, take exit 225 and turn east on Anderson Road. Take an immediate left (north) on Cedarvale Road, which parallels the freeway. In approximately one-half mile, turn right (east) on Blackburn Road. Continue on Blackburn Road for about one mile, then turn right (south) on Little Mountain Road. In approximately one-half mile, make another right on Little Mountain Park Road, which leads to the top. (360) 336-6213.

PLACES TO STAY

Best Western College Way Inn: Dogs are welcome at this Best Western for a nightly fee of $10. People pay between $59 and $80. A heated outdoor swimming pool and hot tub are available to guests, too. 300 West College Way; (360) 424-4287 or (800) 793-4024.

Best Western Cotton Tree Inn: Overnight rates range from $74 to $88, and small dogs (under 25 pounds) are welcome for $10 per stay. 2300 Market Street; (360) 428-5678 or (800) 662-6886.

Days Inn of Mount Vernon: This Days Inn accepts dogs in some rooms for a $5 per-night fee. It's located in north Mount Vernon (Interstate 5 exit 227).

Room rates range from $55 to $65, depending on the time of year of your visit. 2009 Riverside Drive; (360) 424-4141.

Hillside Motel: Small pups (under 25 pounds) are permitted here for a $5 per-night charge. It's located south of Mount Vernon (Interstate 5 exit 218) on a hillside overlooking the Skagit Valley. The room rate is about $45. 2300 Bonnie View Road; (360) 445-3252.

Mount Vernon Comfort Inn: Yay, free local phone calls and free continental breakfast, and access to the indoor swimming pool. Rates for humans range from $49 to $79; dogs cost $10 nightly. 1910 Freeway Drive; (360) 428-7020.

Skagit County Fair RV Park: RV and tent campers can bring their dogs to Mount Vernon's Skagit County Fairgrounds except during the fair (the second weekend in August). It's an easy walk from the fairgrounds to downtown and the riverside. Hookup sites (with water and electricity only) cost $15 per night and tent sites are $11; stays are limited to two weeks. 315 South 3rd Street; (360) 336-9453.

West Winds Motel: Dogs are OK at the West Winds, where there's a one-time $5 dog fee. The winter room rate is $37, and the rest of the year it's $47. 2020 Riverside Drive; (360) 424-4224.

FESTIVALS

Skagit Valley Tulip Festival: You used to be able to see the colorful Skagit Valley tulip fields as you sped by on I-5. But no more. Marketers turned the tulip season into a festival that city folks would drive to and the fields are now on the west side of the Skagit River dike. But it's still beautiful, especially as an increasing number of berry and pea farmers get into the cash crop of tulips. There is more to growing and harvesting tulips than you might imagine, especially in a delta that grows the most tulips outside of Holland. The blooming celebration goes on all over the valley during the first two weeks in April. Most farms have parking lots and shopping opportunities, not to mention photo ops. Festivities include bus tours, river trips, arts and crafts displays, fireworks, a street fair, an ecumenical Easter sunrise service in the tulip fields, volkswalks, a 10-K "Slug Run," and so on. (360) 428-5959, (360) 428-6753 (fax); www.tulipfestival.org.

DIVERSIONS

The well-read canine: Dogs with good manners (you know the kind) are welcome to roam the aisles with you in **Scotts Bookstore,** which stocks more than 45,000 titles (the travel section is particularly good). Scotts is open seven days a week. 121 Freeway Drive; (360) 336-6181 or (800) 532-BOOK.

BELLINGHAM AREA

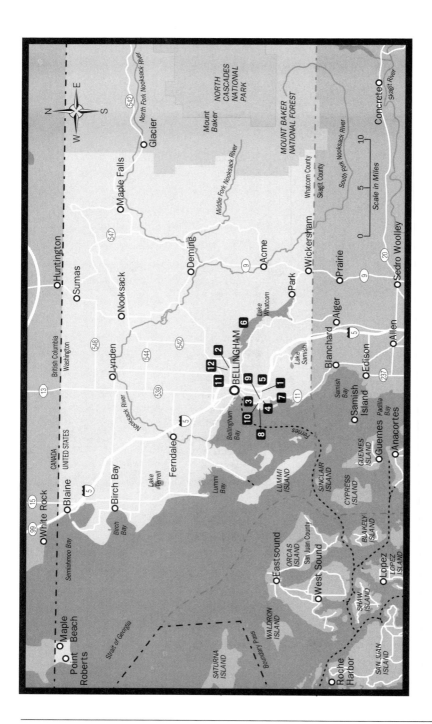

5
BELLINGHAM AREA

Pristine Whatcom County, which shares a 100-mile border with Canada, is where Seattleites would like to live, if it just weren't so far away from Seattle (80 miles). For over a century however, people have moved here, and later figured out a way to earn a living. The county extends 100 miles east into the Mount Baker-Snoqualmie National Forest and North Cascades National Park. The city of Bellingham, home to Western Washington University, hugs the waters of Bellingham Bay, but a Georgia Pacific plant on landfill has the best piece of waterfront. Some people say privately that the mill needs to "go away" for Bellingham to realize its full potential. Downtown has a certain charm, but as a major property developer described it: "The character here is a disorganized area next to a pulp mill." Most of Whatcom County is quite pristine, however.

The city's southside, Fairhaven, is the big draw for bookstore browsers, tourists, and espresso sippers. They all sit at the outside cafés even into winter. Every summer Sunday afternoon, weather permitting, crowds gather in Fairhaven to enjoy free jazz at the intersection of Harris Avenue and 11th Street.

TRANSPORTATION

Fairhaven is also home to the Bellingham Cruise Terminal, the southern terminus of the Alaska Marine Highway System (Alaska Ferry). The cruise terminal is part of a regional transportation hub that links the Alaska Ferry with Amtrak and Greyhound stations and provides moorage for whale-watching boats, salmon charters, foot ferries to the San Juan Islands, and the foot passenger ferry to Victoria on Vancouver Island.

Here is a rundown on the doggie transport options from Fairhaven:

Airporter Shuttle: Dogs are welcome on this shuttle that runs on I-5 between the Canadian border at Blaine south to SeaTac Airport, with stops at Semiahmoo, the Bellingham Cruise Terminal, Anacortes Ferry Terminal, and Whidbey Island. If your fellow passengers agree, Mercury can ride up front with you; otherwise, she must be in a carrier in back with the luggage. (800) 235-5247 in Washington, British Columbia, and Alaska; (800) 423-4219 in all other states and provinces.

Alaska Ferry: Friday sailings to Alaska for people, dogs, and vehicles leave at 6 P.M. from the Bellingham Cruise Terminal at the west end of Fairhaven. It's about a five-minute walk from "downtown." Traveling dogs are required to have a valid health certificate, signed by a vet within 30 days of sailing. The requirement is to satisfy the state of Alaska concerning pets traveling through Canadian waters.

The cost each way, for each dog, is $25. And here's where a traveling duo could get positively grumpy. For $25, Firelia doesn't even get deck privileges.

No. Not. She has to stay either in the vehicle or in dog limbo-land below decks in an "approved carrying container." You are allowed to visit three times a day, and are supplied "cleaning implements." At ports of call you can both escape the boat briefly for a walk. 355 Harris Avenue; (360) 676-8445 (recording) or (800) 642-0066.

Amtrak: Amtrak goes from Bellingham north to Vancouver, B.C., daily at 9:47 A.M. and south to Seattle daily at 10:15 A.M. and 7:35 P.M., but unless you can produce proof that La Guardia at your side is a bona fide service dog, you travel alone. You may be better off crossing the Canadian border in your car, all you need is a rabies and health certificate. 401 Harris Avenue; (360) 734-8851 or (800) 872-7245.

Greyhound: Nyet on canine passengers here too. Buses go north and south from the Fairhaven terminal several times daily, and every now and then a driver will say, "You can ride 'im down below with the baggage, but I wouldn't do that to any animal." 401 Harris Avenue; (360) 733-5252 or (800) 231-2222.

San Juan Island Commuter: Your Odysseus is welcome to ride with you (in a kennel) on this daily commuter boat that runs to 14 San Juan Islands, including four marine state parks. Some of the islands have no docks, so the boat just pulls up to the beach and lowers the ramp. Don't forget the kayak and camping gear. 355 Harris Avenue, Suite 104; (360) 734-8180 or (888) 734-8180.

San Juan Island Shuttle Express: Ah, travel relief for you and yours. Dogs are welcome passengers, at least "small ones in approved carrying devices," but most of the devices are backpacks or satchels. A kennel is available, but call ahead to reserve it. The boat leaves Fairhaven daily at 9:15 A.M. during June, July, August, and September. It stops at Lieber Haven Resort on Orcas Island and at Friday Harbor on San Juan Island. It then takes a three-hour whale-watching cruise before retracing its wake and returning to Fairhaven at 6:15 P.M. 355 Harris Avenue; (360) 671-1137 or (888) 373-8522.

Victoria Star: With daily 9 A.M. summer sailings to Victoria, B.C., from Fairhaven, this is a popular foot ferry. But just like on Amtrak, only service dogs are allowed on board. 355 Harris Avenue; (360) 738-8099 or (800) 443-4552.

West Isle Air: West Isle Air, which flies small planes to the islands from Boeing Field in Seattle and from Bellingham, will happily carry you and yours to, say, San Juan Island. But there's a catch. You have to charter the plane. There is no baggage storage area, so the dog gets a seat all to herself. The airline carries mostly businesspeople, and says it wouldn't be fair to make a guy in a business suit sit next to a hairy beast. In our case, the one-way charter for Quinn, Emma, and me, from Bellingham to San Juan Island, was $93.50. (360) 671-8463 or (800) 874-4434.

Whatcom Transit Authority: This city and county-wide bus service from Fairhaven says "yes" to wheelchairs, "yes" to bicycles and only "if" to your precious Freeberg. That means only if the dog is small and even then only if she is in an approved carrying device. There is no Sunday service. (360) 676-RIDE.

BELLINGHAM

There are five leash-free park areas in Bellingham, among the few between Seattle and the Canadian border. Both Bellingham and Whatcom County are well known for their parks. From mountain woods to bay beaches, the local recreation areas offer miles and miles of trails.

All Whatcom County parks have leash laws, and there are a few restricted areas where dogs are not allowed at all: the soccer fields at the corner of Smith and Northwest Roads, all swimming beaches, and the Roeder Home in Bellingham. Hovander Park near Ferndale, with its farm animals on display, allows dogs but requires leashes at all times. Park staff enforce the leash laws in those places, especially at Hovander, and, as one staffer said, "It's a little difficult to be polite when the free-running dog has peacock feathers in its mouth."

Leash laws are rigorously enforced and there are stiff fines for willful violation. But there are so many miles of county park trails that are so lightly used, no one objects to dogs running free if they don't bother anybody. Dog owners' discretion and sense of appropriateness will help to maintain this lenient approach to the rules. In city parks you can be fined $250 for not scooping after your dog.

PARKS, BEACHES, AND RECREATION AREAS

• Arroyo Park 🐾🐾🐾🐾 🐕 See **1** on page 82.

All of Arroyo's trails are leash-free. The park includes 38 acres of dense, second-growth forest and two hiking and equestrian trails. One trail follows the creek and the other crisscrosses the south side of the canyon. If you and your pooch traverse the second trail through the canyon, you'll discover something big: a little-known cathedral grove, punctuated by shafts of sunlight on clear summer days. A 700-foot-long bridge once crossed this canyon 130 feet up, along the route of the Interurban Railway (a one-car train that ran between Bellingham and Mount Vernon in the early 1900s).

From Fairhaven, drive south on State Highway 11 (Chuckanut Drive) for about one mile, and then turn left on Old Samish Road. Proceed for one-quarter mile on Old Samish Road and then park in either of the graveled lots on the right. (360) 676-6985.

• Bloedel-Donovan Park 🐾🐾 See **2** on page 82.

The Bellingham Parks Department surprised local dog owners with a tactical switch. They were all invited to bring their dogs to Bloedel-Donovan Park on Lake Whatcom during the spring and turn them loose to chase geese and ducks. Unleash? To chase waterfowl? Those are high crimes and misdemeanors most other places. But as elsewhere in the Puget Sound region, freshwater beaches and swimming parks are getting inundated with, uh, poop. There's no nice way to say it, and no nice way to deal with it. It's a problem in lots of parks along the Pacific Flyway in the Northwest. The park department's purpose was to prevent it in the first place by bringing in the canine muscle to get the birds to move elsewhere on the 11-mile-long lake. "We picked up on the thought from the Seattle area," said Marvin Harris, manager of operations for

Bellingham Park and Recreation Department. "One of the cities hired a dog walker to do goose patrol." The program has been a success from the "turf care standpoint." Harris added, "There's been no problem between dogs and park users. We'd like to try it again next year."

To reach the park, take I-5 exit 253 and drive east on Lakeway Drive for nearly two miles. Turn left on Electric Avenue and proceed almost two miles to the park on the right. (360) 676-6985.

•Boulevard Park 🐾 See ❸ on page 82.

Bad news for dogs in this beautiful bayside park: Keep off the grass. It didn't used to be so, back when Emma and Quinn would chase a basketball by the hour. It's a case of too many people spoiling the canine fun. From the parking lot, there are two leashed choices. The path to the left connects to a wooden walkway over the water and eventual access to the railroad tracks and a few trails. At the north end of the park, you can climb a four-story flight of steps (to one of the best island views in Bellingham) to a walkway over the tracks. This leads to more park along the Boulevard, or, instead of climbing the steps, just cross the tracks on foot to get on the wide gravel trail that continues a few miles to downtown Bellingham. Dogs must be leashed.

Boulevard Park is about a half mile north of Fairhaven on the main north-south street. Don't worry about the street signs. Just follow the main drag, because in the space of that half mile its names are, from south to north, Chuckanut Drive, 12th Street, Finnegan Way, 11th Street, and South State Street. Just as it becomes South State Street, turn left on Bayview Drive and continue down into the park. The gate closes at 10 P.M. (360) 676-6985.

•Fairhaven Park 🐾🐾 See ❹ on page 82.

Fairhaven is a 16-acre city park offering a basketball court, softball field, tennis courts, playground, picnic shelter, community building, picnic tables, rose garden, American Youth Hostel, playground, and wading pool. Dogs are allowed throughout the park, with the exception of the wading pool and hostel. You'll also find stream fishing and hiking opportunities here. The Padden Creek Trail connects with Fairhaven Park in at least three places. All dogs must remain leashed.

From Fairhaven, drive three blocks south on 12th Street, which turns into Chuckanut Drive. You'll find the park on the left side of the street. (360) 676-6985.

•Lake Padden Park 🐾🐾🐾🐾 🐕 See ❺ on page 82.

This park is 1,008 acres of fun. You can do the 2.8-mile jog thing around the lake (leashed), go leash-free on the six miles of bridle trails, or leash up on the 10 miles of hiking trails. Or simply go swimming in the canine aquatics zone at the southern tip of the lake. No motorboats are allowed on the 152-acre lake, but it is open to windsurfers, canoeists, kayakers, and others with motorless boats. The park also has ball fields, a 6,700-yard golf course, plus a whole lot of land for just hanging out. Pooches are not allowed on the humans' beach. The leash-free training area is behind the athletic field restroom in the southeastern part of the park, not far from the doggy beach.

To reach Lake Padden Park, take I-5 exit 250. Turn left (if you're driving south) or right (if you're driving north) and proceed two blocks east on Old Fairhaven Parkway to a T in the road. At the T, turn left (north) on 36th Street. Proceed on 36th Street to Samish Way. Turn right (south) on Samish Way and follow the signs to Lake Padden Park's golf course entrance. Bear right and continue to the end of the road. (360) 676-6985.

• Lake Whatcom Trail 🐾🐾🐾🐾 See **6** on page 82.

The Lake Whatcom Trail is a great place to run your dog. Your horse too, for that matter. The pleasant lakeside trail starts at the southern end of North Shore Drive on the northeast side of Lake Whatcom and runs for 3.1 miles. We took my granddogs Emma and Quinn to check it out. The terrain along the trail, opposite the water on the west side of Lake Whatcom, is immense second-growth forest, interspersed with three-story-tall granite walls and waterfalls with pools below. It's as nice a run as anything we've seen, even in British Columbia. Emma and Quinn thrived on the water chases, patrolled some huge downed logs, and sneered at the occasional dog running by with his jogger. "I'm sure glad Grandpa doesn't make us do THAT," Quinn said to Emma. "Like those poor sappy dogs at Greenlake, running their pads off going around in human circles." "Exactly, Emma," answered Quinn. They thought I wasn't listening. "There are too many great smells to chase. We might even find a hedgehog out here."

To reach the Lake Whatcom Trail from northbound Interstate 5, take exit 253. At the stop sign (the Convention and Visitor Bureau is one block straight ahead on your right), turn right on King Street and proceed for one block. Turn left at the stoplight onto Lakeway Drive and proceed for 1.6 miles. Turn left on Electric Avenue. In slightly less than a mile, you'll pass Bloedel-Donovan Park. Continue straight on North Shore Drive for about six miles and watch for the Lake Whatcom Trail sign. (360) 733-2900.

• Larrabee State Park 🐾🐾🐾🐾 See **7** on page 82.

Larrabee, seven miles south of Bellingham, is located on world-famous Chuckanut Drive above Samish Bay. The park contains a picturesque band shell and a grassy amphitheater frequently used for weddings, children's theater performances, and the seven-mile Chuckanut Foot Race's award ceremony. Larrabee is connected to Bellingham by the 5.5-mile Interurban Trail System (see page 88), a former electric-train route between Bellingham and Mount Vernon. The Interurban is well used by hikers, bikers, and Chuckanut Foot Racers. Dogs run with their handlers in this annual race, but they must be leashed in the park. Larrabee's rocky beach and sandstone-bluff waterfront offer some of the best tidepooling around. On the east side of Chuckanut Drive, several trails wind into the Chuckanut Mountains, stopping at places like the Bat Caves. Larrabee was established as Washington's first state park; recent purchases and swaps of land on the mountainside have made it a wonderful area for explorers. With elevations ranging from sea level to 1,940 feet, the park occupies most of the westward side of Chuckanut Mountain in Whatcom/Skagit Counties.

Reservations are required for camping at Larrabee. Open year-round, the park's campgrounds include 26 utility sites ($16 per night), 53 standard sites

($11 per night), eight walk-in sites ($7 nightly), three emergency campsites, and eight primitive tent sites, which tend to fill up quickly on spring and summer weekends. From April 1 to September 30, the park is open from 8 A.M. to dusk and from October 1 to March 31, the hours are 6:30 A.M. to dusk. Dusk is defined as one-half hour after sunset, at which time the day-use area gates are closed. Campground gates are closed at 10 P.M. (800) 233-0321 (information); (800) 452-5687 (reservations, $6 fee).

From I-5 exit 250, Bellingham's southernmost, drive west on Old Fairhaven Parkway (also State Highway 11, which becomes Chuckanut Drive) for just over a mile to a traffic light. Turn left here, south, onto 12th Street, which in one block becomes Chuckanut Drive. Follow it for about five miles to the park entrance on the right. (360) 676-2093 or (800) 233-0321.

•Marine Park at Post Point 🐾🐾 See 8 on page 82.

You'll find parking, restrooms, and a kitchen shelter at this small, grassy Bellingham Bay park. Leashes are required, and dogs are not allowed on the grass or the beach, but it's a good walk-through to the miles of railroad tracks and rocky beaches to the south. Marine Park is set next to the Burlington Northern railroad tracks, which circle the bay and continue south to Seattle. (Unleashed dogs are allowed across the tracks next to the Post Point Lagoon. See page 89.)

And hey, if there's anything a dog loves more than a muddy beach at low tide, I don't know what it is. Whether he's Fido or she's Fiodora, the dog is a big help in the clam digging department. The water is cold, 45°F in winter, 55°F in summer, so neither you nor your buddy will want to get too wet for too long.

A bit less than a mile south along the tracks is a nice Chuckanut sandstone outcropping. It's great for climbing around and checking out the tidepools. Young people waiting for the Friday sailings of the Alaska Ferry camp on the grassy area here. Eagles sometimes perch in the tall twin pines on the point, and herons nest up in the hillside trees. They all negotiate with the seagulls and crows for edibles on the beach. Crows teach their young to break clamshells on nearby streets and houses, and seagulls fly away who-knows-where with starfish in their beaks.

About the railroad tracks: The sound of an approaching train isn't as easy to hear as you might think. These are busy tracks, used 24 hours a day, and while the trains are relatively slow, they're just as deadly as the fast ones. Act as though you're trespassing, since you are, and be alert. Many dogs and their owners regularly use this path, but they walk along it at their own risk.

To reach the park, take I-5 exit 250 and follow signs to the Alaska Ferry. Instead of turning right into the terminal, turn left into the park. (360) 676-2500.

•Padden Creek/Interurban Trail System 🐾🐾🐾 See 9 on page 82.

The Interurban Trail System, which starts at Marine Park (see above) and runs about six miles between Old Fairhaven Parkway and Larrabee State Park (see page 87), connects with various paths; one trail proceeds three miles north through Fairhaven, Boulevard Park (see page 86), and into downtown

Bellingham. The Interurban Trail attracts hikers, bikers, joggers, and equestrians. Your dog must be leashed at all times.

To reach the Padden Creek Trail, take I-5 exit 250 and drive less than a mile west on Old Fairhaven Parkway. You'll see a trail parking lot on the south side of the road. (360) 676-6985.

• Post Point Lagoon 🐾🐾🐾🐾 🐕 See **10** on page 82.

This 30 or so acres of city land surrounding the water treatment plant and bordering Post Point Lagoon is entirely leash-free. It's simply vacant city land that was recently approved as a leash-free dog area, and it's open all hours. Scooping is required; baggies and trashcans are provided. It's not unusual for 10-20 dogs plus their handlers to congregate at the edge of the saltwater lagoon or over in the marsh grass area. Some dogs swim and some chase tennis balls swatted a fair distance with tennis racquets. The lagoon area muddies up pretty good in the rainy season, but it doesn't seem to bother anybody. The owners of rude or aggressive dogs are asked to take them home. Gravel trails crisscross the area, bordered by 4th Street and the railroad tracks. Herons and crows nest high in trees.

To reach the lagoon, take I-5 exit 250 and follow signs to the Alaska Ferry. Just about at the ferry terminal on Harris Street, turn left onto 4th Street, then right onto McKenzie Avenue. McKenzie goes for about a block to the water treatment plant, and you can park anywhere in its lot. (360) 676-6985.

• Sunset Pond 🐾🐾 🐕 See **11** on page 82.

This totally leash-free Bellingham park has a half-mile-long pond that used to be a water-skier lake. It's used now by model boaters weekends and Wednesdays, but it's a good go-fetch-swim body of water for dogs. Surrounding the pond are thick scrubby woods that are perfect for tracking exercises, but only a few of the trails are wide enough for humans. It's strictly for the dogs here, and about a zillion birds.

To reach the pond, which is right behind Kmart, take I-5 exit 255 and proceed one block east on Sunset Drive. Turn left at the James Street traffic light that guides traffic into the Sunset Square shopping center. Take another immediate left (still on James Street) and continue down the hill past Woodstock Way. Two gravel parking lots are on the right, each with a sign for Sunset Pond. (360) 676-6985.

• Whatcom Falls Park 🐾🐾🐾🐾 🐕 See **12** on page 82.

Whatcom Falls Park encompasses 241 acres on both sides of Whatcom Creek, and the entire north side of the creek past the stone bridge is leash-free. Even here, though, your dog must be under your voice control. There are 2.5 miles of hiking trails near the creek and through the woods, plus some horse trails, so keep an eye out. The trails along the cascading creek are the most glamorous, and in summer weather you'll see youths jumping off cliffs into water that they hope is deep enough. No. Don't try it. Check out the stone bridge over the falls instead. It's one of those 1939 Works Progress Administration jobs that's still around. Kids 14 and under can fish the stream, and there's a fish hatchery in the park that releases 1.2 million fish a year. And yes, Her Dogness is welcome to visit the fish, but only on a leash.

The hatchery's hours are 8 A.M. to 5 P.M. daily. Park hours are 6 A.M. to 10 P.M. daily.

To reach the park, take I-5 exit 253 and drive east on Lakeway Drive for nearly two miles. Turn left on Electric Avenue and proceed almost a mile to the park on the left. (360) 676-6985.

RESTAURANTS

Archer Ale House: This Fairhaven underground pub's for you, but Freedonia there has to be tied either to the long railing on the sidewalk or on the shady platform out back. Out back is best, on the grass with the other dogs. This smoke-free pub has great stuff on tap and traditional pub food like pasties (vegetables in a sauce with meat baked in a pastry), soups, and pizza by the slice. Downstairs at 1212 10th Street; (360) 647-7002.

Barnacle's: For a good meal, bring your traveling beast to the outdoor dining area, which offers unimpeded views across Bellingham Bay to the Canadian Coastal Mountains. Barnacle's offers a range of hot and cold sandwiches, desserts, and espresso drinks. The Caesar and Chinese chicken salads are highly recommended. 355 Harris Avenue; (360) 647-5072.

The Bergsma Gallery and Coffee Shop: Outdoor tables are available at this coffee shop, set next to the Convention and Visitors Bureau, from April through September. During those months, you and your pooch can munch outside. Owner and artist Jody Bergsma says, "We'll bring the dogs water and whatever their owner orders for them from the menu." Someone brought in one of those squeally pot-bellied pigs one time, and Jody says it was not a lot of fun. The café is open 7 A.M. to 7 P.M., seven days a week. You know it's a happy place when the waitress talks to the plants as she waters them. Bergsma's serves Caravelli coffees, fresh organic greens, low-fat soups, homemade breads, good baked goods, and deli sandwiches, complete with Grey Poupon. 1344 King Street; (360) 733-1101.

BoZak: New to downtown Bellingham, just like its Vancouver chef of high repute, Bozak strives for high flavor foods in a gracious atmosphere. In warm weather, sidewalk tables are considered an extension of the dining room. You're welcome to be served there and your dog is welcome too. 1309 Commercial Street; (360) 752-1524.

The Calumet Restaurant: Stop by the comprehensive Newsstand next door for reading materials, then relax in the sun at Calumet's sidewalk tables. Dogs are frequent guests here. In case of rain, the awning is waterproof. The Calumet has a daily pasta special for $6.95, a grilled veggie sandwich for $6.50, plus a good variety of soups and salads. Lunch is served from 11 A.M. and dinner from 5 P.M. 113 Magnolia; (360) 733-3331.

Colophon Café & Deli: The Legendary Colophon, which shares space with the just-as-legendary Village Books, which allows polite dogs, by the way, is featured in *Northwest Best Places, Fodor's, Green Cuisine, Bon Appétit,* and now *The Dog Lover's Companion to Seattle.* It's earned its reputation as the most regularly visited eatery in Fairhaven. Ben & Jerry's ice cream is only one reason. Torrefazione coffees are another (although the Postum au lait is very good too), plus Village Turkey sandwiches, African Peanut Soup, and many others. Oh, and Freesia is free to join you upstairs at the sidewalk tables or downstairs on the perimeter of the patio. Bowls of water and biscuits are served on request, daily in summer until 10 P.M. A side note: Notices on the poles out front say, "Tied dogs will be towed." 1208 11th Street; (360) 647-0092.

The Daily Wrap: Sidewalk tables and chairs are available at this centrally located Fairhaven wrappery. Wraps range from Jamaican jerk shrimp to Thai veggie to Greek garden. The espresso-tea bar offers the usual brews plus tasty smoothies. Open daily 9 A.M. to 9 P.M. 1209 11th Avenue; (360) 733-9727.

Doggie Diner & Pet Paraphernalia: Fairhaven's Doggie Diner for people and pets features an actual diner counter with stools, plus a few tables, but don't stall-out there. The outdoor patio area is just a shout from the Colophon Café (same owner), and that's where the human treats come from. Actually, many of the doggie treats do too, baked early in the morning by a pretty serious caninist. My third granddog, Bosco the Pug, hangs out here whenever he's in town. The store also has plenty of doggie necessities, desirables, and, uh, gifts and cards. Don't forget the humans on your list. Among the "popular paraphernalia" is, ahem, Leash Luggage. It's sort of a pocket that velcroes onto any leash, including the retractables, and it holds all your stuff. It even has a hook for keys. The Doggie Diner is open seven days a week from 9 A.M. to 7 P.M. 1007 Harris Avenue; (360) 756-0295.

Fairhaven Station Coffee & News: Coffees, snacks and the news of the day are available next to the Amtrak station, and guess what? Your canine buddy is even welcome inside, since there is no kitchen. She has to be well-behaved though; otherwise she'll be sent to the outside tables. 401 Harris Avenue; (360) 676-7166.

Pastazza: Weekend mornings at the sidewalk tables are especially enjoyable for dogs and their owners. Pastazza's "morning meals" feature frittatas, blintzes, burritos, plus simple scones and lattes. 2945 Newmarket Street, Suite 101; (360) 714-1168.

Skylark's Fountain & Mercantile: Pups are welcome at the café's outdoor tables, just up the cobblestones from the big bus in Fairhaven. Brunch and lunch are popular times for fanciers of good breeding and excellent fare. Meals are made from scratch, plus they offer espresso, ice cream, sodas, sundaes, shakes, and malts. 1308-B 11th Street; (360) 715-3642.

PLACES TO STAY

Hotel Bellwether: Bellingham's newest luxury hotel has its own marina at the northern edge of Bellingham Bay. It has commanding views of the San Juan Islands and Mount Baker. Dogs under 25 pounds are entirely welcome for $65 per stay. Standard water view rooms start at $199. 1 Bellwether Way; (360) 392-3100, (877) 411-1200; www.hotelbellwether.com.

Larrabee State Park camping: See page 87.

Motel 6: As with most Motel 6s, one pooch per room is allowed. This one is close to the freeway exit, restaurants, and gas stations, and Sehome Village shopping center is kitty-corner across the street. The room rate is about $50. 3701 Byron Avenue; (360) 671-4494 or (800) 466-8356.

Quality Inn Baron Suites: Only small pets are accepted at this Quality Inn, and a $25 nonrefundable deposit is required. Rates range from $75 to $1,054. Most suites include a lounge area (with a couch and a desk with two chairs) and a microwave and refrigerator. 100 East Kellogg Road; (360) 647-8000 or (800) 900-4661.

Resort Semiahmoo: This inn, midway between Seattle and Vancouver, is at the end of a mile-long sand spit, which forms the western barrier of Drayton Harbor. It offers a unique place for romping and exploring. You can stroll miles of beaches, see nesting eagles, watch harbor seals at play, and enjoy the views of Mount Baker and the Canadian Coastal Range. Year-round rates range from $149 to $359 (for the honeymoon suite), but ask about discounts. Dogs are welcome for a one-time fee of $50. Children 18 and under can stay for free if they share a room with their parents. 9565 Semiahmoo Parkway; (360) 371-2000 or (800) 770-7992.

Rodeway Inn: Room rates range from $36 to $90, and dogs are welcome for an extra $10 per pet. 3710 Meridian Street; (360) 738-6000 or (800) 228-2000.

Super 8 Motel Ferndale: Rates for two are $56 to $66, including continental breakfast, at this dog-friendly Ferndale motel adjacent to McDonald's and Denny's. Guests must sign a form agreeing to pay $25 if dog damage occurs. Our dogs wouldn't cause any damage, would they? The Super 8 is located just off I-5 exit 262. 5788 Barrett Avenue; (360) 384-8881.

Travelers Inn: Unlike most hotels in this chain, Bellingham's Travelers Inn says yes to dogs, thanks to the large number of dog shows in Lynden, 10 miles to the north. Dog rates are $10 per stay, and people-a-pair pay $49 to $89. 3750 Meridian; (360) 671-4600.

Val-U-Inn: You'll find doggy-accessible rooms on the ground floor of this Val-U-Inn. Small dogs are welcome for $5 per dog per night. The manager defines a small dog as one who rides in the car (up to 40 pounds). Large dogs are those who ride in the back of pickups. Room rates range from $54 to $62. 805 Lakeway Drive at I-5 exit 253; (360) 671-9600.

DIVERSIONS

Strut your stuff: A kids' dog show is held the third weekend in March at Bellingham's Bloedel-Donovan Park. Prizes at this "not serious" event are awarded for longest ears and happiest face. (360) 676-6985.

Drop your nickels in the doggy bank: Dog biscuits are freely given to leashed pups at Key Bank, even if you forgot to bring the dog. She can even visit with the manager. 1200 12th Street; (360) 676-6345.

One-stop pet shop: Let Herculea lead you into Pet Stop (a pet-supply store), where you can meet the daily guest from the animal shelter and peruse the latest in carrier designs. Proprietors Alan and Barbara will be happy to tell you about their "cats allowed, too" policy. 326 36th Street in the Sehome Village shopping center; (360) 738-3663.

Paws Awhile: That's the actual name of this Humane Society store in downtown Bellingham. Merchandise includes new, consigned, and donated pet goods, household items, and other "enchanting" merchandise. 312 West Champion Street; (360) 752-2970.

Welcome mat: At the Bellingham-Whatcom County Convention & Visitors Bureau, stop in for a pan of water and a current list of Bellingham and Whatcom County accommodations that accept dogs. The C&V Bureau is a short block from I-5 northbound exit 253. 904 Potter Street; (360) 671-3990 or (800) 487-2032.

GLACIER

The little town of Glacier abuts the western boundary of the Mount Baker-Snoqualmie National Forest, 17 miles from Mount Baker. It's home to snowboarders, skiers, and other outdoor adventurers, plus weekend warriors who maintain vacation cabins in the area.

RESTAURANTS

Milano's Cafe and Deli: Milano's gives you your daily pasta made fresh on the premises by a world-champion snowboarder. The salmon ravioli and tomato sauces regularly draw raves, and the Puttanesca was so good they kept it on the menu. The Caesar salad may be the best in the region. As for dogs, Glacier may be a wee tad overpopulated with them, but as long as diners tether their furry buddies outside the deck railing they'll still be within a paw's reach for handouts. 9990 Mount Baker Highway; (360) 599-2863.

PLACES TO STAY

Mount Baker Chalet: At Mile Post 33 on the Mount Baker Highway (Highway 542 east from Bellingham), the Mount Baker Chalet has dog-friendly cabins and condos in and around the town of Glacier, itself nearly surrounded by the Mount Baker–Snoqualmie National Forest. Dorothy the manager says that on some holiday weekends, up to 90 percent of her customers bring dogs. My daughter honeymooned in one of the cabins a few years back and was delighted with the woodsy, folksy atmosphere. This is definitely out in the country, in the foothills of Mount Baker itself. Prices range from $60 to $225 and there are no dog fees. 9857 Mount Baker Highway; (360) 599-2405 or (800) 258-2405.

SOUTHERN PUGET SOUND

GRRRRR

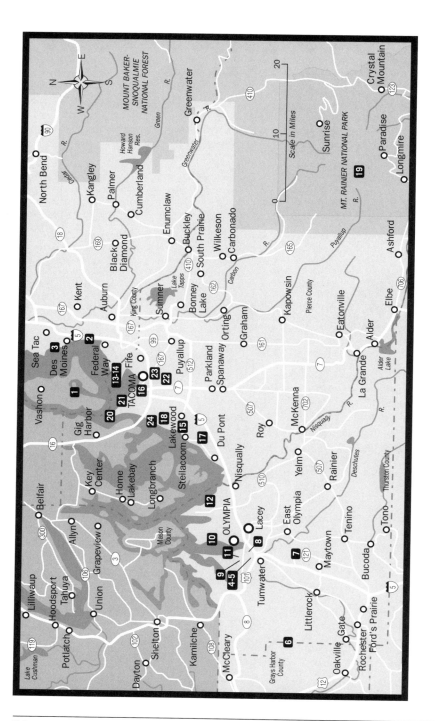

6
SOUTHERN PUGET SOUND

SOUTH OF SEATTLE

PARKS, BEACHES, AND RECREATION AREAS

• **Burton Acres Park** 🐾🐾🐾 See **1** on page 96.

There isn't a Puget Sound park that can be more protected from the elements than Burton Acres. This Vashon Island park sits at the end of a little peninsula in the middle of a harbor at the head of an inlet, on the northeast side of the Burton Peninsula in Quartermaster Harbor. The park has a small beach that, because the inner harbor waters are reasonably warm, is OK for swimming in the summer months. Be careful though—it's nothing but silty mud at low tide. Your leashed hiking buddy will particularly enjoy the 68 acres of walking and horseback riding trails. These woods contain a lot of never-cut old-growth cedars. The trailhead is across the street from the boat launch parking lot.

Take the Washington State Ferry from the Fauntleroy dock in West Seattle to Vashon Island (approximately 15 minutes) and drive straight south on Vashon Highway Southwest for almost eight miles and turn left (east) into the park. (206) 463-9602.

• **Saltwater State Park** 🐾🐾🐾 See **2** on page 96.

Nineteen miles south of downtown Seattle near Des Moines, 90-acre Saltwater State Park feels like a month in the country. There are 52 campsites for tents or self-contained RVs ($11 to $17 per night), two miles of woodsy trails, and 150 feet of beach for romping. Dogs are welcome, of course, but as in all state parks, they must be leashed. The campground has full restrooms with showers. Because of the unusual underwater park with its sunken barge and tire reef, this campground is a favorite of scuba divers. The park was started by the CCC in the 1930s, and later on, McSorely Creekbed was actually moved north to enlarge the parking area and extend the beach. The campground is open late March through early September.

From I-5, 15 miles south of downtown Seattle, take exit 149 onto Washington Highway 516 west. Drive two miles, then turn south onto Highway 509 south (Marine View Drive). The park is in two miles at 8th Place South. (800) 233-0321.

• **Seahurst Park** 🐾🐾🐾 See **3** on page 96.

Seahurst Park was a King County Park until 1996 when it was given to the new city of Burien. It's a lovely, peaceful park, a wilderness surrounded by city, and its beach is a favorite among sunset watchers. The beach itself is about 2,000 feet long. If you and Suzuki (leashed, of course) take a close look and sniff at low tide, you may find, all on one rock, barnacles, mussels, whelk, limpets, chitons, moon snails, and sea pens. Then check out a crevice for red rock crabs, sea stars, and maybe even a sea cucumber.

The park is open from 8:00 A.M. until 9:00 P.M. Seahurst Park is in Burien at Southwest 140th Street and 16th Avenue Southwest. To get there from I-5 at Southcenter, take Highway 518 west for about 3.5 miles to its end, where it becomes Southwest 148th Street. Continue straight west on Southwest 148th Street for a little over half a mile. Turn right (north) onto Ambaum Boulevard Southwest and drive for two long blocks to Southwest 144th Street. Turn left (west) and drive for three short blocks, where you turn right (north) onto 13th Avenue Southwest. Stay on it as it becomes Southwest 140th Street. The park entrance will be on your left. (206) 244-5662.

OLYMPIA

With 47,000 acres of public parks, including 108 lakes and several streams and rivers, not to mention Puget Sound waterfront, Thurston County offers dogs and their owners a range of exploring opportunities. If you're more interested in legislative affairs, visit Olympia, the attractive capital city, just 60 miles south of Seattle. Although you can't let Rover romp inside the stately Capitol—one of the tallest masonry-domed buildings in the world—you and your leashed pooch can play on the Capitol's beautifully landscaped grounds while your partner takes a quick tour of the politicos in action.

Olympia has a tough caveat for visiting dog owners. "It is unlawful to allow or permit any animal to run at large, without a restraining device in any park, or to enter any lake, pond, fountain or stream therein." So states Olympia's not-so-dog-friendly law. It's also unlawful to "conduct a circus" in any park without a permit, but that probably doesn't concern you—unless your four-footed friend looks good in a tutu and you've taught her lots of big-top tricks!

PARKS, BEACHES, AND RECREATION AREAS

•Capitol Campus 🐾🐾 See **4** on page 96.

Seasonal floral displays contribute to the beauty of the Capitol's 30 landscaped acres. Emma and Quinn show a strong preference for dogwood but are also partial to the fragrant cherry blossoms. The flowing fountain—a replica of Copenhagen's Tivoli Garden fountain—lights up the area at night, and the grounds are a popular venue for leashed dogs taking their owners on evening strolls.

The park is between 11th Avenue and 14th Street on the right (west) side of Capitol Way. (360) 753-5686.

•Capitol Lake 🐾🐾 See **5** on page 96.

Capitol Lake (actually a dredged and filled basin) is just a block from downtown Olympia. Dog walkers and runners can choose between a one-mile and five-mile trail. The one-mile path passes bridges spanning the Deschutes River and Percival Creek, which collectively drain into Budd Inlet to the north. The path connects with Marathon Park on the western boundary. The five-mile trail heads counterclockwise from Capitol Park, passes through Marathon Park on the west side, and turns on Tumwater, which connects with Capitol Boulevard at the Miller Brewing Company. Finally, the path heads back north on Capitol Boulevard, which becomes Capitol Way when it crosses I-5, on the east side of the lake.

An occasional seal has been seen under the gates of the dam, and in the lake itself you may see otters, ospreys, eagles, deer, and geese. All we saw was a lot of goose poop and signs suggesting the water was unfit for swimming. Emma reads better than Quinn, so she stayed on shore.

Capitol Lake is located at the intersection of 5th Avenue and Water Street. (360) 753-8380.

• Capitol State Forest 🐾🐾🐾 See **6** on page 96.

This Washington Department of Natural Resources (DNR) working forest park is full of campgrounds, plus lots of trails for people with hiking shoes, people with mountain bikes, people with horses and, naturally enough, people with dogs. The forest is 91,000 acres in the Black Hills southwest of Olympia, and since it's a working forest, watch out for logging trucks. Most of the roads are dirt and gravel, with soft shoulders. The speed limit throughout the forest is 25 miles per hour. About dogs: They're welcome in the forest, and as on all DNR lands, they are requested to be on a leash.

The forest has seven camp/picnic grounds with a total of 81 sites. A couple of those, Porter Creek and Middle Waddell, are favored by the loud crowd: motorbikers. This is a multiple-use site at its best. The Middle Waddell parking lot is the trailhead for the motorbikers. Probably the quietest camps would be Sherman Valley and North Creek, both in the southern section of the forest on Bordeaux Road. Sherman is 5.7 miles west from the Mima Road entrance, and North Creek is 2.5 miles farther. The Sherman Valley campground, on Porter Creek, has seven primitive tent sites, tables, grills, water, and vault toilets. The North Creek campground has five primitive sites on Cedar Creek, with picnic tables, grills, water, and vault toilets. These two campgrounds are open all year and there is no fee to stay in them. They're first come, first served. No reservations are taken.

For hiking, a good starter trail is the McLane Creek Nature Trail, a 1.1-mile loop with a couple of beaver ponds, some boardwalk trail, and all kinds of birds and spawning salmon in McLane Creek. If you can't stand the smell of skunk cabbage, avoid March and April.

To reach the McLane Creek access point, take the I-5 exit 104 east, on U.S. 101. Keep right and exit at Black Lake Boulevard, in less than a mile. Go south three miles to Delphi Road and turn right. The McLane Creek Nature Trail starts just shy of a mile ahead, on the left.

Alternatively, for Bordeaux, drive south from Olympia on I-5 and take exit 95. Turn west (right) and go 3.8 miles to Mima Road. Turn south (left) and go for 1.3 miles to Bordeaux Road. Turn west (right) and the Bordeaux Entrance is in just over two miles. (360) 748-2383 or (800) 528-1234.

• Millersylvania State Park 🐾🐾🐾 See **7** on page 96.

Emma and Quinn say that, for their Milk-Bones money, this Deep Lake state park is the region's best. The usual leash rules apply, but this park is so big and uncrowded that most park officials don't even give a howl if you let your dog off the leash. It just doesn't fit the image of the packed and noisy campgrounds that have influenced so many people to take up RVing. In 1921

Fredrick Miller gave the land to the state as a perpetual park and included maintenance money. Millersylvania has old-growth forest crisscrossed by a fitness trail that is accessible for wheelchairs, a big lake for stick-fetching or duck-chasing and some old CCC buildings made of logs and Tenino sandstone that lend the park some real charm. There are plenty of plain old hiking trails too, replete with scents that you and I can only guess about. You'd think this must be dog heaven, chasing down all the bear and deer trails. Not for Quinn, though. He gave his all to the gopher piles of dirt. He dug four of them down almost a foot. He poked his nose in the tunnels, snorted, and then looked for another pile. He can't help it. Digging is in his terrier genes.

Millersylvania has 132 tent sites ($11 per night) and 47 more with hookups for water, electricity, and sewer ($16 per night).

The park is about 10 miles south of Olympia. To get there, take the I-5 exit 99. Head east on 93rd Avenue for just over a mile to Tilley Road South. Turn right on Tilley Road South, and you'll find the park entrance about three miles ahead, on your right. (360) 753-1519 or (800) 233-0321.

•Olympia Watershed Trail Park 🐾🐾 See 🎱 on page 96.
This park is 171 acres of wild woods just east of downtown Olympia. It's bisected by Henderson Boulevard. Moxlie Creek is the main water source in the watershed, and the trails cross it in several places. Dogs must be leashed.

The park, bisected by Henderson Boulevard, borders I-5 at exit 105. To get there from downtown Olympia, go south on Plum Street, which becomes Henderson Boulevard. Henderson goes through the park for about a mile. (360) 753-8380.

•Percival Landing Park 🐾🐾 See 🎱 on page 96.
Captain Sam Percival built the first Puget Sound dock on this location in 1860, when the area was the business, transportation, and social center of Olympia. Today, Percival Landing is a 1.5-mile recreational boardwalk close to downtown and the marina. It's a very popular stroll. There's a neat observation tower at the north end of Water Street between Thurston Avenue and 4th Avenue. One minimalist grassy patch is available for your leashed buddy.

The park is located between Thurston Avenue and 4th Avenue. (360) 753-8380.

•Priest Point Park 🐾🐾🐾 See 🔟 on page 96.
Priest Point is a 324-acre city park with open fields, outdoor kitchen shelters, trails through the woods, and access to the beach. Enjoy the graceful glider swings, wading pool, and wheelchair-accessible playground before your dog drags you (and his leash) to the waterside. The Ellis Cove Trail, a three-mile self-guided interpretive loop, has four beach access points: at the shoreline north of Ellis Cove, below the swamp, at Ellis Creek Interpretive Station, and at Ellis Bar.

Head north on East Bay Drive from the intersection of Plum Street and State Avenue. The park abuts Budd Inlet on your left and lies on both sides of East Bay Drive. (360) 753-8380.

•Sylvester Park 🐾 See 🈫 on page 96.
Events at this downtown Olympia park tend toward the musical and politi-

cal, but you and your pooch can simply enjoy the grassy public square. Concerts are played on Wednesday evenings and Friday afternoons during the summer. The Shakespeare Festival/Renaissance Faire runs daily the last half of August. Romeo and Juliet must be leashed at all times.

The park borders Capitol Way, Legion Way, and Washington Street. (360) 753-5686.

•Tolmie State Park 🐾🐾🐾 See **12** on page 96.

This 106-acre day-use park, just eight miles north of Olympia at Big Slough, is well famed for scuba diving in the 40- to 45-degree waters of Puget Sound. Three barges were purposely sunk several hundred yards offshore to form an artificial reef 60 feet down. Unfortunately, Emma and Quinn left their flotation devices at home. There are 3.4 miles of forested trails in the uplands, and the lowland sand spit and lagoon are prime spots for bird-watching. This park has 1,800 feet of waterfront, with great views of Pitts Passage, McNeil, and Anderson Islands. Dogs are welcome in Tolmie Park, but scooping and leashing are required.

Tolmie is eight miles east of Olympia at Big Slough. To get there, take I-5 exit 111, and drive north on Marvin Road Northeast for about five miles to 6227 Johnson Point Road Northeast. (206) 456-6464 or (800) 233-0321.

RESTAURANTS

Capitale Espresso-Grill: Desserts are a specialty at the Capitale, plus there is a full range of pastas, antipasti (the polenta is especially good), and salads, not to mention the espressos. Capitale features Batdorf & Bronson coffees, roasted just one block away. Some customers think the coffee puts Starbucks to shame. You and Niçoise can sit at a sidewalk table and enjoy the lifestyle of lingering over the finer foods in life. 609 Capitol Way South; (360) 352-8007.

Starbucks: Starbucks stores always seem to welcome dogs at their outside tables, and this one across from Sylvester Park is no exception. It features Schwartz Brothers Bakery goods. 550 Capitol Way South; (360) 753-7771.

Sweet Oasis Mediterranean Cafe & Bakery: You and Yassou had better save your appetites for the Oasis. If you can hold out until dinner, Emma and I suggest the Eman Paldi, an eggplant affair guaranteed to make you a repeat customer. Call ahead and hostess Jill will cheerfully reserve a sidewalk table for you and yours. The Oasis also favors Greek salads, hummus dishes, and creations with abundant garlic. Lunches are available for $5 and dinner prices range from $7 to $10. The Oasis is not open for breakfast. 507 Capitol Way South; (360) 956-0470.

PLACES TO STAY

Alder Lake Campground: This 231-acre campground on the lakeshore is wooded and relatively peaceful, but for the water-skiers who start early in the morning. That's multiple-use for you, but you and Ziggy will enjoy this place a lot. This is a Department of Natural Resources site, so there is no charge, and dogs are requested to be leashed. The campground has 27 sites, drinking water, picnic tables, fire grills, tent pads, pit toilets, boat launch, and a dock.

To get to the campground from Olympia, drive south on I-5 for 38 miles and take exit 68. Go east on U.S. Highway 12 for 30 miles to Morton, and turn north onto Washington Highway 7. Drive for 15 miles and turn left onto Pleasant Valley Road. Continue for 3.5 miles to the campground. (360) 748-2383.

Best Western Aladdin Motor Inn: The centrally located Aladdin Motor Inn welcomes small dogs on the ground floor for a one-night stand only (and there's a limit of one dog per room). The congenial hosts at these pleasant digs request that you call them ahead of time rather than show up unannounced with your pooch. Room rates range from $71 to $82 (but ask about discounts), and there's a $5 per-night doggy fee. 900 Capitol Way; (360) 352-7200 or (800) 528-1234.

Best Western Tumwater Inn: The Best Western Tumwater permits dogs weighing under 50 pounds to sleep here. Rates are $68-$88, with an additional $5 per-night fee for your dog. 5188 Capitol Boulevard; (360) 956-1235 or (800) 528-1234.

Capitol State Forest camping: See page 99.

Millersylvania State Park camping: See page 99.

Mima Falls Trailhead camping: The Mima Falls Trailhead campground has five primitive campsites with drinking water, picnic tables, fire grills, tent pads, pit toilets, and a horse-loading ramp which you won't need to use. There is no fee, as with most Department of Natural Resources campgrounds. This is a very quiet and peaceful site. The Mima Mounds Natural Area Preserve is about a mile away to the northwest.

To get there from Olympia, drive south on I-5 for 11 miles. Take exit 95 and drive west on Washington Highway 121 for three miles to Littlerock. Continue on 121 for one more mile, then turn left on Gate Mima Road Southwest and drive for 1.5 miles to Bordeaux Road Southwest. Turn right and drive for three-fourths of a mile to Marksman Street Southwest, where you turn right and drive for two-thirds of a mile. Turn left into the campground, about 200 yards. (360) 748-2383.

Shalimar Suites: There's a four-day minimum stay at the Shalimar, a two-story, L-shaped apartment building-turned-motel. "The longer the better," says management. Towels are changed twice a week and linens once a week. The suites are studios, one- and two-bedrooms, and all are fully furnished, including kitchens and all utensils. Dogs are welcome, but it's smart to call first. Rates are $37 to $49. For a week, rates are $31 to $44 per night, and for a month, they're $28 to $37 per night. Dog fees are $6 each, per night. 5895 Capitol Boulevard South; (360) 943-8391.

FESTIVALS

Capital Lakefair: This mid-July city fair, held at Capitol Lake, gets into summer with booths staffed by local organizations, carnival rides, entertainment, fireworks, and a parade. It's not a special attraction for dogs, but they're certainly welcome to watch—leashed, of course. (360) 943-7344.

Super Saturday: The Evergreen State College's commencement festival kicks off on the third Saturday in June. The fair is free and open to everybody, including leashed dogs. You and your canine companion should keep in mind that Super Saturday is a busy, noisy, crowded event, although it's possible to take a break from all of the hustle and bustle by sneaking off to one of the several quiet trails that snake through the woods on campus.

Super Saturday is held entirely outdoors—it hasn't rained on this parade in more than 15 years. Five stages, including one featuring clowns and puppeteers, offer shows from 11 A.M. until 7 P.M. Food and craft vendors ply their wares during the same hours. After 7 P.M., a dance band, playing on the library's fourth-floor balcony, takes over. The entire day is free, except for what you buy. 2700 The Evergreen College Parkway Northwest; (360) 866-6000.

DIVERSIONS

Sick puppy? Critter Calls: In the Olympia, Lacey, and Tumwater areas, Dr. Christina Lasrado, DVM makes small animal house calls for vaccinations, check-ups, skin problems, and internal medicine. She'll make a house call anywhere "within reason," including hotels, motels, and campgrounds. Operations must be done at the hospital. The doctor is associated with Farmhouse Veterinary Hospital, and both are reached at the same phone number. 7602 Steilacoom Road Southeast; (360) 456-5684.

TACOMA

The crest of the Cascade Mountains defines the eastern borders of all of the Washington counties that look westward to Puget Sound, including Pierce County. And while national wilderness areas, parks, forests, and recreation areas make up as much as half of Pierce, King, Snohomish, Skagit, and Whatcom Counties, Pierce County has the distinct privilege of enclosing all of 14,400-foot Mount Rainier within its boundaries. Pierce County also encompasses Tacoma, home to the two-mile Ruston Way waterfront walk, where dog-walkers, runners, and in-line skaters join the crowds gathered to try out the many popular restaurants.

Every park in Pierce County and the Metropolitan Park District of Tacoma requires dogs to be leashed at all times. But they shouldn't feel discriminated against, because cats face the same rule and other pets are not allowed in the parks. You may even be asked to show evidence of intent to scoop. A Tacoma city ordinance requires you to scoop your dog's (or cat's) leavings and to carry the appropriate equipment (plastic bags will work just fine). In fact, Pierce County dog owners are required to carry litterbags in their automobiles! Neither dogs nor cats are allowed on beaches or in fountains or swimming areas, including lakes, ponds, and wading pools. The parks in Tacoma and Pierce County are largely world-class in design and maintenance, and all are open from dawn to dusk. The only downside is that none of the parks have off-leash areas, a handicap for the romping spirit of happy dogs and their handlers.

PARKS, BEACHES, AND RECREATION AREAS

• Dash Point Park and Pier 🐾 See 🔢 on page 96.

Tacoma's Dash Point and its two-acre park lie just west of Dash Point State Park (see 104) that straddles the King/Pierce County line separating Tacoma from Federal Way. There are some hiking trails (be sure to keep the leash on), a fishing pier, and swimming for those who can brave the cold saltwater, but please remember dogs aren't allowed on the beach.

To get to Dash Point Park and Pier from downtown Tacoma, go east on

South 11th Street, which becomes South 11th Street East and then Highway 509. Stay on Highway 509 as it turns northwest onto Marine View Drive. On Dash Point, turn left (west) on Northeast Markham Street. (253) 305-1000.

•Dash Point State Park 🐾🐾 See **14** on page 96.

Rumor has it that the fish are easily duped by baited hooks at Dash Point. So try casting your line for cutthroat trout, sea perch, salmon, and rockfish. More important for your four-pawed buddy are the park's 7.4 miles of hiking trails—but don't forget the leash, because some of those trail miles are for mountain bikers, too. The wooded trails are mostly gentle and heavily used, but there are plenty of new scents to puzzle over. Dash Point offers 109 tent sites ($11 to $12 a night) and 30 utility sites for RVs ($16 to $17 a night; with water and electricity only). There is Puget Sound beachfront (3,300 feet) to enjoy as well, and you're never far from civilization—just walk a bit north to Federal Way or south to the Tacoma city line. It's basically an urban state park, and therefore very well used. It's open year-round.

Dash Point State Park is on South 11th Street East, five miles northeast of downtown Tacoma via Highway 509. From I-5 in Tacoma, take exit 136 and drive north for two blocks, passing Washington Highway 99 (Pacific Highway) to Highway 509 (East-West Road). Turn right onto Highway 509 and drive eight miles to the park. (253) 593-2206 or (800) 233-0321.

•Fort Steilacoom Park 🐾🐾 See **15** on page 96.

Some of the trails here are amazingly primitive for a place mostly dedicated to field sports, fitness, and play. This is probably because there's no swimming or boating at Waughop Lake, which occupies the middle of this 342-acre park between Steilacoom and Tacoma. The lake shores are beautiful, serene, and undeveloped. The central feature of the Fort Steilacoom Park trail system is a stroll around the lake—it can't be beat. Horse trails wind around here too, so keep the leashes on. The west side of Pierce Community College borders the trail system. The park's new manager, the City of Lakewood, intends to set aside a leash-free area soon.

The park entrance is off Steilacoom Boulevard at 87th Avenue Southwest (Elwood Drive). To get there from I-5, take exit 127 and go north on South Tacoma Way for eight-tenths of a mile. Turn left (west) on Steilacoom Boulevard (a state historical road), and stay on it for 3.2 miles until you reach the park entrance on your left. (253) 589-2489.

•Franklin Park 🐾🐾 See **16** on page 96.

A 22.5-acre sportspersons' paradise, with fields and courts for just about any game you might want to play, Franklin is a great big place for pooches to romp—leashed, please, so the "ball terriers" don't ruin everybody's games. There's even a fitness course for people in wheelchairs.

From I-5, take exit 132 and head north on Union Avenue for one mile. Turn right (east) onto South 12th Street. The park is one block up on your right. (253) 305-1000.

•Harry Todd Park 🐾🐾 See **17** on page 96.

This 13-acre park, which includes American Lake, is practically surrounded by the Fort Lewis Military Reservation, which is itself joined to McChord Air Force Base on the north. Keep your pooch leashed at all times and carry a scooper or plastic baggy.

To reach Harry Todd from I-5, take exit 123 and head west on North Thorne Lane Southwest to the park entrance. (253) 589-2489.

• Minnitti Park 🐾 🐾 See **18** on page 96.
Tacoma Community College owns this large undeveloped tract of land, which offers some easy trails (don't forget the mandatory leash and scooper) in a peaceful, uncrowded setting with good views of the mountains. There are three small lakes, but remember, dogs aren't allowed to swim in Tacoma.

Minnitti is located east of Tacoma Community College (TCC) between South 12th and 19th Streets. Just get on South 11th Street downtown (since 12th is a one-way street, in the wrong direction) and drive west. South 11th Street shortly joins South 12th Street; continue on South 12th Street for 2.5 miles to the college. Turn left (south) at Mildred Street, the first street after TCC, and Minnitti Park will be on your right. (253) 566-5152.

• Mount Rainier National Park 🐾 See **19** on page 96.
The National Park Service prefers that you leave your dog at home while you visit Mount Rainier National Park, or at least down in the lowlands with someone else. It's technically OK for your leashed dog to be in the park, but not on any of the trails. That restricts you to drive-throughs and parking-lot walks. The general rule is that your dog may be anywhere your car is. The bonus? That includes campgrounds. There are 689 campsites within the park's five campgrounds. One of them, Sunshine Point Campground, is open year-round. The others follow a seasonal schedule that varies with the weather. Wilderness camping with dogs is not allowed.

Bad weather may lead to the closure of some Mount Rainier National Park services. The road to Sunrise, the visitor area on the east side of the park, closes for winter, as do Cayuse Pass and Chinook Pass on the east side of Mount Rainier and the campgrounds of Ohanapecosh, White River, and Cougar Rock. The road to Paradise from the Nisqually entrance on the southwest side of the park stays open all year, while the Henry M. Jackson Memorial Visitor Center opens only on weekends and holidays from mid-October to mid-April. The Paradise Inn closes for winter, but the National Park Inn at Longmire stays open year-round; dogs are not allowed in either of the inns.

To get there from Seattle (87 miles) or Tacoma (65 miles), take I-5 south to exit 127 and head east on Highway 512. After 2.5 miles, turn right (south) onto Highway 7. At Elbe, turn east onto Highway 706 and continue to the Nisqually entrance to the park, the only entrance that's open year-round. (360) 569-2211; Mount Rainier Guest Services: (360) 569-2275.

• Point Defiance Park 🐾 🐾 🐾 ◀🐾 See **20** on page 96.
The big pup park in Tacoma's Metropolitan Park District offers about 700 acres of old-growth forest, along with a top-notch zoo and aquarium, formal gardens, a restored Hudson's Bay trading post, a commendable restaurant, a logging museum with steam-train rides, and "Never Never Land," a 10-acre children's storyland (no dogs, please). Dogs, of course, think everything is a

storyland, especially when they're exploring wooded trails, and Point Defiance Park has plenty. If that isn't reason enough to visit, the five-mile park drive is closed to automobiles on Saturday mornings. Remember to bring your leash and scooper; they're mandatory.

Take exit 132 off I-5 and drive west on Highway 16. Exit on 6th Avenue and turn right (north) onto Pearl Street (State Route 163), which ends at the park entrance. (253) 305-1000.

•Ruston Way Parks 🐾🐾 See **21** on page 96.

A public-access waterfront is hard to come by in Puget Sound cities, making this collection of waterfront parks on Commencement Bay fairly unique. The two-mile path along the harbor often teems with leashed dogs, joggers, walkers, and skaters on summer afternoons. On weekends, doggie scoop bags are handed out with a smile by volunteers for the parks department and Humane Society. Restaurants, old docks, a fishing pier, and a sandy beach dot the stretch. From downtown Tacoma, go west toward the waterfront on any of the numbered streets. Turn north (left) onto Pacific Street, which will become Schuster Parkway and then Ruston Way. (253) 305-1000.

•Swan Creek Park (Metropolitan Tacoma) 🐾🐾🐾 See **22** on page 96.

Trails galore run through this 250-acre paradise, which follows a more generous swath of Swan Creek (more than a mile long on both sides of the creek) than the Pierce County Swan Creek Park listed below. You can stick close to the creek (you do have a spare pair of shoes in the car, don't you?) or try some of the steeper dirt and scree on the side slopes. Either way, plan on your dog getting muddy. Don't neglect the leash.

From I-5, take exit 130, the East 56th Street exit, and head east on East 56th Street for approximately three miles, until you reach Roosevelt Avenue. (253) 305-1000.

•Swan Creek Park (Pierce County) 🐾🐾🐾 See **23** on page 96.

This Pierce County park contains 40 acres of undeveloped land on the Swan Creek waterfront. Sections of the trail call for a bit of a scramble, but it's no problem for dogs and the spectacular scenery is worth the effort. We got to the gravel bar beside the stream and Emma and Quinn liked it a lot. Keep an eye out for stinging nettle, which grows here in abundance. As we climbed a steep hill in the canyon near the 56th Street end of the park, it occurred to us that this is a pretty remote area. Just to be safe, we recommend trekking about Swan Creek Park with friends. Leashes, of course, are required.

The park is on the eastern edge of Tacoma, south of the Puyallup River and two miles southeast of the Tacoma Dome. You'll find plenty of parking at the lower end at the intersection of West Pioneer Way near the foot of Waller Road East. (253) 798-4176.

•Titlow Park 🐾🐾🐾 See **24** on page 96.

On the saltwater of the Tacoma Narrows, just south of the famous bridge, Titlow Park is our favorite Pierce County park, with 49 acres of lagoons, grassy meadows, forests, and wildlife. We saw a heron standing among ducks as we crossed a small footbridge spanning a picturesque stream. We kept the granddogs leashed out of respect for the wildlife (not to mention the fact that leashes are required). The trails are wide and the fresh sea breezes invigorating, although they did more for me than they did for the dogs, who kept their noses close to the ground.

Titlow Park is located at the west end of Tacoma's 6th Avenue Extension, about five miles from downtown. (253) 305-1000.

PLACES TO STAY

Best Western Executive Inn: This inn says yes to dogs, for a $25 fee. The Best Western's sensible list of House Pet Rules is worth keeping in mind whenever you travel: 1) Keep your pet's kennel on a plastic sheet at all times. 2) Please do not bathe your dog in the bathtub. 3) Please do not use ice buckets for pet water. 4) Please keep your dog happy and quiet.

Rooms average $89 per night for a double. 5700 Pacific Highway East; (253) 922-0080.

Best Western Tacoma Inn: Dogs of any size and number are welcome here. Rates for a double average $69 to $79 and the cleaning surcharge is $20 per stay. 8726 South Hosmer Street; (253) 535-2880 or (800) 938-8500.

Dash Point State Park camping: See page 104.

Econo Lodge of Fife: Its location near the Tacoma Dome and Port of Tacoma keeps the Econo Lodge busy. Dogs are welcome . . . you don't even need to call ahead. Room rates are $45 for a double. A $50 refundable damage deposit is required, plus there is a daily $10 pet fee. 3518 Pacific Highway East; (253) 922-0550 or (800) 424-4777.

Evans Creek Campground: Leashed dogs are welcome to camp with you at this 6-acre creekside campground in the Mount Baker-Snoqualmie National Forest. It's well into the foothills (at 3,400 feet elevation) of Mount Rainier, with plenty of hiking and fishing. There are some nearby off-road vehicle trails, so it's not entirely quiet. Camp water is from a hand pump, and there are picnic tables, fire grills, vault toilets, and firewood, but no showers. Campsites cost $11 to $17.

Evans Creek Campground is located near the town of Buckley. From Tacoma, drive east on Washington Highway 167 for nine miles, then east on Highway 410 to Buckley. From Buckley take Highway 165 south for 19 miles. Take a left on Forest Service Road 7920 and drive 1.5 miles to the campground. (360) 825-6585.

Motel 6 Tacoma/Fife: Pooches are allowed at this Motel 6 north of Tacoma, two miles from the Tacoma Dome. A room for two costs $46. 5201 20th Street East; (253) 922-1270 or (800) 466-8356.

Mount Rainier National Park camping: See page 105.

Saltwater State Park camping: See page 97.

Sheraton Tacoma Hotel: Riding up and down the 24 floors several times a day in the Sheraton Tacoma Hotel elevator, you're sure to encounter other riders. Most are visibly alarmed when they start to walk into the elevator and spy the dogs. Some choose to wait for another ride, a few want to know all about the dogs, and occasionally one will come on in for the ride but keep his back to the door. Their effort at a smile looks more like a grimace, with equal parts anger at being placed in an awkward dangerous circumstance mixed with "can't wait to tell my buddies" about new dangers of city life. As for the granddogs, Quinn and Emma thrill to whatever their next venture might be. In the Sheraton's lobby they hustled us to the elevator. Inside, they faced the mirrored doors, hunkered down a bit on all fours for balance, and waited for the doors to slide open and reveal the next plane of fun.

The Sheraton Tacoma is very hospitable to dogs. It only requires a credit-card imprint for possible damages (or a $250 refundable cash deposit) and that you put a "Dogs Inside" sign on the outer doorknob whenever the dog is in the room. A double will cost $94 to $127. 1320 Broadway Plaza; (253) 572-3200.

Shilo Inn: The Shilo welcomes dogs, one or two per room, but restricts them to ground-floor smoking rooms. There's a grassy pet area south of the parking lot, and an indoor pool, exercise room, and complimentary continental breakfast for the humans. Doubles average $119; the cost per night for a dog is $10. 7414 South Hosmer Street; (253) 475-4020.

Tacoma Comfort Inn: Only two rooms are set aside for people with dogs, so call ahead for availability. Doubles are $65 to $69, plus a $15 per stay surcharge for dogs. 5601 Pacific Highway East; (253) 926-2301.

FESTIVALS

Dog-A-Thon: The registration fee is $5 on the day of the event to simply walk the course of this pledge-type fund-raiser held in Point Defiance Park (located at 5400 Pearl Street). Proceeds go to the Humane Society's Cinderella Fund and the Park District's Youth Scholarship Fund. The Dog-A-Thon is held annually on a Sunday in the middle of July. Leashes are required. (253) 383-2733.

KITSAP PENINSULA

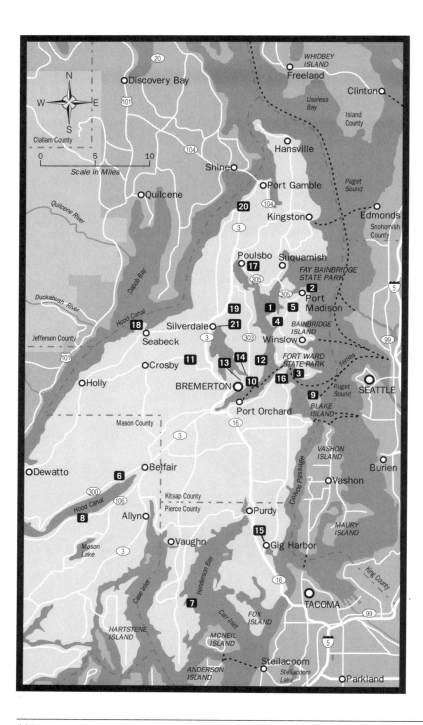

7
KITSAP PENINSULA

The Kitsap Peninsula is nearly surrounded by 236 miles of shoreline, with the 63-mile Hood Canal on one side and Puget Sound on the other. Its picturesque waterside towns attract day-trippers who want to take a scenic ferry ride from Seattle, indulge in a leisurely lunch, and gander at the many touristy antique and knickknack shops. Washington State Ferries link Seattle and Bremerton on the western Kitsap Peninsula (dogs can come aboard, although they have to stay below on the car deck). The ride takes one hour, and ferries leave in each direction nearly every hour. The floating Hood Canal Bridge connects the northern Kitsap and Olympic Peninsulas.

Kitsap County had five of the world's largest sawmills in the 1850s, when it may have been the richest county in the United States. By the 1890s Kitsap County was the most populous in the state, although the smallest geographically. (The population of King County, with Seattle on its waterfront, easily surpassed Kitsap County early in the 20th Century.) The county, which includes the Kitsap Peninsula, Bainbridge Island, and Blake Island, has enjoyed an economic boom in the past decade, thanks to the Bremerton Navy Shipyards and the Bangor Trident Nuclear Submarine Base, which have beefed up the number of military personnel in the area. The county's population growth is supplemented by the steady stream of folks moving to the pastoral, ferry-accessible bedroom community of Bainbridge Island, a 35-minute commute on the water from Seattle.

The Kitsap Peninsula's terrain is fairly flat, making it ideal for bicycling—if you've got a dog who jumps at the chance to ride Toto-style. If you prefer to let someone else do the navigating, various enterprising boat tours and a fleet of mosquito boat taxis whisk commuters and tourists (many with their bikes and dogs in tow) across Bremerton's fjords and inlets.

When Kitsap dogs aren't on their own property, they must be accompanied by someone able to keep them under physical restraint or at the very least voice control. They also have to wear a collar with a license tag at all times (even on private property). Bear in mind that a dog found guilty of biting anyone will be quarantined for a period of 10 days (and his owner will have to foot the bill for the not-so-fancy accommodations at the hound pound, with a minimum $40 fine to boot). Outlaw canines convicted of a misdemeanor (i.e., the naughty pooch has a list of prior violations) will cost their owners plenty: a maximum fine of $1,000 and as many as 90 days in the doggy penitentiary.

BAINBRIDGE ISLAND

Bainbridge Island was popular with the summer-home elite for decades, until Seattle workers discovered they could commute on the ferry and live on the pristine island year-round. The truck farms, largely strawberry, are fewer in number now, a consequence of both the World War II internment of Japanese-American farmers, whose farms reverted to forest, and the construction of homes and businesses. But the progress issue is one of scale; compared to most other communities within commuting range of Seattle, Bainbridge Island is still highly desirable. It's circumscribed and crisscrossed with narrow country lanes, houses are often hidden from view and face the water, and some truck farms are making a comeback. State Highway 305, beginning in Winslow where the Washington State Ferries from Seattle dock, bisects the northern two-thirds of the island and connects with the Kitsap Peninsula via the Agate Passage Bridge. In about six miles from the bridge crossing, Highway 305 runs into Highway 3, which continues north to connect with the Olympic Peninsula via the Hood Canal Floating Bridge.

Dogs are welcome at all Bainbridge Island parks as long as they are leashed. Opinions differ as to whether there is a scooper law or not, but just in case, scoop.

PARKS, BEACHES, AND RECREATION AREAS

• Battle Point Park 🐾🐾 See ❶ on page 110.

Battle Point, a former military installation encompassing 90 acres, two ponds, and a 1.5-mile walking trail, is Bainbridge Island's most popular park. To facilitate PC pooch behavior, the county provides a doggy-bag dispenser for those who "forget" to bring their own. Dogs must be leashed. The park sits on Arrow Point between Manzanita and Port Orchard Bays.

To reach the park from the Winslow ferry terminal, take State Highway 305 north to Koura Road. At Koura Road turn left (west) and continue to the stop sign at Miller Road. Turn left (south) on Miller Road and make a quick right (west) turn on Arrow Point Drive. Proceed on Arrow Point Drive to the park. (206) 842-2306.

• Fay Bainbridge State Park 🐾🐾 See ❷ on page 110.

Located on northeastern Bainbridge Island's waterfront, Fay Bainbridge is the only local park with camping facilities. Dogs must be leashed at all times, and there's an eight-foot leash length maximum. In summer, the tree-shaded hiking trail is the one to walk. It winds past old bunkers and sword ferns under a conifer forest. The park offers a sandy beach (subject to a leash requirement), kitchen shelters, and a boat launch. Dogs are not allowed on designated swimming beaches. You'll find plenty of clam-digging opportunities for the clam terriers; fisherfolk can keep busy here, too. Campsites include 26 standard tent sites ($11 per night) and 10 rather primitive vehicle sites ($6 to $8). The camping facilities are closed from October through March, but the park is open year-round.

From the Winslow ferry terminal, take State Highway 305 north until it intersects with Bay Road. Turn right (east) on Bay Road, continue to its end, then turn left (north) on Sunrise Drive. The park is at the northeastern end of Sunrise Drive. (206) 842-3931 or (800) 233-0321.

• Fort Ward State Park 🐾🐾 See ❸ on page 110.

Fort Ward State Park, an old coastal artillery fort on Rich Passage, is known for its scuba diving, fishing, and picnicking. The park includes a mile-long beach, an offshore scuba-diving park, and a boat launch for you and your first mate. If water sports aren't your thing, there's a 1.5-mile wooded trail. "Leash and scoop" is the law.

The park, open year-round, is four miles southwest of the Winslow ferry dock on Pleasant Beach Drive Northeast. (206) 842-3931 or (800) 233-0321.

• The Grand Forest 🐾 🐾 See 4 on page 110.

You and Wilbur will share this park's trails with Mr. Ed, so leash up your dog or he might get flattened by something with a bigger nose and a longer tail. The forest is a 240-acre cross-island greenway with an old evergreen forest and a wetlands habitat.

To reach the Miller Road trail access, drive north from Winslow on State Highway 305 for almost a mile and turn left (west) on High School Road. Follow High School Road for just about two miles until it comes to a T with Bay Road. Turn right (north) on Bay Road, which becomes Miller Road, and continue for 1.3 miles to the intersection with Tolo Road. Park across the street from the trail, which is on the right. (206) 842-2306.

• Manzanita Park 🐾 🐾 🐾 See 5 on page 110.

Horse and pedestrian trails crisscross this 120-acre day-use park. In fact, it's primarily an equestrian park, but hikers and their leashed dogs are welcome too. Make sure to stand aside as a courtesy when horses pass and keep your dog tightly leashed. Horses are quite a bit bigger, you know, but that doesn't stop antsy dogs. I was holding Quinn, my fox terrier, in my arms one time, and he tried to bite a pony in the neck—nearly jumped out of my arms to do it. I'm glad Quinn missed, because that same pony kicked me in the ribs once. But about Manzanita—it's long and relatively narrow, so you're never far from the road. It's moderately hilly and thickly forested off the trail, but it's not challenging. The two-mile nature trail is the easiest. It starts off the parking lot near the caretaker's home.

From the Winslow ferry terminal, take State Highway 305 north to Bay Road. Turn left (west) on Bay Road, and when you reach the Y, keep to the right. The park is one-quarter mile from the intersection of the Y, on the right. (206) 842-2306.

RESTAURANTS

Bainbridge Thai Cuisine: There is "no problem" here about dogs, but like everyone else, you have to tie yours up out front and keep an eye on things from the sunny deck. It's just a few feet to the marina, so you could tie up your boat, too. You can eat on the deck or choose takeout. The prices are very reasonable. It's located at 330 Madison Avenue; (206) 780-2403.

The Harbour Public House: Here on the Winslow Waterfront, where the Seattle to Bainbridge ferry docks, the Harbour Public House says, "Yeah, a lot of people tie up their dogs outside of the deck railing, or out in front. People do it all the time." Not only that, but there's a place to tie up your dinghy too. Dogs may not go inside, of course, nor onto the deck, and humans must be at least 21. But about the beers: 12 Northwest microbrews on draught. Not many pubs can say that. The food's good too; homemade, they say. It's open daily 11 A.M. to midnight. 231 Parfitt Way Southwest; (206) 842-0969.

Madrona Waterfront Cafe: The Madrona says dogs are usually pretty happy outside the fence on the sidewalk. Here too you can eat on the deck overlooking the marina. The cafe features pasta and salads, seafood and steaks, and vegetarian sandwiches and dishes. It's open daily for lunch and dinner. 403 Madison Avenue South; (206) 842-8339.

PLACES TO STAY

Fay Bainbridge State Park camping: See page 112.

DIVERSIONS

To market, to market, to buy a big bone: Bainbridge Island Farmers' Market offers lots of organic vegetables, ranch eggs, herbs, homemade jams and syrups, fresh cut flowers, food booths, and the work of local artists. This market shows its stuff as a historical island hotbed of high-yield truck farming. Your pup can hope for a handout, but she must be leashed. The market is open on Saturday, 9 A.M. to 1 P.M., April 15 through September 30. It's located next the Bainbridge Island City Hall in downtown Winslow, on Winslow Way. (206) 855-1500.

BELFAIR

PARKS, BEACHES, AND RECREATION AREAS

•Belfair State Park 🐾🐾🐾 See 6 on page 110.

You and your pooch will find 134 tent sites ($11 per night) and 47 utility sites ($16 nightly) at this waterfront park, near the inside end of Hood Canal. This 62-acre campground has 3,720 feet of saltwater shoreline. The 300-foot swimming beach is in an enclosed man-made saltwater basin, controlled by a tide gate. Because of the many arrowheads found during construction, this beach was determined to have been a meeting place for many generations of Indians. Two creeks run through the campground, Big Mission and Little Mission, in which salmon spawn during the fall. The park offers a kitchen shelter, too, with tables and stoves. Dogs must be leashed to explore the trails along the creek and shoreline, as well as those that crisscross Tahuya State Forest, just southwest of the park. And near Belfair itself, there is a 3.8-mile walking trail around Theler Wetlands.

From the town of Bremerton on the Kitsap Peninsula, take Washington Highway 3 southwest for 12 miles to the town of Belfair. From Belfair, drive three miles west on Washington Highway 300 to the campground. (800) 233-0321 for information or (800) 452-5687 for reservations.

•Penrose Point State Park See 7 on page 110.

The local community played an important part in the development of this park. It was built out of a swamp that is now the large day-use area. Early Native American activity is evidenced by a petroglyph located on the spit in the inner cove. The majority of the park is natural forest with a network of trails offering access. The beach is 1,700 feet long. There are 83 tent/self-contained RV sites ($11 per night, $12 in summer) and one primitive tent site. The campground has piped water, picnic tables, a dump station, coin-operated showers, toilets, eight mooring buoys, and 2.5 miles of hiking trails. As at any Washington state park, leashed dogs are welcome.

Penrose is on the Key Peninsula 26 miles from Tacoma. You have to drive all around Henderson Bay and Carr Inlet, but it's worth the drive. From I-5 at Tacoma, drive 16 miles north on Highway 16. Just before the town of Purdy, turn left onto Washington Highway 302/Key Peninsula Highway. It's also called the Gig Harbor-Long Branch Road. Be sure to stay on Key Peninsula Highway when it bears left in about five miles. Continue through the towns of Key Center and Home to Lake Bay. (800) 233-0321.

• Twanoh State Park 🐾 🐾 See **8** on page 110.

Twanoh State Park has 182 acres on 3,167 feet of beautiful saltwater shoreline, ideal for dogs who love to swim. Dogs will enjoy the good hiking trails, and fisherfolk will appreciate the proximity of oysters, crab, and perch. There are 38 tent sites ($11 per night) and nine RV sites with sewer hookups ($16 nightly). The park buildings were constructed by the CCC in the early 1930s and are still preserved in their natural beauty. Because of the wealth of wild-life, early Indians here were among the few hunting and gathering societies in the world which produced wealth beyond their needs. The basis for their economy was fishing, with salmon the main fish.

Twanoh has drinking water, picnic tables, fire grills, restrooms with show-ers, store, playground, tennis court, horseshoe pits, boat dock, seven mooring buoys, boat pumpout facility, two boat launch ramps, 580 feet of swimming beach, and kiddies wading pool (sorry, no pups in the pool). To get there from Shelton on U.S. Highway 101, drive north on 101 for 10 miles, then turn east on Washington Highway 106. Continue for 11 miles to the park. (800) 233-0321.

PLACES TO STAY

Belfair State Park camping: See page 114.
Penrose State Park camping: See page 114.
Twanoh State Park camping: See above.

DIVERSIONS

We'll take the macramé collar: Belfair Farmers' Market features crafts and ceramics, handmade jewelry, woodwork, honey, a variety of baked goods, and several types of plants. Your pooch must be leashed or hand-carried. This farmers' market is held on Saturday, 9 A.M. to 3 P.M., June through mid-October. It's located on State Highway 3 at the Belfair Elementary School play shed; (360) 275-3848.

BLAKE ISLAND

PARKS, BEACHES, AND RECREATION AREAS

• Blake Island State Park 🐾 🐾 🐾 See **9** on page 110.

Lots of luck getting here, since Blake Island is only accessible to dogs and their owners by private boat. Ferry service is not available. Blake Island State Park encompasses the entire 476-acre island and is home to many deer. There are 48 primitive campsites, kitchen shelters, tables, stoves, moorage, and swimming beaches. The island's Tillicum Village is a popular tourist destination; traditional native dances and a salmon dinner are part of the experience. The park has a three-quarter-mile loop trail and 15 miles of foot trails. The campsites are primitive, and there are 23 moorage buoys (moorage time is limited to 72 hours and no reservations are possible). Campsites and buoys cost $5 per night. Canine companions must be leashed.

Sail or power two miles south from Bainbridge Island, or three miles due west from Seattle. (800) 233-0321.

PLACES TO STAY
Blake Island State Park camping: See page 115.

BREMERTON

Bremerton has been a Navy town for a century, and the shipyard is the largest local employer. You're of course too young to remember President Truman's "Give 'em Hell Harry" speech, which he gave here. But you can study up on it at the commemorative plaque on the corner of 5th Street and Pacific Avenue in downtown Bremerton.

The waterfront (formerly a wasteland of rocks, dirt, and the skeletons of industry) is now a delightful four-block-long promenade. Bremerton also offers a pier, restaurants, tour boats, a guest marina, and a colorful Sunday farmers' market. These days Bremerton fosters its 1940s look and promotes it as nostalgia, minus the wartime ladies of the evening.

PARKS, BEACHES, AND RECREATION AREAS

•Evergreen Park 🐾🐾 See **10** on page 110.
Leashes are required here, and violators are definitely cited, so you and your pal should be on your best behavior. The six-acre park sits along a waterside stretch of Washington Narrows between the city's two bridges, Manette and Warren Avenue Bridges. The park includes broad fields, a rose garden, and a picnic area.

Located on Park Avenue between 14th and 16th Streets, turn east toward the Narrows from Park Avenue; the entrance is one-half block down. (360) 478-5305.

•Green Mountain 🐾🐾🐾 See **11** on page 110.
Green Mountain offers eight miles of hiking and biking trails, and the mountain-top view is worth the effort to get there. The Department of Natural Resources, which administers the park, requests that you stay on the trails and keep your dog leashed. The park allows walk-in access only. There are places to camp, but they require a four-mile walk to reach.

From Bremerton, take Kitsap Way west, then turn left (west) onto Northlake Way just past the entrance to Kitsap Lake. After one mile on Northlake Way, turn left (west) again on Seabeck Highway. Continue for three miles to the park. (360) 825-1631.

•Illahee State Park 🐾🐾🐾 See **12** on page 110.

This park has 75 acres and 1,800 feet of saltwater frontage on Port Orchard Bay, set amid the fringes of suburban Bremerton. The camping area is set on a bluff above the mostly rocky beach in a second-growth forest. The views across nearly a mile of water to Bainbridge Island are lovely. The park offers 25 standard tent sites ($11 a night), eight primitive sites ($8 a night), a pier, a concrete breakwater for swimming and scuba diving, and a fishing dock. You can dig for oysters and clams, or fish for salmon, flounder, perch, and trout. A hiking trail offers diversion for your dog (leashes are required), while a baseball field provides entertainment for the kids.

From the Bremerton ferry terminal, flow with the traffic to the right (north) onto Washington Avenue and then left (east) onto 11th Street. After proceeding for six blocks on 11th Street, turn right (north) on Warren Avenue, also known as State Highway 303. Continue north on Warren Avenue as it crosses the Warren Avenue Bridge and becomes Wheaton Way, also considered part of State Highway 303. Turn right (east) on Sylvan Way and continue nearly two miles to the park entrance on the left. (800) 233-0321.

•Kiwanis Park 🐾🐾 See **13** on page 110.

Kiwanis Park's three acres are known locally as Kiwanis Field, probably because the park offers softball and soccer fields, tennis courts, and a playground. All dogs must be on a leash.

The park is located between 4th and 5th Streets, west of Veneta Avenue. (360) 478-5305.

•Lions Community Playfield 🐾🐾🐾 See **14** on page 110.

Leashes are required at this park, too, which sits on 15 waterfront acres on Washington Narrows' north side. There is a path along the water; a fishing pier next to the boat launch at the west end; and, as the name suggests, plenty of playing fields. The park entrance is at the intersection of Lebo Boulevard and Hefner Street. (360) 478-5305.

PLACES TO STAY

Best Western Bremerton Inn: This inn has 102 units, 66 with kitchens. It takes small dogs only, under 25 pounds, and a $50 deposit is required. The deposit is normally returned. In fact, it's been withheld only once, because of a long-haired dog at the height of shedding season. The Inn has a heated pool and hot tub. $81 is the standard rate for a room for two people, one bed.

It's located 3.5 miles west of the ferry terminal, one-half mile east of Highway 3; from Highway 3 take the Kitsap Way exit west to 4303 Kitsap Way; (360) 405-1111 or (800) 228-5151.

Dunes Motel: The Dunes has 63 rooms (five with kitchens) and allows small pets only (weighing under 20 pounds). Rates are $50 per night for one bed, $60 for two, with an additional per-visit fee of $20 for your dog. 3400 11th Street; (360) 377-0093.

Flagship Inn: Dogs weighing 15 pounds and under are welcome at the Flagship, which offers 29 units equipped with a refrigerator, a microwave, and a TV and VCR. Many rooms also offer a great view of Oyster Bay. A continental breakfast is included in the rate, which ranges from $65 to $75, in addition to a $6 per-night dog fee. There's a swimming pool, too. 4320 Kitsap Way; (360) 479-6566 or (800) 447-9396.

Illahee State Park camping: See page 117.

Midway Inn: The Midway takes small dogs only, by which the owner means one that you can easily carry in your arms. It has 60 rooms with microwaves and refrigerators. Rates range from $59 to $64, in addition to a one-time fee of $10 for your doggie babe in arms. 2909 Wheaton Way; (360) 479-2909 or (800) 231-0575.

Oyster Bay Inn: If your dog weighs less than 30 pounds, she's welcome here. Of Oyster Bay Inn's 78 rooms, five have kitchens. Rates range from $55 to $65, plus a $20 per-stay doggy fee. 4412 Kitsap Way; (360) 377-5510.

Super 8 Motel: Yay, free local phone calls at the Super 8. Two pooches per room are allowed, but a $25 deposit is required at check-in. Rates for one person range from $47 to $56. Extra people pay $4 each. The motel is located next to a Dairy Queen. 5068 Kitsap Way; (360) 377-8881 or (800) 800-8000.

FESTIVALS

Bremerton Blackberry Festival: A celebration of the area's ubiquitous bramble bush is the raison d'être for this fun-filled waterfront festival. In addition to paying homage to all things berry (and examining your pup's purple-stained tongue), you'll find ethnic food booths, lots of blackberry delights, local artists and craftsfolk, pony rides for the kids, and live entertainment for all. Leash up your pup. The blackberry festival takes place on Labor Day weekend, at the Bremerton Boardwalk. (360) 377-3041.

GIG HARBOR

Gig Harbor, across the Narrows Bridge from Tacoma, has a snug harbor discovered by New Yorkers. It's cheaper for them to moor their boats in Gig Harbor and fly out twice a year for a sail, than it would cost to keep them at home.

PARKS, BEACHES, AND RECREATION AREAS

•City Park at Crescent Creek 🐾 See **15** on page 110.

The best part about this small, tidy, green park is that it's next to a field of cows. Doggy delight! Watch your cow terriers spring to life. There's also a playground and covered picnic tables. Dogs must be leashed and you must scoop.

Once in Gig Harbor, go north on Harborview Drive (the road closest to the water) and turn right twice, first onto North Harborview Drive and again onto Vernhardson Street. The park is at the very head of the harbor. (253) 851-8136.

KINGSTON

PLACES TO STAY

Smiley's Colonial Motel: Smiley's offers 18 rooms, with one set aside for you-know-who. The rate for a stay in the aptly named "Pet Room" is about $49. 11067 State Highway 104; (360) 297-3622.

DIVERSIONS

Kingston Farmers' Market: The Kingston market is good for produce, baked goods, shellfish, homemade crafts, and local artworks. Dogs who behave are welcome, but they must be leashed. The Kingston market operates Saturdays between 9 A.M. and 2 P.M. early May through mid-October at the Marina park; (360) 297-7683.

PORT ORCHARD

Port Orchard, the Kitsap County seat, is antique central. The selection from the many shops vies for being the best in western Washington, but the town of Snohomish probably wouldn't agree. There are plenty of good bicycling opportunities in the Port Orchard area.

PARKS, BEACHES, AND RECREATION AREAS

• Manchester State Park 🐾 🐾 See 🔟 on page 110.

Manchester is a stop on the Cascadia Marine Trail system. It has 111 acres with 3,400 feet of saltwater shoreline on Rich Passage. Well off the beaten track for campers, it's usually not crowded at all. You and your dog (who'll be on a mandatory, eight-foot maximum-length leash) will enjoy the view from Middle Point Overlook. The park features a 1.5-mile, self-guided interpretive foot trail, as well as the Middle Point Trail, which follows the waterfront along Rich Passage. The camp has 53 tent/self-contained RV sites costing $11 to $16 per night ($12 to $17 in summer). There's plenty of hiking, fishing, clamming, and scuba diving. Amenities include drinking water, picnic tables, fire grills, and restrooms with coin-operated showers. It's just six miles from Port Orchard. Constructed at the turn of the 20th century as a U.S. Coast Artillery Harbor Defense installation for the protection of Bremerton, this area was converted to a Navy Fuel Supply Depot and Navy Fire Fighting Station during World War II. From I-5 at Tacoma, take exit 132 onto Washington Highway 16 toward Bremerton. In 24 miles, take Highway 160/Sedgwick Road exit and follow the signs to the park.

If driving from downtown Port Orchard, proceed east on Bay Street, also known as State Highway 166. Continue on State Highway 166 until it becomes Mile Hill Drive. Proceed for 3.2 miles on Mile Hill Drive until it ends at Colchester. Turn left (north) on Colchester and drive three miles to the park, on the right. (800) 233-0321.

PLACES TO STAY

Manchester State Park camping: See above.

Vista Motel: Deep down inside, most of us think we might be just a tad excessive with our dogs and granddogs. We treat them pretty nice, after all, and take them to some swell places. But who among us would have the nerve to travel with five Rottweilers? One woman did exactly that, and the Vista Motel, regretfully, had to say, "No, please." The Vista welcomes small, well-behaved dogs, and charges a $10 nonrefundable deposit in exchange for the favor. There are 28 rooms, and five have kitchens. Rates for two people start at $45. 1090 Bethel Avenue; (360) 876-8046.

DIVERSIONS

Calling all salty sea pups: Dogs are always welcome, no charge, on Kitsap Harbor Tours. They offer a 45-minute narrated excursion of Bremerton's Puget Sound Naval Shipyard and its mothball fleet of decommissioned ships. Adults pay $8.50, seniors $7.50, and kids 5 to 12 $5.50. The tour office is located on the Port Orchard waterfront, 110 Harrison Avenue; (360) 876-1260.

Custom doghouses and produce, too: Whimsical is the best word to describe the craftwork for sale at the Port Orchard Farmers' Market. Custom doghouses are among the best of these offerings, and the fancifully decorated mailboxes are fun, too. Leashed pooches are welcome. The outdoor farmers' market is held on Saturday, 9 A.M. to 3 P.M., May through October 31, behind the Peninsula Feed store on Bay Street. (253) 857-2657.

POULSBO

Poulsbo, on the shores of Liberty Bay, is known as Little Norway, a nod to the heritage of the original settlers—fishers, loggers, and farmers who arrived in 1890—who could have easily mistaken the local geography for that of their homeland. The Norwegian settlers were followed by Swedes, Finns, Danes, and Lapps. Some Lapp herdsmen imported reindeer to Seattle and then herded them all the way north to Alaska. That's a good example of the ends to which pioneers went in the Northwest, and most people here are still pretty industrious. The Scandinavian theme extends to the town's storefronts and murals, and at annual events where colorful ethnic costumes become the haute couture of Poulsbo.

King Olav himself came here in 1975, looked across the bay toward the Olympic Mountains and said, "This looks just like home." Poulsbo has a temperate climate common to shoreline villages, and the waterfront here enjoys a fleet of fishing and pleasure boats. Poulsbo has a law requiring industrious scooping.

PARKS, BEACHES, AND RECREATION AREAS

• **American Legion Park** 🐾🐾 See **17** on page 110.
It's an easy walk from downtown Poulsbo's waterfront to this five-acre bay shore park. It's what bay shore land used to be like before it was developed. Start on the boardwalk that begins in front of the Sons of Norway Hall, and follow it along Liberty Bay to enjoy the wooded trails. Dogs must be leashed.

In Poulsbo, turn west on Horstmark Street from State Highway 305. Continue on Horstmark Street to Front Street. Turn right on Front Street, which leads to the park. (360) 697-8271.

RESTAURANTS

Sluys Poulsbo Bakery: In the morning, join the locals for a latte and a great array of breads and pastries fresh from the oven. Poulsbo Bread is sold in grocery stores, but it's not the same at all. You'll have to leave Carnivora outside while you pick your bagfull, but there's a bench in front of the barber shop next door where you can share some of the goodies. 18924 Front Street; (360) 779-2798.

PLACES TO STAY

Poulsbo Inn: At the Poulsbo Inn, you and your canine companion will find 73 rooms (one is an exercise room and 22 have kitchens), a heated pool and spa, and a view of the Olympics. Rates are from $70 to $99, including continental breakfast. Dog fees are $10 per night for each canine. 18680 State Highway 305; (360) 779-3921 or (800) 597-5151.

FESTIVALS

Poulsbo Viking Fest: Held in conjunction with Norway's Independence Day, this event takes place on the third weekend in May. Poulsbo's version has been going on for more than a quarter of a century. The festivities include a traditional Norwegian smorgasbord (Thor can hope for a helping of lutefisk) and pancake breakfasts, as well as a parade and waterskiing event. Dogs are welcome, but the festival becomes crowded, so keep your four-legged friend leashed. You'll find the fun on Front Street, at the Poulsbo Boardwalk. (360) 779-4848.

SEABECK

Seabeck sits on the Hood Canal and faces Dabob Bay, on the Olympic Peninsula. The town has plenty of B&Bs, quiet beaches, and dense forests. Best of all, Seabeck has an air leading you to believe that, if you stretch out far enough, you just might be able to reach out and touch the Olympic Mountains. The pizza is very good in Seabeck, a fine attraction for pizza terriers.

PARKS, BEACHES, AND RECREATION AREAS

• **Scenic Beach State Park** 🐾 🐾 🐾 See **18** on page 110.

Near Bremerton on the Hood Canal, Scenic Beach State Park is one of the loveliest in the state park system. With 1,500 feet of gravelly saltwater frontage, it sits on the bluff in a forest and has great views of the Olympic Mountains. Among the Western red cedar, madrona, and Western hemlock at the park, there is a 450-year-old Douglas fir. With so much to explore, this is an ideal park for leashed dogs. There are 50 tent/self-contained RV sites ($11 to $16 or $12 to $17 in summer) and two primitive tent sites. There is plenty of hiking, fishing, boating, and oyster harvesting. Remember to keep your dog leashed as you both bird-watch. The park is home to varieties of thrushes and waterfowl, willow goldfinches, and pileated woodpeckers. Orcas and pilot whales roam the waters. The site was originally developed as a homesite and later purchased for development as Scenic Beach Resort with cabins, campground, boat rentals, and picnic facilities.

From Bremerton, drive north on Washington Highway 3 for about five miles. Before the town of Silverdale, take the Newberry Hill Road exit and drive west for three miles to the end of the road at Seabeck Highway. Turn right to the town of Seabeck. Just past the Seabeck Elementary School, turn right onto Stavis Bay Road and drive one mile to the campground at the end of the road. (800) 233-0321.

PLACES TO STAY

Scenic Beach State Park camping: See above.

SILVERDALE

PARKS, BEACHES, AND RECREATION AREAS

•Island Lake Park 🐾🐾 See **19** on page 110.

Although this is the only lake park on the peninsula that allows dogs, leash laws are in effect, so there's no swimming for Bunky (though you might want to jump in the lake). The park is pretty remote and is used mostly by fishers, but it's a nice place to relax and enjoy the countryside.

From Silverdale, drive north on Chico Way, which becomes Silverdale Way. About 1.3 miles past Waaga Way, turn right (southeast) on Northwest Island Lake Road. The lake is less than a half-mile ahead at 1087 Northwest Island Lake Road. (360) 337-4595.

•Kitsap Memorial State Park 🐾🐾🐾 See **19** on page 110.

Set near the northern end of Hood Canal, this park has 43 standard tent sites ($11 per night, $12 in summer) and a nice mile-long wooded trail. The trail system to the beach offers a sweeping view of the Hood Canal and Olympic Peninsula. Bottom fishing is supposed to be good. Bring the binoculars for bird-watching, a fishing rod for bottom-fishing, and a shovel for clamming. And be sure to keep your clam terrier on a leash at all times.

To get there from Bremerton on the Kitsap Peninsula, drive north on Washington Highway 3 for 19 miles. The entrance is located on the left four miles before the Hood Canal Bridge. (360) 779-3205 or (800) 233-0321.

•Waterfront Park 🐾🐾 See **20** on page 110.

Located in Silverdale's Old Towne, this waterfront beach park has a pier, marina, boat ramps, picnic areas, and playgrounds. Leashed dogs are welcome. There's free parking and a paved walkway along the beach.

From Bremerton, take State Highway 3 to the first Silverdale/Newberry Hill exit, turn right on Newberry Lane, follow the roadway to the left (Chico Way), turn right on Byron Street, and turn right on Washington Avenue. (360) 337-4595.

PLACES TO STAY

Kitsap Memorial State Park camping: See above.

FESTIVALS

Fathoms O' Fun: Port Orchard puts everything there is to celebrate during the year into one 10-day fun fest that includes things like barn dances, softball tournament, fun run, and, most important, a children's pet parade. Emma and Quinn recommend avoiding the fireworks, unless your pooch has nerves of steel. The festival starts in late June. Dogs must be leashed. For more information, write to: P.O. Box 312, Port Orchard, 98366; (360) 876-3505.

Pets Highway LK: In mid-May, any animal who is not "fractious" is welcome to join the fun at this Humane Society fund-raiser. Each year there are hundreds of people and hundreds of animals, including potbellied pigs, goats, and, of course, the usual barking beasts. They all have to be leashed too. (360) 692-6977.

Silverdale Whaling Days: Always held on the last weekend in July, the days are full of live entertainment, street fair throughout the weekend, an artwork competition with prizes, and a foot race. Leashed dogs are welcome. (360) 692-6800.

DIVERSIONS

Silverdale Farmers' Market: There is often live entertainment at the Silverdale Market, which is held Saturdays (between 9 A.M. and 2 P.M.) and Sundays (10 A.M. to 3 P.M.) early May through mid-October, at Silverdale Waterfront Park. Leashed dogs are welcome. (360) 876-3073.

OLYMPIC PENINSULA

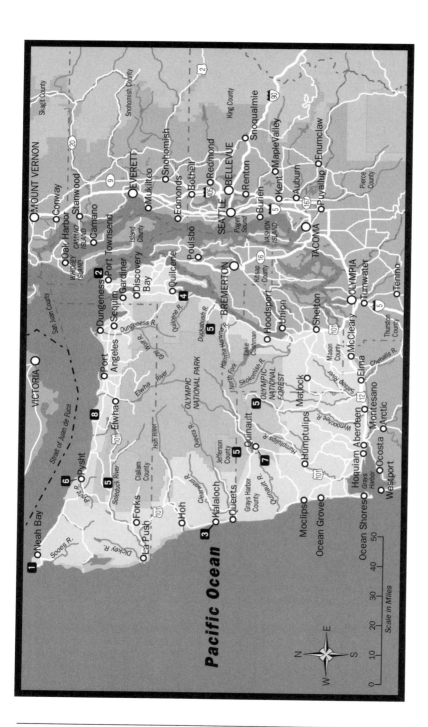

8
OLYMPIC PENINSULA

There are two subjects to master before having a good time with your dog on the Olympic Peninsula. The first is Olympic National Park, administered by the National Park Service for the U.S. Department of the Interior. The second subject is Olympic National Forest, administered by the U.S. Forest Service for the U.S. Department of Agriculture.

Think of them this way: the Park, Park Service, and Department of the Interior keep parks to preserve nature; the National Forest, Forest Service, and Department of Agriculture grow crops, like trees, and provide recreation.

Got it?

Let's try again.

Olympic National *Park* does not like dogs.

Olympic National *Forest* thinks they're OK, mostly.

Now check your map of the Peninsula. The great huge dark green area in the middle (and another thin piece down the west coast) is 900,000 acres of Olympic National Park, mostly off-limits to dogs, with exceptions noted below.

The lighter green area that almost surrounds the park is Olympic National Forest, mostly on-limits to dogs, with certain exceptions noted below.

People of the peninsula are a varied lot, but in general, they don't pay much mind to the comings and goings of the government. That's been to their economic detriment. Because of varied government decisions of late, many people who used to be loggers and commercial fishers are now reinventing themselves as tour guides and travel hosts. Espresso carts are popping up all over. One logger sold off a few million dollars' worth of logging equipment for ten cents on the dollar, and considered himself lucky. On beach treks he collects washed-up glass fishing globes from Japan, and must have nearly a thousand in his front yard. Whale-watching tours use former fishing boats and loggers lead camping treks through dense forest land to Pacific beaches where deer graze and eagles soar and people camp just within the tree line up from the beach.

So excuse the locals if they seem a bit grumpy for a few years. I once bought a packet of plastic forks in Forks, and the clerk saw no humor in that whatsoever.

And about the rain: It's more than you can imagine. It's measured in feet on the Olympic Peninsula. Ferns, trees, and everything else grow to monster proportions. Where does all that rain go? The peninsula has 12 major rivers and 200 smaller streams, renewed almost daily.

There's a lot of watching to be done on the Olympic Peninsula: storm-watching, whale-watching, storm-watching, bird-watching, storm-watching. July through September, though, are relatively dry, and temperatures get into the 70s. But the Olympic Peninsula is basically a temperate rain forest, nearly a million acres of it, and much of what there is to do concerns water: fishing, boating, river rafting, beach walking, oystering. Even just going for a walk can mean wet feet. Good water-resistant boots and raingear will keep you a happy camper.

Highway 101 is the only way around the peninsula. It makes a loop, starting just west of Olympia, but there are enough side trips to keep you busy for days. Westport is well known for charter fishing and whale-watching and Ocean Shores is a bit of beach resort paradise. On the north end, Neah Bay charter fishing is a big attraction, but don't forget the Makah Tribal Museum. It exhibits the best of the Ozette archaeological digs.

Olympic National Park was recognized by UNESCO as a biosphere reserve back in 1976. The recognition was for its primo temperate rain forests and the large protected ecosystem. The park was also selected as a world heritage site in 1981. The park is open all year, but some roads and facilities close in the winter. Much of the Olympic Peninsula consists of sharp and steep ridges over 4,000 feet high. The mountains are a mass of folded and metamorphosed rock, never-melting snowfields and several small glaciers.

So about those 900,000 acres of Olympic National Park and your dog. Dogs are not permitted on trails, in public buildings, at naturalist walks, or in the backcountry, including boats on rivers. My own opinion is that the park can't control its own goat population, so it shouldn't worry about a few well-behaved dogs. But to continue the rules, dogs may be carried in your car or led on a leash (six feet maximum) in parking areas, on paved roads, at Rialto Beach one mile north to Hole in the Wall, and on the Kalaloch Beaches. You can take your dog camping in the park, but only in the public campgrounds reached by road. There are 11 parks accessible by RVs and trailers. The recommended maximum trailer length is 21 feet. The dog must be leashed or under physical restraint at all times and he cannot be left unattended. That means neither of you can go on a hike, because the dog can't go on the trail and you can't leave him in camp.

Oddly, there are 300 miles of trails in the park for stock use, meaning horses, burros, mules, and llamas. The park takes a lot of flack for prohibiting dogs on these rides, but the fact remains, they're not allowed. In one case, a ranger discovered two guys with horses and dogs 13 miles inside the park boundary, in the Enchanted Valley. The ranger sent them packing, in late afternoon, and wrote some expensive tickets into the bargain.

The Olympic National Forest, which grows trees as a crop, does allow dogs for the most part. You and your dog are allowed to camp anywhere for up to 14 days. Dogs are OK in the campgrounds, as long as they're tethered and don't annoy other campers. Dogs may go on hikes with you on Forest Service lands, but when on the trail they must be leashed. Off-trail, in the backcountry, the attitude is, "Wither thou goest, who knowest?" That's not the rule, just the attitude. As for scooping, there's no need to pack it out to a trashcan, but you might consider taking a shovel. The dog poop rules are the same as for humans: Bury it six to eight inches deep, at least 100 feet from trails, water, and campgrounds. There are 19 developed campgrounds on the Forest Service lands, plus five boating sites, four nature trails, and one viewpoint. There are 201 miles of trails in the forest, some of which lead into the national park.

Dogs are not allowed on Forest Service wilderness lands; the rules are exactly the same as for National Park Service parklands. There are five wilderness areas totaling 88,481 acres. These are only accessible by foot or horseback.

PARKS, BEACHES, AND RECREATION AREAS

•Cape Flattery Trail 🐾 🐾 🐾 See **1** on page 126.

The Cape Flattery Trail is a half-hour boardwalk trail that will take you through dense swampy woods to the most northwestern part of the continental United States. You can't get to the beach here because there isn't any. The trail ends on a bluff a few hundred feet above the crashing waters. From here you can see sea caves, Tatoosh Island, gray whales, and orcas on a good day. Dress for windy cold weather year-round. Dogs are welcome but they must be leashed.

In the town of Neah Bay, turn right at the IHS Clinic/Presbyterian Church. Go for one block, then turn left and follow the signs to the Tribal Center. This road is paved. Drive about 2.5 miles to the Makah Tribal Center and continue past it for one-quarter mile to a gravel road. Continue on the gravel road for approximately four miles. You will see a "Cape Trail" sign. Stay left and travel a short distance to the trailhead.

•Fort Worden State Park 🐾 🐾 🐾 See **2** on page 126.

Within the town of Port Townsend, this big magnificent year-round park has 434 acres with two miles of saltwater shoreline on Admiralty Inlet and the Strait of Juan de Fuca. The park is listed in both the State and National Register of Historic Places and has been designated a National Historic Landmark. The old military buildings house conferences like the Sea Kayak Symposium held in September. The campground itself is very popular with sea kayakers and scuba divers. Your leashed dog will like it too. The camping area is on a sand peninsula that can get quite windy. The abandoned concrete bunkers and artillery vaults are a real curiosity. Wildlife includes black-tailed deer, great blue herons, bald eagles, gray whales, and orca whales. There are six miles of hiking trails and huge grass areas above the bluff at the old parade grounds.

There are 80 campsites for tents and self-contained RVs, plus three primitive, hike-in/bike-in tent sites. Fees are $8 to $17. For a $6 fee, you can make reservations through Reservations Northwest at (800) 452-5687.

The park is within the city limits of Port Townsend at the north end of town. The directional signage from downtown is good. (800) 233-0321.

•Kalaloch Campground 🐾 🐾 🐾 See **3** on page 126

This is one of the few campgrounds with Pacific beach access. On the west coast of Olympic National Park, 35 miles south of the town of Forks, Kalaloch Campground is almost a city. It has 177 campsites for tents and RVs. It's large enough that a walk around camp is an actual excursion. Some of the campsites have an ocean view, and most of the sites are shielded from each other by growth. Be prepared for wet weather, both fog and rain, in any season. The big fun here for dogs, who are most welcome when they're leashed, is the stretch of beach that's so long you shouldn't leave your campsite without a backpack full of lunch. I wouldn't suggest much water play for you or the dog. Besides it being rough water, lots of logs (see all those up on the beach?) get tossed onshore by the waves. You can't always see 'em coming. The campground is open year-round. It has drinking water, picnic tables, fire grills, and restrooms. Cost is $11 to $17 per night.

From the town of Forks on U.S. Highway 101, drive 35 miles south to the campground. (360) 452-4501.

•Mount Walker Observation Area 🐾🐾🐾 🐾 See ❹ on page 126.

Mount Walker's 2,759-foot summit offers spectacular views of about five million acres, including a large portion of the Olympic Peninsula, Hood Canal, Kitsap Peninsula, southern Puget Sound, and the Seattle/Tacoma area. The summit is accessible via a two-mile walking trail, which leads to the south viewpoint. On a clear day you can actually see Seattle's Space Needle, 28 miles away. Dogs must be kept on a leash at all times, and the maximum leash length is six feet.

The Mount Walker Observation Area parking lot is located one-quarter mile from the trailhead. To reach the park from Quilcene, drive approximately five miles south on U.S. Federal Highway 101. Turn left (east) on Forest Service Road 2730, a gravel road that steeply ascends to Mount Walker's summit. (360) 956-2300.

•Olympic National Forest 🐾🐾🐾 See ❺ on page 126.

In the Olympic National Forest, you'll find trees growing to monster proportions and ferns too big for even an elkhound to pee on. The 632,000-acre forest encompasses 201 miles of trails, some of which lead into the national park; keep in mind, however, that Olympic National Park is largely inaccessible to your canine companion. Everyone will be happier exploring in the forest, where you and your dog can even camp (except in the U.S. Forest Service wilderness area) for up to 14 days. In all, there are 24 campgrounds in the national forest, with a total of 498 campsites. Seven of the campgrounds charge no fee at all, and the rest range from $4 to $13.

From I-5 at Olympia, take exit 104 onto U.S. 101 north. U.S. 101 circles the entire Olympic Peninsula and provides access to several of the national forest's entrances. From the town of Hoodsport, 34 miles from I-5, Highway 119 leads past Lake Cushman (with a couple of good campgrounds) through the Mount Skokomish Wilderness into Olympic National Park. Farther up Hood Canal, 25 miles from Hoodsport, a good access road leads from the town of Brinnon into Olympic National Forest along the Dosewallips River. The best view into the Olympic Mountains is from Hurricane Ridge, reached by an access road leading south from Port Angeles. (360) 956-2300.

•Pillar Point County Park 🐾🐾🐾 See ❻ on page 126.

Thirty-five miles west of Port Angeles on the Strait of Juan de Fuca, Pillar Point contains 4.3 acres of land, 35 primitive campsites, a full service restroom (no showers), two vault toilets, picnic shelter, and lots of saltwater beach access. There's plenty of beach room to romp, and the beachcombing is good.

Dogs are welcome, but they must be on a leash no longer than eight feet. Park users can fish, crab, gather shellfish, walk the beach, and look in wonder across the Strait of Juan de Fuca. The campground is open May 15-September 15. Campsites cost $11 to $17, and there is an on-site park manager during the camping season. Reservations are accepted by calling the park after May 15th.

Follow Highway 101 west from Port Angeles. Turn right onto Highway 112, follow Highway 112 until you see signs for Pillar Point. (360) 417-2291.

•Quinault Loop Trail 🐾🐾🐾 🦴 See **7** on page 126.

This trail extends four miles along the shore of Lake Quinault and deep into the rain forest. As you wander through these primordial woods, your dog will discover unique places to sniff and explore, including swamps, trees standing on stilt-like roots (the result of nurse logs rotting away), and some of the tallest trees your pooch will probably ever see. Dogs must be leashed; the loop takes two to three hours to hike. You can access the trail at several points, including the Quinault Ranger Station, Lake Quinault Lodge, Willaby Campground, Falls Creek Campground, and the Quinault Rain Forest Nature Trail parking lot.

From Port Angeles, drive 121 miles west on U.S. 101. Turn left (east) on South Shore Road and then proceed for approximately two miles to the trail. (360) 288-2525.

•Salt Creek and Tongue Creek Recreation Area 🐾🐾🐾🐾 See **8** on page 126.

Tongue Point juts into the Strait of Juan de Fuca toward Vancouver Island, about 12 miles north. Nearby Agate Bay is named for the treasures still found on local beaches. This is one of the few parks and/or campgrounds on the Strait, and it's a good one for a time-out on a drive around the Olympic Peninsula or for an extended stay (two-week limit). It's open year-round. There is no day-use fee, and the gate closes at dark. Pets are allowed on leashes no longer than eight feet.

Activities include hiking, fishing, swimming, horseshoes, beachcombing, and horseback riding. The 196-acre park includes upland forests, rocky bluffs, tidepools, sandy beaches, Salt Creek River access, hiking trails, and five beach access walkways with interpretive signs. The park also serves as a hiking trail access to the Department of Natural Resources trails which accesses the Striped Peak area.

The tidepools in front of Salt Creek Recreation Area are rich with marine life and are designated as a Marine Life Sanctuary. This means "look but don't touch."

The park has 92 campsites for tents or self-contained RVs. There are no hookups for electricity or water; however, water is available in several locations throughout the park. Camping is on a first-come, first-served basis; reservations are not available. Campsites start at $8 per night.

From Port Angeles on the Strait of Juan de Fuca take U.S. Highway 101 west for five miles. Then turn right (west) onto Washington Highway 112 and continue about seven miles to Camp Hayden Road. Turn right (north) on Camp Hayden Road. The campground is about three miles from the turnoff. (360) 928-3441.

PLACES TO STAY

Cape Motel and RV Park: You can bring your friendly pooch to the Cape Motel, but you'll have to pay an additional $7 per night for the pleasure. Rooms range from $48 to $68. Reservations are welcome year-round and are highly recommended during the fishing season. At the RV park (which usually closes in the winter), rates are $17 per night for one person, plus $2 for each additional person. Tent sites cost $12 per night. There is no doggy charge at the RV park. Box 136, Neah Bay, WA 98357; (360) 645-2250.

Falls Creek Campground: Falls Creek offers 15 tent sites ($7 a night) and 16 trailer sites ($13 a night) on the south shore of Lake Quinault. The maximum allowable RV length is 16 feet. This campground is set on a rocky beach and offers a boat-launch ramp and a swimming area. You must keep your dog physically restrained and quiet at all times. Campsites are available on a first-come, first-served basis. From Hoquiam, take U.S. 101 north for 38 miles to South Shore Road. Turn right on South Shore Road and drive 2.6 miles to the campground. (360) 288-2525.

Hard Rain Cafe & Mercantile: Hard Rain Cafe is a long-standing Hoh River Valley business with a new name, although the former name was better: R&R Sports Center & RV Park & Burger Shack & Wooley Packer Llama Company, which said it all. Fortunately, Hard Rain still covers all of the recreational bases with RV sites, groceries, fast food, and fishing supplies. Of the 13 RV sites, seven offer full hookups ($15 per night) and six come with water and electricity ($13 per night). Dogs are welcome and leashes are optional, but beware of the llamas in the nearby pasture, which have chased away coyotes and a cougar and have actually stomped on pesky dogs. Deer and elk frequent the pasture too. Hard Rain is often full, so reserve your spot in advance, particularly during the hunting season. (360) 374-9288.

Kalaloch Campground: See page 129.

Kalaloch Lodge: A long-favored Pacific Northwest getaway, Kalaloch is busy even in the winter, when storm-watching is a popular pastime. The lodge is part of Olympic National Park, and one of the few park locales that allows dogs. Lodgings consist of a motel unit with ten rooms, a main lodge with eight rooms, and 40 housekeeping cabins on the bluff above the beach. A dining room and coffee shop serving pretty good chow are located in the lodge.

Kalaloch is set on a bluff directly above a long, sandy beach that's perfect for runs with Spot. Dogs must be leashed and are only allowed in the cabins. A two-person cabin ranges upward from $93 and $135 per night, depending on the location, view, and season. Dogs cost an extra $10 each per night. (360) 962-2271.

Lake Quinault Lodge: A grand, national park-style affair, this lodge overlooks the lake. Dogs are not allowed in the lodge, but they may stay with you in the one-story annex with a wrap-around porch. The comfortable lobby is beautiful, albeit dark, and periodically filled with the hubbub of people passing through. Annex rates for a double range from $68 to $120, depending on the season and view; the doggy fee is an extra $10 each per night. 345 South Shore Road; (360) 288-2900 or (800) 562-6672.

Olympic National Forest camping: See page 130.

Pillar Point County Park camping: See page 130.

Port Angeles–Sequim KOA Kampground: This campground boasts a dog exercise area (bring a leash). Your dog cannot stay in the cabins, but you can keep her in your RV or tent and she must be leashed. The campground is midway between Port Angeles and Sequim, and offers 90 sites, a grocery store, heated pool, free hot showers, and a rec room. Campsites are $22 per night. RV rates are $28 for a site with full hookups and $26 for a site with water and electricity only, no sewer. (360) 457-5916.

Salt Creek and Tongue Creek Recreation Area camping: See page 131.

Sol Duc Hot Springs Resort: Sol Duc, located within Olympic National Park, was originally built as a health spa in the European tradition. Today it offers giant hot tubs full of mineral water. The resort is closed in the winter. Dogs are welcome in the RV park (but not in the cabins) as long as they obey national park rules: they aren't allowed on trails and must be leashed and accompanied at all times. RV sites are $16 per night. Pool use is extra: $7.50 per day. (360) 327-3583.

South Fork Hoh Campground: This free Department of Natural Resources campground has just three sites for tents or self-contained RVs. It's so remote it's almost your own personal wilderness site. The year-round campground is in the Olympic Experimental State Forest, also known as the Bert Cole State Forest. It's 30 miles southeast of the town of Forks on the Hoh River. Bring your own water, but there are picnic tables and vault toilets. The Olympic National Park South Fork Trailhead is two miles beyond the campground.

About 16 miles south of the town of Forks at milepost 176 on U.S. Highway 101, turn east onto Hoh Mainline. Drive for 6.6 miles, then turn left onto H-1000 Road, which becomes one-lane gravel for the last few miles. The campground is in 7.4 miles on the right. (360) 374-6131.

Willaby Campground: There's room for seven tents and 14 trailers in this wooded campground set on a rocky beach on Lake Quinault's south shore. The swimming is good, although chilly, and there is a boat launch. Dogs must be leashed at all times; the maximum leash length is six feet. The nightly fee is $13. From Hoquiam, take U.S. 101 north for 38 miles to South Shore Road. Turn right on South Shore Road and drive one mile to the campground. (360) 288-2525.

DIVERSIONS

Doggie deliverance: Olympic Raft and Kayak provides rafting trips down the pristine and gentle Hoh River from April through September. "I take my black Lab, who's quite a river dog, on raft trips," says owner Dave King. And he says your dog is welcome, too, for a $10 fee. Dave asks that you clip Ahab's claws to protect the rubber raft. Rates for humans are $44 for adults and $39 for children under 12. Bring a doggy personal flotation device, available at stores such as REI in Seattle. The Hoh, a Wild and Scenic River, is rated a Class I and offers a few easy rapids. It's a main peninsula river, fed by four tributaries from Mount Olympus. Raft trips take place outside of the park and meander through Oxbow Canyon. Lucky rafters will see river otters, grazing elk, bald eagles, and harlequin ducks. Call or write for more information about rafting on the Hoh or other Olympic rivers: 123 Lake Aldwell Road, Port Angeles, WA 98363; (360) 452-1443.

Port Angeles Waterfront Trail: This eight-mile paved trail runs from the site of the old Rayonier Mill along the Port Angeles waterfront to the end of Ediz Hook, where picnic sites and restrooms are available. For a good short walk you can start on the trail at the Port Angeles City Pier and walk to the site of the Old Rayonier Mill and return on the same path. This walk is 1.5 miles along sandstone cliffs. Your dog must be leashed, and watch out for bicyclists and in-line skaters. (360) 452-2363.

SAN JUAN ISLANDS

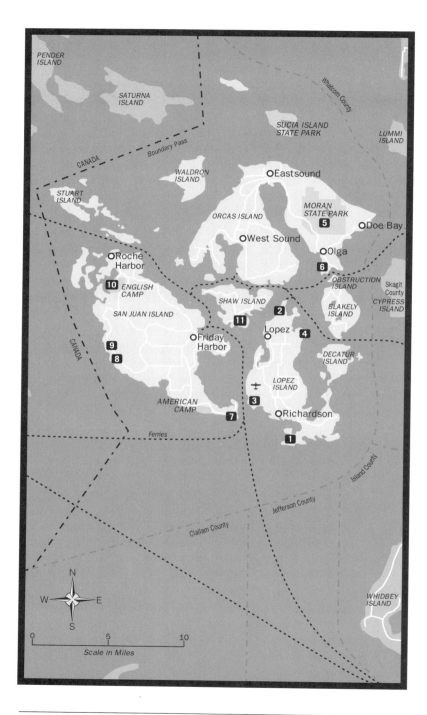

9
SAN JUAN ISLANDS

Known to locals as the "Magic Islands," the San Juan Islands form a bit of a banana belt: San Juan Island averages 55 more sunny days a year than Seattle (70 air miles to the south), and Lopez Island actually has a profusion of cacti on its southern reaches. With resort names like Deer Harbor and Doe Bay, the islands cast a spell on visitors that makes them ask themselves, "How can I retire 20 years early so I can live here?" The old-time hippies figured it out in the 1960s, and have lived on the islands ever since. But of all the enchanting islands that exist in San Juan County (hundreds of which don't appear until low tide), only 172 have names, and Washington State Ferries (see To Reach the Islands at the end of this chapter) serve only four of them: Orcas, San Juan, Lopez, and Shaw. On weekends, holidays, and throughout the summer months, prepare for huge lines of people waiting to catch the popular ferries.

People reside on 60 of the islands, while another 83 belong to the San Juan Islands National Wildlife Refuge and Wilderness Area (and, except for Matia and Turn Islands, these wilderness islands cannot legally be trod upon). Tourists, bicyclists (who love the flat terrain that characterizes Lopez Island), and summer-home owners from throughout the United States inundate the few vacation destinations. San Juan County is one of the best places in the world for sighting whales, bald eagles, and English skylarks. Sea kayaking is another primary recreation, with boats and tours offered nearly everywhere. For more information on the islands, call the *San Juan Islands Visitor Information Service:* (360) 468-3663.

LOPEZ ISLAND

Lopez (population 1,500) is mainly a farming and fishing island, rediscovered in recent times by boaters and bicyclists. Agate Beach County Park, at Outer Bay, is a great place to see cormorants and puffins. Great blue herons, geese, kingfishers, rabbits, deer, and raccoons frequent Spencer Spit State Park. Stop by the Richardson General Store, formerly a steamer shop, which is listed on the National Register of Historic Places. Currently, the general store caters to boaters.

Lopez residents are some of the friendliest in the San Juan Islands. Whether you're on a bike or in a car, you'll learn to wave at everyone who extends a greeting. Unfortunately, the island's innkeepers are not as welcoming to our canine friends; there are 60 guest rooms here, but dogs are not permitted in any of them. So to spend more than a day here, you'll have to camp with Fido.

PARKS, BEACHES, AND RECREATION AREAS

• **Agate Beach County Park** 🐾 See ❶ on page 136.
Located on the southwest tip of Lopez Island, Agate's beach is very rocky, but

it's a nice stop for hikers, bikers, and kayakers. There is no camping. Leash your pooch.

To reach the park, drive south from the ferry dock on Ferry Road. Proceed on Ferry Road until you reach Lopez Sound Road. Turn left (east) on Lopez Sound Road, then turn right (south) on Mud Bay Road. At Mac Kaye Harbor Road, turn right (south) and continue to the park. (360) 378-8420.

•Odlin County Park 🐾 🐾 See **2** on page 136.

This park has 30 campsites on 80 wooded acres. There aren't many sandy beaches in the Northwest, but this park offers a mile of sandy shoreline. You can swim in the chilly water if you dare. Odlin County Park also offers a pier, float, mooring buoys, ballparks, and a covered cook shack. Dogs must be leashed and attended at all times.

From the ferry landing, take Ferry Road one mile south to the park. (360) 378-2992 (park); (360) 378-1842 (reservations mid-February to mid-September), (360) 378-8420 (County Parks).

•Shark Reef Park 🐾 🐾 🐾 See **3** on page 136.

Shark Reef's wild ground, a parcel of Washington State Department of Natural Resources (DNR) land, includes a forest that ends at a scenic promontory. Hundreds of seals hang out on the big rocks offshore (your pooch will thrill to barks of a different sort). As on all DNR lands, dogs are requested to be leashed. From the Lopez Island Airport, drive nearly two miles on Shark Reef Road to the park. (360) 856-3500 (regional DNR), (800) 527-3305 (state DNR); (360) 378-8420 (County Parks).

•Spencer Spit State Park 🐾 🐾 See **4** on page 136.

Twenty-five vehicle-accessible campsites, 10 walk-in sites, two group camps, and a mile of sandy beach are available at this 129-acre park on the sunrise side of the island. The campsite fee is $11 per night and reservations are recommended. Showers are not available. Please bring your own firewood. Leashes are required, and rangers patrol on mountain bikes to enforce this regulation.

From the ferry landing, drive south on Ferry Road for just over one mile. Turn left (east) on Port Stanley Road and continue for nearly two miles, around Swifts Bay, to the park. (360) 468-2251 or (800) 233-0321.

PLACES TO STAY
Odlin County Park camping: See above.
Spencer Spit State Park camping: See above.

ORCAS ISLAND

Stunning, 54-square-mile Orcas Island is the largest of the San Juans and offers comprehensive tourist services. Getting around the summer traffic on this horseshoe-shaped island takes some time, unless, of course, you have a boat. Bicyclists have to contend with hilly terrain, but Orcas is so beautiful you'll be glad of any mode of transport that provides a tour of the island.

PARKS, BEACHES, AND RECREATION AREAS

• Moran State Park 🐾🐾🐾 See 5 on page 130.

In 1920, Robert Moran, a shipbuilder and a former mayor of Seattle, donated 2,600 of Orcas Island's acres to the state for use as this park. Moran State Park has since expanded to more than 5,000 acres and includes two mountains, five lakes, 30 miles of foot trails, and 300 acres of old-growth forest. Visitors can camp, picnic, fish, swim, boat, and hike here. Most trails run through the woods, but you will find paths with views of Lopez, Lummi, Blakely, Matia, Barnes, Cypress, and Clark Islands. The park is open year-round, but it's busiest on summer weekends. Cold Springs is a particularly pleasant picnic spot, set in an isolated stand of timber. Dogs must be kept on a leash (eight feet in length or less) at all times, and they are not allowed to annoy other park visitors. Scooping is also required.

Aside from its many trails and lakes, perhaps Moran's greatest attraction is its views from Mount Constitution (elevation 2,409 feet) and Little Summit Lookout (elevation 2,039 feet). You can drive, bike, or hike to either. From the park's only road, there's a cutoff to Mount Constitution. The cutoff veers left just before Mountain Lake, but it's closed at dusk and during winter snowfall. The summit of Mount Constitution offers a spectacular 360-degree view. On a clear day, you can see Vancouver, B.C., Vancouver Island, Mount Garibaldi (north of Vancouver), Mount Baker, Mount Rainier, and the Olympics. The 52-foot tower at the top of Mount Constitution was designed by renowned architect Elsworth Storey, patterned after the 12th-century watchtowers in the Caucasus Mountains, and built in the 1930s by the Civilian Conservation Corps (CCC). CCC workers built the tower with sandstone blocks from an island quarry and forged and shaped its decorative wrought-iron gates, railings, and barriers.

Moran State Park has 151 campsites, open year-round. You'll find sites at the north end of the park (on a wooded slope above the road, across from Cascade Lake), in the middle of the park at the south end of Cascade Lake, and at Mountain Lake. Mountain Lake is a reservoir, so swimming is not allowed, but fishing is permitted. Camping fees range from $5 to $11.

From the Orcas Island ferry landing, turn left (west) on Orcas to Olga Road and continue for 15 miles to the park. (800) 233-0321 (information), (800) 452-5687 (reservations, $6 fee).

• Obstruction Pass Recreation Site 🐾🐾 See 6 on page 136.

Obstruction Pass is a Washington State Department of Natural Resources park, with nine free campsites and two picnic sites. There are outdoor toilets, three mooring buoys, and good access to the shoreline. Potable water is not available. Dogs are requested to be leashed, and quiet hours are in force from 10 P.M. to 6 A.M.

From the ferry landing, turn immediately left (west) on Orcas to Olga Road. Proceed on Orcas to Olga Road for approximately 16 miles. Turn left (east) on Olga to Point Lawrence Road (also known as Doe Bay Road). Drive on Olga to Point Lawrence Road for just over one-half mile, then turn right (south) on Obstruction Pass Road and continue to the park. (360) 856-3500.

RESTAURANTS

The Starfish Grill: This Deer Harbor restaurant, recently renovated, is strong on local seafood steaks, teriyaki salmon with a nice touch of Mediterranean flavorings, and an exquisite grilled New Zealand spring lamb. It also has a deli and plenty of outside tables during nice weather. Well-behaved dogs are welcome. (360) 376-2482.

PLACES TO STAY

Doe Bay Resort & Retreat: Doe Bay provides a great, retro-hippie-1960s weekend. And dogs are welcome during the off-season for a $10 per-night fee. Dogs are not allowed between June 16 and September 16. Stay leashed on the premises. Loose dogs are a real problem with the sheep raised on the island, plus most of the deer are almost tame in their disregard of humans and their dogs. Doe Bay calls its cabins and retreat facilities "rustic," but "funky" might be more apt. You'll find light bulbs hanging from ceiling fixtures, and you can hang your gear on nails stuck in the bedroom and bathroom walls. But, hey, it's basically clean, the bathrooms have those 5,000-foot rolls of toilet paper, and the price is right. Rates for a cabin range from $49 to $110. The larger ones have three bedrooms with a kitchen and utensils. There's a $10 charge for each additional person. Campsites are available too, ranging in cost from $12 to $24.

Doe Bay Resort & Retreat has a good natural-foods restaurant (open for breakfast and dinner) as well as guided kayak trips (the $40 per-person fee covers a three-hour guided trip, kayak, and all required gear). As we paddled away one morning, we watched a man doing his tai chi. When we paddled back in to the beach, an accordionist playing slow, wistful, melancholic polkas serenaded us.

Doe Bay's clothing-optional mineral baths and sauna are a big attraction, too. Two hot tubs hold about 10 people each if you're willing to rub, uh, elbows. The same principle applies to the cold tub, which accommodates around 20 folks. Dogs are not welcome in the tubs, but they like to watch the fun. 86 Star Route; (360) 376-2291.

Moran State Park camping: See page 139.

North Beach Inn: A tip from Sandy, my first girlfriend and a lifelong friend, led us to Orcas Island's North Beach Inn. The inn offers pleasant cabins, each with a kitchenette and fireplace, facing north toward Sucia and Matia Islands. The owners have dogs of their own, and they allow visitors to bring a maximum of two well-behaved pooches. There's a two-night minimum-stay requirement. Summer rates are $105 for a one-bedroom unit, $160 for a two-bedroom unit, and $185 for a three-bedroom unit. Off-season rates are lower. Each dog costs $10 per night or $50 per week. (360) 376-2660.

Obstruction Pass Recreation Site camping: See page 139.

West Beach Resort: A stay at Eastsound's West Beach Resort, like travel in the San Juans, resembles a journey back in time. "We try to keep West Beach Resort as much like the 1920s as possible," says the owner of the resort, which was built in 1928. Dogs are allowed in some of the one- and two-bedroom cabins, which are equipped with kitchens (including dog-friendly linoleum flooring) and a great location—right on the beach. Upon check-in, dog owners are required to sign a "pet agreement" specifying that there will be "no evidence of a pet" in your cabin when you leave. Common sense will prevent any problems. The deposit has been withheld only twice: once when the dog had obviously slept on the couch, and again when an owner tied his dog up to a tree and left for the day. Imagine the barking. Dogs tend to run around here and swim a lot in the President Channel between Orcas and Waldron Islands. There's also a handy lake, so bring a lot of your own towels. The owner says that, "We're looking for the perfect dog with no fleas who doesn't shed." Let her know if you've made any discoveries.

The dog fee is $10 a night, in addition to a $50 deposit. The room rate at West Beach is seasonal: during the high season, July through August, cabins rent only by the week for $1,025 for up to four people; from mid-September to mid-June, nightly rates are $100 for up to four people; and in the winter, rates drop to $90 a night. West Beach also has 40 summer campsites, some equipped with RV hookups. Rates are about $30 for RV sites and $25 for standard sites, which accommodate up to three people. Route 1; (360) 376-2240 or (877) 937-8224; www.westbeachresort.com.

SAN JUAN ISLAND

San Juan is the most heavily populated of the four islands served by the Washington State Ferries. Nearly half of its 4,000 inhabitants reside in the town of Friday Harbor (the county seat), home to a fishing fleet and several hundred pleasure craft. It's the only incorporated village in all of the islands and hosts the only whale museum in the U.S. dedicated to the interpretation of whales living in the wild.

PARKS, BEACHES, AND RECREATION AREAS

•Cattle Point Interpretive Site Park 🐾🐾🐾 See **7** on page 136.
Cattle Point is a 10-acre Department of Natural Resources (DNR) park at the very southeast point of San Juan Island, reached by Cattle Point Road which goes through American Camp, or simply by walking south of American Camp. You'll find sand dunes, a rarity in the islands, and bald and golden eagles. Cattle Point is a day-use area only (no fee), and includes eight picnic sites, a shelter, drinking water, and outdoor toilets. Dogs are requested to be on leashes. There's a lovely, hidden cove just beyond the park's last rise (but don't tell the locals I shared this secret with you).

From Friday Harbor's waterfront, drive southwest on Spring Street. Turn left (south) on Argyle Road and continue for approximately 2.5 miles. Turn left (south) on Cattle Point Road and proceed for 6.5 miles to the park. (360) 856-3500 or (800) 527-3305.

•Lime Kiln State Park 🐾🐾 See **8** on page 136.
This 39-acre day-use park is the only one in the world intended specifically for whale-watching. The park, set on a rocky headland with a lighthouse built in 1919, serves as a prime whale-watching site. It overlooks Haro Strait, on the west side of San Juan Island, and has 2,500 feet of shoreline. From June to September, whales pass about three-quarters of a mile offshore. Orcas are a common sight, swimming in pods of up to 30. Leashes are required on your pooches.

From Friday Harbor's waterfront, drive southwest on Spring Street. Turn left (south) on San Juan Valley Road. Turn left (south) on Wold Road, then right (west) on Bailer Hill Road. Bailer Hill Road becomes Westside Road and leads into the park. (360) 378-2044 or (800) 233-0321.

• San Juan County Park 🐾🐾 See 🮲 on page 136.

San Juan Island's only public camping park includes 20 campsites and a boat launch. Leashed dogs are welcome. It's located at Smallpox Bay, on the western-central shore of the island. Campsites are available on a first-come, first-served basis in the off-season. Car-camping rates are $15 per night, for up to four people. Hikers, kayakers, and walk-in campers pay $5. There are no hookups or showers, but you'll see plenty of eagles and orcas, and there's a great view.

From the ferry landing, turn left (southeast) on Front Street. Drive on Front Street for two blocks, then turn right (southwest) on Spring Street. Spring Street becomes San Juan Valley Road near the western city limits. From San Juan Valley Road, turn left (south) on Wold Road, then turn right (west) on Bailer Hill Road. Bailer Hill Road becomes Westside Road and continues north up the coast. Once you've passed Lime Kiln State Park, look for San Juan County Park Road, which leads into the park. (360) 378-2992.

• San Juan Island National Historical Park 🐾🐾 See 🮳 on page 136.

This park allows leashed dogs. It's a wonder and a rarity that the National Park Service permits dogs to enter at all, since there is so much wildlife here, including foxes. However, the rangers are rigorous about issuing $75 tickets to the handlers of unleashed dogs, and dogs are not allowed at all on the guided summer tours.

The park is composed of two areas, about 15 miles apart. American Camp is set on the southern tip of the island, and English Camp is near Roche Harbor, on the island's northwest corner. Both the British and the Americans laid claim to the San Juans, and their former encampments are the historic sites of the Pig War of 1854—an altercation between an American settler and his British neighbor, which led to the shooting of the Brit's pig. After a 12-year standoff, arbitration favored the Americans. Park staff give excellent narrated tours on weekends from Memorial Day to Labor Day, and you'll find numerous opportunities for hiking, beachcombing, and bird-watching. There's a 1.25-mile trail with fine views of the water that leads fromm English Camp to Mount Young. At an elevation of 590 feet, Mount Young is the highest accessible point on San Juan Island.

To reach American Camp from the ferry landing, drive on Spring Street to Mullis Road. Turn left on Mullis Road, and drive for approximately six miles to the park. To reach English Camp from the ferry landing, proceed on Spring Street to 2nd Street. Turn right on 2nd Street, and drive approximately nine miles to the park. (360) 378-2240.

PLACES TO STAY

Animal Inn: Co-owner Milene Henley cautions that while her and her husband's Animal Inn is a very nice place for animals to stay, "We don't board people." The inn is one of only two boarding facilities in Washington state that is accredited by the American Boarding Kennels Association. In addition to dogs, they board cats, birds, rabbits, guinea pigs, and horses. Services include grooming, shipping, taxi pickup and delivery, and carrier rental. For dogs to stay over, proof of vaccinations is required for rabies, distemper, parvo, and Bordetella. Checkout time is 9 A.M. The Inn is located about four miles out of town at 497 Boyce Road; (360) 378-4735.

Blair House Bed and Breakfast Inn: Blair House accommodates dogs and their humans at a private cottage, only four blocks from the Friday Harbor ferry dock. For $165 to $185 per night (there is no minimum stay, which is a rarity on the island), you get a stocked kitchen, hot tub, deck, barbecue, and nearly two acres of running room for Fido. A full breakfast is included. You'll share the swimming pool with guests staying in the main house. 345 Blair Avenue; (360) 378-5907 or (360) 378-3030 (B&B hot line).

The Inn at Friday Harbor: Located in Friday Harbor one-half mile from the ferry dock, this 72-room inn welcomes dogs but requires a $50 deposit. It has an indoor swimming pool. Low season prices are $69 and $79. Summer rates are $109 and $249. 410 Spring Street; (360) 378-4000.

Lakedale Resort: You can bring your leashed dog to Lakedale for a fee of $1 per night. This chummy, 82-acre campground bordered by two lakes includes 125 campsites. You'll find excellent swimming, hiking, canoeing, and trout fishing here. Fishing licenses are not required, but there is a daily fishing fee. The campground also has a small grocery and coin-operated showers. Lakedale is open from March 15 to October 15. Car-camping rates are $24 per night (for two people) during July and August, and $19 per night the rest of the year. In July and August, bicyclists pay $8 per night, and $7 for the remaining months.

From the San Juan Island ferry landing, turn left (southeast) on Front Street. Drive one block on Front Street and turn right (southwest) on West Street. Proceed on West Street for two blocks and turn right (northwest) on 2nd Street. Turn left (west) on Guard Street (at the Friday Harbor High School) and continue for one block. Turn right (north) on Tucker Avenue. After four blocks on Tucker Avenue, turn left (northwest) on Roche Harbor Road. Lakedale is four miles ahead on your left. (360) 378-2350 or (800) 617-CAMP.

San Juan County Park camping: See page 142.

Snug Harbor Marina Resort: Pooches are allowed throughout Snug Harbor Resort, but they must be approved in advance. The resort is located on Mitchell Bay, north of Lime Kiln State Park and San Juan County Park. High-season rates for this marine resort's bungalows range from $80 to $205, and dogs are $5 extra per night. Nine tent sites are available for $15 per day; 25 RV sites cost $40 per day. 1997 Mitchell Bay Road, Friday Harbor; (360) 378-4762.

SHAW ISLAND

Almost exclusively a residential island, Shaw is the smallest of the ferry-served islands, and it's a great place to tour by bike. It has just 11 miles of public roads, so bicyclists like it. They really feel like they've gone somewhere after exhausting the possibilities. Franciscan nuns operate the ferry dock and run the island's only grocery store. There are no restaurants, hotels, motels, or B&Bs here, so if you wish to spend the night, prepare to camp at Shaw Island County Park.

PARKS, BEACHES, AND RECREATION AREAS

• Shaw Island County Park 🐾 See 11 on page 136.

All pups must be on a leash at this park. Campsites for car campers cost $10 and $12 per night; hikers, bikers, and kayakers pay $3 nightly. Hookups and showers are not available. From the ferry dock, take Blind Bay Road south and then west for approximately two miles. Turn left on Hoffman Cove Road and drive 1.5 miles to the park. (360) 738-8420 (information), (360) 378-1842 (reservations).

PLACES TO STAY

Shaw Island County Park camping: See above.

TO REACH THE ISLANDS

"About taking dogs on ferries," said the ticketer for Washington State Ferries, "you're supposed to keep them on the car deck." But she has seen dogs once in awhile on the other decks. They were well behaved and leashed. It largely depends on the crew of the particular boat, so it never hurts to ask.

The official version is that you can take a leashed dog on any car ferry, but you must remain both with your dog and on the car deck for the duration of the crossing. Small dogs in carriers are welcome upstairs.

To get to the Washington State Ferry dock in Anacortes from Seattle, take I-5 north for 66 miles to Burlington/Exit 230; turn west onto State Highway 20 and follow it for 12 miles to where it splits into Highway 20 and Highway 20 Spur. Take the spur for the last five miles by continuing straight, through Anacortes, to the ferry terminal. The signage is good.

The ferries depart at regularly scheduled intervals, but the schedule changes seasonally. The lineup lot for the ferry has a picnic area with a sign for pet area, pointing to the grass about mid-way at the edge of the parking lot. It's east of lane one of the lot. Pets must be leashed. Don't forget that when you and Fido get on the ferry, you bark. And when you get off, you debark, or is it disembark? (888) 808-7977 (Washington only), (206) 464-6400, (800) 84-FERRY (recording, Washington only).

Most islands are also accessible to private boats and commercial air flights are scheduled regularly from Bellingham and Seattle.

Paraclete Charters: Skip, the skipper of Paraclete Charters at the Skyline Marina 24 hours a day in Anacortes, provides marine transportation throughout the San Juan Islands. Most of his customers are homeowners, and he says most of them are "multiple dog owners. Their pets are just part of the luggage, and sometimes we carry more dogs than people." With 24-hour notice on a scheduled run, the charge can be as low as $20 per person each way, depending on the island. If you want to charter the boat (it's warm and dry inside, and holds 34 people) for yourself the cost is $150 per hour, two-hour minimum. Paraclete operates seven days a week from the Skyline Marina. (360) 293-5920; (800) 808-2999; www.paracletecharters.com.

Getting there from Bellingham: See various travel options on page 84.

ABOUT CANADA AND BRITISH COLUMBIA

More than ninety percent of British Columbia's 366,000 square miles is commonly owned by the people of the province. Consequently, British Columbia has one of the most extensive publicly owned park systems, and they're still building. A total of 356 parks covers 13.2 million acres (20,700 square miles)—an area larger than all of Switzerland.

In addition to six national parks and four national historic parks and sites, British Columbia has 346 provincial parks. Within the provincial parks are wildlife areas, old-growth forests, beaches, alpine meadows, 11,000 individual public campsites, and marine environments—and many of these areas are open to canine visitors.

Coastal British Columbia, including Vancouver Island, is known as the Pacific Coast Temperate Rainforest. It's now being studied as never before in an attempt to justify closing out logging in perpetuity. For example, in Carmanah Pacific Park on Vancouver Island, there is a research station 200 feet up in the forest canopy. New ecosystems and life forms have been discovered there that only exist high off the ground. Hikers can enjoy these temperate rain forests from trailheads within a 20-minute drive of downtown Vancouver, and there are many others north to Whistler and west on Vancouver Island.

As Vancouver writer Steve Threndyle said, "B.C. is one of the few places in the world where people can still seek out an endless amount of recreational challenge in a vast, uncompromising wilderness setting."

Please note that all prices listed in the following chapters are in Canadian dollars.

REGULATIONS FOR YOU AND YOUR POOCH

United States or Canadian-born citizens need only a valid driver's license to cross into Canada. If you are not a United States or Canadian-born citizen, you must carry proof of citizenship. Airlines may require a passport to board a flight from the U.S. into Canada. A passport and visa may be required of non-United States citizens. Children and infants must also have identification or proof of citizenship for entry into Canada. You may be required to prove "adequacy" of funds in your possession for the duration of your visit. You may not enter with handguns, stun guns, automatic weapons, chemical protective devices, like Mace or pepper spray. If you have a felony on your record, you may be denied entrance into Canada, and Canada considers a D.W.I. to be a felony. Other U.S. crimes may be considered felonies in Canada.

TEN HIKING ESSENTIALS

On any hike, if you go far enough from your car to lock it, take the ten essentials recommended by mountaineering instructors:

1) map of the area
2) compass
3) knife
4) flashlight
5) first-aid kit
6) extra clothing
7) something to drink, preferably water
8) something to eat
9) waterproof matches
10) a wind break, or shelter

To bring a domestic dog with you into Canada, other than a service dog, you must have a certificate issued by a veterinarian in Canada or the United States that clearly identifies your dog and certifies that a rabies vaccine has been given in the last 36 months. In addition, British Columbia requires a canine health certificate filled out by a vet within 30 days of entry. Puppies under three months of age and service dogs accompanied by their owners may enter Canada without certification or further restriction. For further information, write: Director, Animal Health, F.P.&I. Branch, Agriculture Canada, 2-620 Royal Avenue, New Westminster, British Columbia, Canada V3L 5A8; (604) 666-0575.

United States state driver's licenses are valid in Canada. Vehicle insurance is compulsory in Canada, and visiting motorists are required to produce evidence of financial responsibility should they be involved in an accident. The minimum liability insurance requirement in Canada is $200,000 (except in Quebec, where the limit is $50,000).

Upon reentering the United States, travelers who have spent less than 48 hours in Canada have a $25 exemption. That is, they can bring back, free of duty and tax, $25 worth of articles for personal use. For a stay in Canada of more than 48 hours, the exemption per person is $400.

Most retail transactions in Canada suffer an additional seven percent Goods and Services Tax. Americans can apply to get this seven percent back on most goods purchased, but, alas, not on most services. Most shops and hotels have the official pamphlet that explains the rules and a form to fill out when you return home.

Just so you have it with you, here's the address and phone number of the United States Consulate in British Columbia: 1095 West Pender Street, Vancouver, British Columbia, Canada V6E 2M6; (604) 685-4311.

The nearest Canadian Consulate in the Pacific Northwest is: Canadian Consulate General, 412 Plaza 600, 6th and Stewart, Seattle, WA 98101-1286.

BEAR CAUTION

Black bears in British Columbia number some 120,000, with an estimated 1,000 just between Squamish and Whistler. The bears reside in almost every type of terrain from coastal beaches to forests, dry grassland and subalpine

BEAR PRECAUTIONS

- Be aware of your surroundings, and be especially alert near berry patches and streams. Keep an eye out for fresh bear signs such as footprints or freshly overturned rocks.
- Make noise as you hike to alert bears. Affix a bear bell to your pack, talk loudly and clap from time to time.
- If you see a bear, do *not* approach it. Either back away slowly or wait for it go away.
- Stay away from all animal carcasses.
- Cook well away from your tent.
- Store all food and toiletries well away from your tent. Carry and use a long rope with which to hang your stuff between or from trees.
- Avoid littering, especially meal leftovers.

meadows. In the forest, they like open spaces where berries can be found but they also go fishing in shallow streams for spawning salmon. Bears generally try to avoid human contact and will retreat upon the sight of humans. A few, however, acquire a taste for the food they find among humans' garbage, and they become "problem bears," too familiar with human ways. In spring, bears can sometimes be seen from the Whistler ski lifts grazing on the lush green ski runs below.

Any fair-weather hiking in British Columbia, or anywhere in the Northwest for that matter, exposes you to the possibility of bear sightings. Black bears are everywhere, and they're always hungry. If you are outdoors anywhere in British Columbia, camping, hunting, fishing, or hiking, even the most casual search for information will net you some tips. Pay attention to signs, the back of maps, and pamphlets that are in nearly all info racks for tourists. Following the guidelines will help to avoid nasty confrontations.

VANCOUVER, BRITISH COLUMBIA

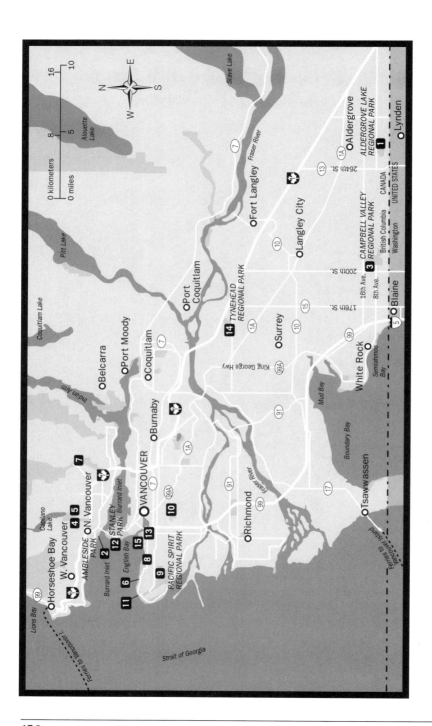

10
VANCOUVER, BRITISH COLUMBIA

Vancouver is an internationally acclaimed tourist destination, noted for its distinct cosmopolitan neighborhoods, cultural sophistication, and natural beauty. Eastern Canadians often retire here for the warm weather; many young people come for the economic opportunities. It's a fun, outdoorsy kind of city, with lots of bicyclists, joggers, and folks who frequently walk their dogs on the city streets and through the lush parks. Those who prefer to commune with nature will be happy to hear that escaping the city and its 1.8 million regional residents is remarkably easy, since the north side of Vancouver abuts a few thousand miles of spectacular wilderness.

No freeways have ever been cut through Vancouver, and getting there requires one or two bridge crossings, depending on the route. Vancouver is basically a peninsula, with water traffic on three sides. Steep mountains on the north side and the Fraser River on the south keep Vancouver's city limits defined. There is also Burrard Inlet, English Bay, and False Creek, just to maintain the nautical feeling.

There are 2.75 acres of park per thousand people in Vancouver (New York City has 1.5 acres per thousand). In general, Vancouver's parks allow leashed dogs, although you have to scoop up their calling cards. Unfortunately, dogs are not allowed on most of the beaches, especially in the summer.

People who don't have dogs, but are sympathetic to those who do, often direct you to parks that they think are leash-free. They've seen the park signs with the silhouette of a dog, and assume that means it's a dog park, one that doesn't require leashes. Those signs go on to say that leashes and cleanup are required. All of the city of Vancouver's 174 parks are officially open from daybreak to dusk, meaning that no overnight parking is allowed, but people are free to use them anytime. All the parks on both sides of English Bay are connected by a wide trail that is in use at all hours.

In addition, the Greater Vancouver Regional District (GVRD), a federation of 21 municipalities and electoral areas, administers 17 parks that total more than 23,000 acres. Leashed pups are the GVRD rule except for areas in four of the city parks, detailed below (Aldergrove, Campbell Valley, Tynehead, and Pacific Spirit, the last of which is entirely leash-free). A sign seen now and then in GVRD parks says that vehicle break-ins occur and that people should protect their valuables.

The Dog Lover's Companion to Seattle will list all prices in Canadian dollars and do the metric math for you, but if you're new to Canada, you'll have to get used to doing it for yourself. Parks are measured in hectares, and each hectare is roughly two and a half acres.

PARKS, BEACHES, AND RECREATION AREAS

• **Aldergrove Lake Regional Park** 🐾🐾🐾 🐕 See **1** on page 150.
Grassy meadows and canopy-covered trails dot the thick forests of 617-acre Aldergrove Lake Regional Park, which sits right on the border of the United States and Canada. At the northeast corner of the park, there's an off-leash area of mowed grass that has woods on both sides of it. It's a bit hilly, but offers about five acres of running space. It would have made a great round-ball field for Emma and Quinn if we had only remembered to bring the ball. Instead, a few gopher mounds caught Quinn's attention. A well-beaten path cuts across the field to the wooded trailhead and 2.5 miles of hiking paths.

To get to the park's lake, follow the entrance road past some houses on the right and through the woods; you will eventually pass a roofed picnic area and a wooden bridge. A sign indicates you've reached the lake, but after September, when it's drained, it looks more like a large circular sand dune with a shallow puddle in the middle. During the summer, however, the puddle is transformed into a full-fledged swimmable lake surrounded by a huge sandy beach.

One of the park's oddities is the gravel pits around the east and north sides. It looks like somebody mined half of Canada for gravel. In fact, nearly 30 acres of Aldergrove is a gravel pit. Why? The Greater Vancouver Regional District (GVRD) bought this land in 1969, unaware that the gravel rights were separate from the land title. British Columbia courts upheld the separate titles, so the GVRD worked with the owners to develop a reclamation plan that maximizes recreation and conservation. Fortunately, the plan hasn't disrupted the Salish Sucker, an endangered fish that lives in the park's Pepin Brook. We held back Emma and Quinn, since the GVRD cautions that fish, even in tiny creeks, are endangered by shallow mud holes created by playful dogs.

The best way to get here from stateside is via the Aldergrove/Lynden border crossing (Washington Highway 539 north from Bellingham through Lynden). Continue straight north on 264th Street (B.C. Highway 13) and turn right at the first intersection onto 8th Avenue (also called Warner Avenue, and also called Huntingdon Road. Don't ask; it depends on which free map you use and which street signs you read.). The park entrance is in the middle of the second long block on the right. For the leash-free area, continue on 8th Avenue past that entrance to the next intersection at Lefeuvre Road (also called Cottonwood Street). Just around the corner on your right is the parking area for the leash-free range. (604) 530-4983.

• **Ambleside Park** 🐾🐾🐾🐾 🐕 See **2** on page 150.
This West Vancouver park has quite a large leash-free run, which includes grassy areas and a long paved stroll along the waters of Burrard Inlet. And the waters are available for swimming! No, not in the duck pond, the pristine fowl haven on your left beyond the ball fields. The salt water, on your right across the path, is where you guys want to go. We herded the duck terriers over to the small beach ahead and practiced their skills as stick terriers. There is no nasty keep-off-the-beach rule here, and the supply of sticks to throw is endless since they're refreshed with every incoming tide. Down the path a

ways is a doggie watering station and a baggy dispenser for poop scooping. The bags are black, so you needn't dwell on your chore before you find a trashcan.

There's a large grassy field for serious romping and Frisbee chasing. Dogs thrive in this leash-free area, and the people do too. They stop to chat and introduce their dogs to each other, and new friends are made all the way around. If you continue on the path in the direction of the Lions Gate Bridge (east), it will turn left and up at the Capilano River mouth and enter Capilano Park.

Like Luther Burbank Park on Mercer Island east of Seattle, Ambleside Park is a semi-secret resource to the people of West Vancouver. In both cases, the people of the higher-density cities have to cross a bridge to get to the leash-free park area. To reach Ambleside Park from downtown Vancouver, take B.C. 99 North (Georgia Street west), pass through Stanley Park and cross over First Narrows on the Lions Gate Bridge. Go west on Marine Drive past Taylor Way and past the Park Royal shopping center and turn left into Ambleside Park via 13th Street. The street sign is hard to spot, but just before it there is a large wooden "Ambleside Park" sign on the left side of the street. Park as far past the soccer field as you can and walk east on the path along the water's edge. We made the mistake of stopping within sight of a soccer game and almost lost Quinn to the melee. He really wanted to join the 22 humans chasing down the round black and white hedgehog. (604) 925-7200.

•Campbell Valley Regional Park 🐾 🐾 🐾 🐕 See 🖪 on page 150.

This park is A-1 for sure. In the waist-high grasses of the off-leash area, Quinn and Emma tore through like they were bounding on water. They treed a snake, or more accurately, weeded a snake, a two-foot long dark snake with a green stripe down its back. It played dead, but it's not that easy to fool Emma. Knowing that there are no poisonous snakes west of the Cascade Mountains, I acted bravely and rescued the snake, putting it farther away in the weeds. But the dogs kept up their bounding with big smiles across their faces. When they were more than a few feet away, all I could see of the dogs were tails wagging out of the grasses. A frog croaked and the place felt like a swamp but without the annoying water. A Frisbee attempt here would be counterproductive.

The whole park has 1,321 acres that contain 12.5 miles of walking trails and nine miles of horse trails. It's open for day use only. At the equestrian center off the 8th Street entrance, there is a sign for dogs on leash, as you would expect around horses. The immense field is a cross-country training course for horses.

Out on the trail, one could see that horse people have not yet learned to scoop up after their pets. There are horse leavings all over the trails and fields in Campbell Valley Park, which can be very attractive to dogs who love to roll around in it and perfume themselves. It's a nasal hazard to humans, who have to ride in the same car as their dogs. And to top off the equine insult to the canine world, their pass-through silage is a favorite snack when dogs are on the trail.

Just like near Bellevue's Bridle Trails State Park in the Seattle area, many people who live on the park borders have horses, and need only ride them across the street to enjoy the park. The flat roads are used a lot by groups of cyclists.

The easiest access to the park for the first-time visitor is the South Valley Entrance, at the intersection of 8th Avenue and 204th Street (also called Pepin Road). The Visitor Centre and demonstration wildlife garden are here, as is the restored farmstead site. This will get you along the Shaggy Mane (horse) Trail to the dog fields. The trail abuts both the seasonal (September to April) and year-round off-leash areas. We had more fun at the seasonal, which you can drive to directly by turning right off the end of 8th Avenue onto 204th Street (also Pepin Road), then left onto 4th Avenue (also McBurnie Road) and continue for one mile to a walk-in entrance on the left. The off-leash area is to your immediate left. The year-round off-leash area is back on the corner of 4th Avenue and 204th Street. There is no parking there, so you have to walk the Shaggy Mane Trail from the South Valley Entrance to get to it. The walk to the year-round area is about a quarter of a mile, and continuing to the seasonal area would be another third of a mile. That's not too awful, but you are required to use a leash. The year-round area is mostly grassy, mowed maybe once a year, bordered by trees on two sides and roads on the other two.

To get there from the States, take I-5 exit 275, which takes you directly (via Highway 543) to the truck crossing, known officially as the Pacific Highway Border Crossing. Continue north on B.C. Highway 15 (which is also 176th Street) for nine-tenths of a mile and turn east on 8th Avenue. Continue for 3.6 miles and you're there. There's very good signage near the park entrances. The park is open daily from 8 A.M. to 6 P.M. (604) 530-4983.

•Capilano River Regional Park 🐾 🐾 🐾 See ▣ on page 150.

Remember Rambo? The helicopter shots in the first *Rambo* movie were filmed on the stark granite cliffs across Capilano Canyon. Capilano Pacific Trail, the main path through the park, will be easier on your dog than on you. It's not really tough, but there is about a 500-foot elevation gain and parts of it stay muddy in the rainy season. The trail is well marked through the thick rain forest. Allow plenty of time for Mercuria to check her p-mail at every fern. The trail leads to a good vantage point below Cleveland Dam, which holds back Capilano Lake. From there, you can either continue to the dam or cross the river on the Shinglebolt Trail to the Capilano Salmon Hatchery. Visitors are not allowed into the rearing facilities (where the fish are raised) or holding ponds, but you and Urso can watch the fish ladder through the outside windows and take an excellent self-guided tour of the outdoor displays. The hatchery is open year-round; call (604) 666-1790 for more information. For the return trip to Ambleside Park, you will have to retrace your steps on the trail or walk down the road. Vancouver buses serve the hatchery, but they do not allow dogs on board.

Many people are familiar with this park because of the famed Capilano Suspension Bridge (see next entry), which you can swing when you cross it for a price (the privately owned bridge crosses over the canyon, but not into the park). Capilano Park, which lies on the border between North and West Vancouver, north of Lions Gate Bridge, begins near the north side of Burrard Inlet at the mouth of the Capilano River and stretches for about three miles to Cleveland Dam. It offers 16 miles of trails; 4.7-mile Capilano Pacific Trail is the longest single trail in the system, provided you start at Ambleside Park at the river's mouth. It's a three-hour stroll to the hatchery. The walk begins at the river mouth, goes under bridges, and passes Park Royal South (a bit like Granville Island Market inside), a car wash, and apartment buildings before it leaves civilization behind.

To get to the Capilano River Regional Park from downtown Vancouver, take B.C. Highway 99 North (also known as Georgia Street) through Stanley Park and cross over First Narrows on the Lions Gate Bridge. Go left (west) on Marine Drive past Taylor Way and the Park Royal shopping center and turn left (south) on 13th Street into Ambleside Park. Park as far past the soccer field as you can get and walk east on the path along the water's edge. (604) 224-5739.

• Capilano Suspension Bridge and Park 🐾 🐾 See 5 on page 150.

"You could land a 737 on the Capilano Suspension Bridge if there was room," said the lifeguard at the Capilano Suspension Bridge. Well, this isn't the beach or pool, but the lifeguard sits under a sun umbrella at the east end of the 450-foot walking bridge and makes sure nobody gets hurt.

"Please don't run on the bridge," she announces through the PA system. She makes the request in up to six languages until the boy hears his own and stops running. The swaying bridge is totally safe (the cables at each end are embedded in 13 tons of concrete), but it can be pretty unnerving 25 stories above the Capilano River.

Most dogs don't like it a bit. They're too scared. In fact, very few cross on their own. Some get dragged across; most get carried. Dogs can be left with the lifeguard, just like the baby strollers and canes.

But dogs are totally welcome in the 22-acre park just the same, as is the caretaker's dog Jiro. If you can get your Odysseus to the other side of the bridge, there are 15 acres of forest to explore. There are some Douglas fir trees at the interpretive display at the west end of the bridge, three of them being 400 years old. Up the short trail are trees that are 500-600 years old, and down the short trail are trout ponds. Keep your trout terrier leashed.

A naturalist is on duty to answer any questions. Like, what about the bears and cougars? The park is fenced, so the animals that live in the mountains don't bother visitors. The naturalist, when hiking in the mountains, says when she sees a bear she simply stands still until it goes away.

Capilano Park's Dog Bar, a watering hole for dogs, is actually a sort of dish carved out of the concrete walkway next to the drinking fountain for humans. It's on the east side between the Little Big House and the Canyon Cafe, which serves coffee, tea, salads, muffins, and lasagna. The Loggers Grill, across the patio, serves BBQ, mushroom burgers, and buffalo burgers. Aarff!

Native Tsimshian and Tlingit totem pole carvers work their craft at the Little Big House. The red cedar pole standing in front took a year to carve. There are 25 more around the park.

Interpretive tours of the park are complimentary, live singers stroll the grounds, and the Trading Post has an imaginative collection of native crafts, jewelry, clothing, and leather goods.

The park and bridge are open to people and their dogs every day except Christmas. Summer hours are 8:30 A.M. to dusk. Adult entrance fees are $11.95 Canadian plus GST in the summer, and $9.35 in the winter. Children 6 to 12 pay $3.50 in the winter and $3.25 in the summer. Children under six get in for free. There is no charge for dogs.

To get there from downtown Vancouver, go north over the Lions Gate Bridge, then turn left on Capilano Road and go one mile to the entrance on the left. (604) 985-7474.

•Jericho Beach Park 🐾🐾 See 6 on page 150.

On the southern waters of English Bay, tucked in between Locarno Park and Hastings Mill Park, this 134-acre park has grasslands for football, rugby, and volleyball, as well as tennis courts. The whole front of the park is beach front, part of the continuous trail that goes from False Creek clear around the Endowment Lands and Pacific Spirit Park. You'll see a lot of huge loose dogs, with their humans following along behind "in control." Park rules require leashes at all times. You can be fined $75 for having an off-leash dog, and $125 if the dog is not licensed. Emma and Quinn thought this was a pretty cool park, and were sorry we had left the basketball/hedgehog at home. The eastern section of the park has a large lagoon, off-limits to dogs.

From downtown Vancouver, take Burrard Street southwest across the Burrard Street Bridge. Turn right (west) onto 4th Avenue; the park entrance is 2.5 miles ahead. If you take a half-right turn onto Northwest Marine Drive, which cuts a gorgeous swath through the park. You'll reach a number of part-time leash-free city parks—such as Locarno Park—along the south shore of English Bay. A sign advises that "no overnight residing" is allowed. (604) 257-8400.

•Lynn Headwaters Regional Park 🐾🐾 See 7 on page 150.

Nearly 10 miles of walking trails course through this 12,000-acre North Vancouver park. The starter trail for a first-time visit is the three-mile Lynn Loop Trail, which passes through some thick forest biomass alongside Lynn Creek. It's the easiest of the hikes in the system, and your (leashed) companion will thank you for the experience.

From downtown Vancouver, drive west on Hastings Street (which becomes Hastings Street East) and follow the signs for northbound Highway 1 and the Second Narrows Bridge. Take the Lynn Valley Road exit off Highway 1, and drive about two miles. Trail maps are posted at the park entrance, and individual maps are usually available at the parking lot kiosk. (604) 432-6350.

•McBride Park 🐾 See 8 on page 150.

This is a pleasant 4.8-acre park on 4th Avenue in the Kitsilano neighborhood. It's two blocks long, with grounds for soccer, softball, and tennis, and a playground for the kids. The dogs? you ask. Whatever they can do on leashes can be done in McBride Park. It's good for a bit of romp room if you're in the neighborhood.

From downtown Vancouver, take Burrard Street southwest across the Burrard Street Bridge; turn right (west) onto 4th Avenue and continue for 1.5 miles to the park on the southeast corner of Blenheim Street. (604) 257-8400.

• Pacific Spirit Regional Park 🐾🐾🐾 🐕 See 🟦 on page 150.

Here's a big bonus for dogs and dog lovers: This entire park is leash-free! As part of the Fraser River Estuary, the whole of this big Greater Vancouver Regional District park surrounding the University of British Columbia Endowment Lands allows unleashed dogs, except for environmentally sensitive areas like marshes and one large southern section that doesn't even allow people.

The stats are impressive: 1,885 acres, 31 miles of walking trails, 22 miles of bicycle trails, and four miles of clothing-optional beaches reachable only by trail. It's the third largest regional park in the GVRD.

As the park manager explained it, each GVRD park manager has the authority to assign park areas for certain uses, to bend the rules a bit. Pacific Spirit Park only became official in 1989, and the park manager wanted to respect the earlier users who for decades had walked and run their dogs without leash restrictions. So off-leash dogging was historically a common practice. The management plan for the park included free-running dog usage, but stipulated that the dogs must be "under control" and that they respect the park's wildlife. That's the bottom line, according to the manager. On request, park officers will require of a particular dog owner that he leash his pet. There are rarely any dog "incidents" of any concern.

The park's foreshore, where people swim and sunbathe, is off-limits to dogs between April 1 and mid-October, but they're welcome on its beaches the rest of the year. You'd think the water would be too cold for swimming, but many people and dogs do it. Trails wind throughout the park, and the signage is very good. The Heron Trail runs through the remains of an old-growth forest, a cedar grove, an alder grove, and then passes a golf course.

Although you can hear cars driving on nearby roads, the park's interior feels like a primeval forest. Emma and Quinn clearly liked the woods better than the path, so we turned them loose. Livestock gates, which mark the beginning of the foot-traffic trails, separate equestrians and bicyclists from pedestrians. These foot trails might provide a better experience for you and yours, because some of the bicyclists on their trails clearly seem to feel they have the right of way and don't slow down when they pass you.

Pacific Spirit offers a Multi-Terrain Wheelchair Hiking program, which includes use of the Spirit, a modified golf cart with a roll cage and a joystick control system. Membership in the British Columbia Mobility Opportunities Society (BCMOS) covers one free ride on the Spirit (you have to pay a small fee for membership and all subsequent trips). For more information, call the BCMOS at (604) 688-6464.

From downtown Vancouver, drive south on Granville Street or Burrard Street over False Creek. Stay on either street until 16th Avenue, then turn right (west) and continue to the park offices, on your right.

To drive to the park from south of Vancouver, take B.C. Highway 99 North and cross the Oak Street Bridge over the North Arm of the Fraser River. Take the second right from the end of the bridge. It's called exit 41b, Marine Drive West, and 99 North. You are shortly on Granville Street going north, but get in the left lane quickly because Marine Drive West takes an unnatural turn to the left on west 70th Avenue. Only a teeny sign on the left warns you. The scenic road is now called Southwest Marine Drive and you stay on it for 5.5 miles through estate-type housing and the University of British Columbia Endowment Lands. At 16th Avenue turn east (right) for 1.1 mile and the park offices are on your left. From downtown Vancouver, go south over False Creek via Granville Street or Burrard Street. Stay on either street until 16th Avenue, where you turn right and continue to the park offices on your right within the park.

The official Pacific Spirit Park Centre is open Monday through Friday from 8 A.M. to 4 P.M. There are plenty of maps and brochures inside, and there is one brochure dispenser on the outside of the trailer/building. The restrooms are open on the weekend and there is a pay phone outside. Call (604) 224-5739 for information about Pacific Spirit Park. The GVRD 24-hour emergency number is (604) 432-9483.

•Queen Elizabeth Park 🐾🐾 🐾 🐕 See **10** on page 150.
Queen Elizabeth Park (known affectionately as QE Park) has a terrific view of the city. If you arrive early, you'll also see large numbers of martial-arts practitioners gathered at the park's Bloedel Conservatory. Below the conservatory is the Quarry Gardens, known for its spectacular waterfall. The Conservatory, which does not allow animals inside, has about 500 varieties of tropical and subtropical plants, and the gift shop sells potted plants at very reasonable prices.

This park is beautiful but formal; you may feel guilty if you run on the grass. Since dogs have to be leashed, it's not as much fun for them as it may be for you. The middle of the park, with the restaurant and conservatory, and the beautiful sunken gardens, is where the tourists congregate. More to Fido's liking is QE's grassy backside, which abuts a Frisbee-golf course. It begins at the corner of West 37th Avenue and Ontario Street and continues south along Ontario Street. Two little lakes are attractive to rambunctious dogs and their owners. While the park does not have an official leash-free zone, this section of the park seems by convention to be a local's let-the-dog-run-free area. A sign, however, reminds us all that there is a $500 fine for not being attached to your dog by a leash and for not cleaning up after him. Dogs are not allowed at all in QE's Nat Bailey stadium.

From downtown Vancouver, drive southeast on Nelson Street to the Cambie Bridge. Proceed south on Cambie Street after you cross the bridge and turn left (east) on 29th Avenue. Make a half-right (southeast) turn onto Midlothian Avenue West and follow the signs to the park. (604) 257-8400.

•Spanish Banks Beach 🐾🐾🐾🐾 🐕 See **11** on page 150.
This Vancouver city park has the westernmost beach on the south side of English Bay. Spanish Banks eventually connects with Wreck Beach, which is famed among the locals for its clothing-optional policy. In the summer, volunteer doctors cruise Wreck Beach looking for skin cancers while passing out sunscreen. But back to Spanish Banks Beach. It got its name from famed explorer George Vancouver, who found that he had been preceded by the Spaniards, whom he met here in June of 1792. The beach is dotted with huge driftwood sea logs that look like they are arranged in a binary code of some sort. They're all separated into lines and sections, like a mass art project for an enterprising graduate student. It's illegal to take the logs for firewood, but not

to rearrange them. Parks department tractors set them in order every morning. As of mid-1999, the area west of the concession is leash-free during specific times of day: between the hours of 6 A.M. and 10 A.M. and from 5 P.M. to 10 P.M. There's a $2,000 penalty for littering, so pack your baggies. No overnight residing is allowed in the Spanish Banks West parking lots. The beach is closed from sunset to 8 A.M.

From downtown Vancouver, head south on Highway 99 (also known as Howe Street) and cross the Burrard Street Bridge. Take the 4th Avenue West exit and turn right (northwest) on Northwest Marine Drive. (604) 257-8400.

• Stanley Park 🐾🐾🐾🐾 See **12** on page 150.

A famous 1,000-acre park on the tip of the Vancouver peninsula, Stanley Park contains about 800 acres of coniferous forest, cedar, hemlock, and fir. Those woods are home to 22 rarely-seen coyotes, but stay leashed just in case. The rest of Stanley Park is devoted to recreation and includes the Vancouver Aquarium, gardens, a children's farmyard, a pitch-and-putt golf course, lawn bowling, and a cinder jogging track at the Brockton Oval. The Stanley Park Seawall, which stretches for 5.5 miles from Coal Harbour to English Bay, winds past shipwreck sites, a pioneer cemetery, lava flows, seabird colonies, kelp beds, and the sites of former native dwellings. Bronze kilometer markers are embedded in the stonework along the seawall. If you cross back to your starting point, the trek is about 6.1 miles. It's cool to fish from the Stanley Park Seawall as long as your gear doesn't protrude into the foot and wheel traffic on the path. There are two six-week smelt runs: May 1 to June 15 and August 16 to September 30.

The Nine O'clock Gun is located between Hallelujah and Brockton Points, about a mile along the wall. This cannon fires a blank every evening as it has for a hundred years. Cover Rover's ears if you're anywhere in the vicinity around 9 P.M. The original purpose was for sailing ships entering the precarious tidal waters to set their chronometers accurately.

Stanley Park is a Vancouver city park, which means leashes and cleanup are required. A horse-borne police officer hands out tickets to unleashed malefactors; the fine is $75. Dogs are not allowed on sandy bathing beaches or "areas adjacent thereto."

To get to Stanley Park from downtown Vancouver, just go northwest on Georgia Street, which is the main drag in addition to being B.C. 99 and B.C. 1A. The park entrance is 3.5 miles from Granville Street. (604) 257-8400.

• Sutcliffe Park 🐾🐾 See **13** on page 150.

Granville Island's five-acre Sutcliffe Park is well off the beaten path, a grassy piece of serenity at the water's edge. This is where island employees come to enjoy a quiet takeout lunch and maybe do some reading. Leashed dogs are welcome, but it's not a place to chase a Frisbee. The park adjoins Alder Bay, a narrow side inlet of False Creek, and acts as a buffer between the hubbub of Granville Island and the high-rise residences on the mainland. The park is long and narrow. A park walkway runs behind the Kids Only Store and the False Creek Community Centre, both on Cartwright Street. Pass the Pelican Bay Marina and you'll come to The Mound, a pyramid-shaped outdoor grass amphitheater that's almost too steep to climb, but not quite. A paved path takes you to the top of this structure, which offers a good seagull's-eye view of the surroundings. Noontime jazz concerts sometimes take place here. The giant golf ball affair that you see down at the end of False Creek is a leftover from Expo 86 that now houses an Imax theater and a science center that's a terrific hands-on experience for kids. There are other smaller grass parks on Granville Island, each a bit of a refuge for our country dogs.

From downtown Vancouver, drive southwest on Burrard Street and cross the Burrard Street Bridge. Stay on Burrard as it makes a half-left (south) turn after the bridge, then make a hard left (east) turn on West 2nd Avenue. Follow the signs to Granville Island and turn right on Cartwright Street, in front of the brewing company. Sutcliffe Park is just ahead on your right, next to the False Creek Community Centre. (604) 257-8400.

•Tynehead Regional Park 😊 😊 🐾 See **14** on page 150.

Tynehead is a popular park, largely because it's the closest to civilization of the four big parks with off-leash areas. It has 642 acres, and there were 30 cars in one of the parking lots on a weekend afternoon. The off-leash area is mostly trails through grasslands, blackberries, and scrub trees.

The following etiquette rules are posted in the off-leash area:
1) Dogs must be under the care and control of the person who brought them to the park. It is this individual's responsibility to control the animal's behavior.
2) Be familiar with the extent of the off-leash area. Do not allow your dog to roam into the adjacent Serpentine Loop Trail, where the leash bylaw is enforced.
3) For the comfort of all park users, please pick up your dog's droppings and deposits.
4) The Greater Vancouver Regional District (GVRD) is experimenting with off-leash areas. Comments and suggested improvements are welcome. Phone (604) 530-4983.

Tynehead Park is a nice combination of meadowland, scrub brush, and small trees, with 3.1 miles of walking trails. The roar of the Trans Canada Highway at the north border of the park can be heard. But it's still a nice huge park and lots of dogs enjoy themselves here. There are piles of stuff at frequent intervals, so watch your step. The only lakes and ponds are in the dirt parking lot. There is no other water access for off-leash dogs. The creek running through the park is in the leashed area.

Tynehead is a day-use only park, open from 8 A.M. to 6 P.M. It's near the intersection of the Trans-Canada Highway (Highway 1) and B.C. Highway 15 (176th Street), which runs straight north from the U.S. border truck crossing (cars are allowed too). To get there from B.C. 15, turn west on 96th Avenue and the park is at the first intersection (168th Street) on your right. You can get to the leash-free area faster by turning north on 168th Street to the next entrance. It's a fairly large area off to the left, next to the parking lot. (604) 530-4983.

•Vanier Park 😊 😊 😊 😊 🐾 See **15** on page 150.

What fun to sit in the rain and watch the sunset. We saw a fellow and his dog doing just that in Vanier Park and were reminded of a regular occurrence in the Pacific Northwest. Toward evening, western skies often clear, and the sun on the horizon briefly and brilliantly illuminates the bottoms of the clouds that are dumping on you. Things like that happen in 38-acre Vanier Park on the south edge of English Bay. As of mid-2000, part of Vanier Park is leash-free: west of the Maritime Museum parking lot between the hours of 6 A.M. and 10 A.M. and from 5 P.M. to 10 P.M. The wonderful sandy beach is the best new meet 'n' greet scene in the city for both people and dogs. There's a lot of stick retrieval going on too, from the water. The park is right in the middle of the jogging/in-line skating/bicycling/dog-walking/watch out! path that pretty much starts near the Simon Fraser Memorial Monument at the southern tip of the University of British Columbia campus and runs for nearly 20 miles along or near the water. The route goes clockwise around the University Endowment Lands, along the south and north shores of English Bay (connected by the walkway on the Granville Island Bridge) and around Stanley Park. Vanier Park is a primo spot to watch the human, canine, and boating worlds go by. You can easily walk to Granville Island from here. Just walk the path toward the big bridge to the east, and in about 10 minutes you're there. Vanier Park is open dawn to dusk, and there is no parking 11 P.M. to 6 A.M. To drive to the leash-free area by the Maritime Museum, take Burrard Street southwest, cross the Burrard Street Bridge, and as Burrard turns south, continue southwest onto Cornwall Avenue for less than a block. Turn right (north) onto Chestnut Street and drive straight ahead for four blocks to the museum's parking lot. (604) 257-8400.

RESTAURANTS

Benny's: Benny closed his Yaletown bagelry, but his West Broadway and University of British Columbia campus locations are thriving. The folks at Benny's are so doggone friendly that professional dog walkers, some with several pups in tow, frequently stop for bagels and beverages on the huge patio with the, uh, interesting furniture. Best of all, Benny's is open until 2 A.M. Sunday through Wednesday and until 4 A.M. Thursday through Saturday. Leashes are required. 2503 West Broadway and 5278 University Boulevard; (604) 731-9730.

Big News Coffee Bar: There are plenty of tasty treats at this coffee house on the corner of West Broadway and Granville Street, five blocks south of the Granville Street Bridge. There is plenty of outdoor seating. 802 West Broadway; (604) 872-3315.

Bistro! Bistro!: This trendy Gastown bistro does well with its grills, pasta, and seafood in competitive Gastown. Try the roasted Cornish hen with rosemary, pork au jus, or the braised rabbit with a white-wine mushroom sauce. The crab cakes were judged to be the best in Vancouver. There are two tables outside, at which dogs are totally welcome. Inside, Bistro! Bistro! has the original cedar beams and brick walls of a heritage building. It's open daily from 11 A.M. to 11 P.M. 162 Water Street at Cambie Street; (604) 682-2162.

Blenz Coffee: This coffee spot on the corner of Bute and Robson Streets is terrific for people-watching. Out on the sidewalk are five tables in the fenced-off area, with umbrellas to avoid the rain or sun. The cappuccino foam has so much integrity you have to eat it with a spoon. There are seven other Blenz's around the city, but this one is located at 1201 Robson Street; (604) 681-8092.

Bridges: Bridges is a popular meet market that can be a real swingles scene in warm weather. Actually, it may be more of a fish market, since Bridges advertises itself as the place "Where Kindred Sole Meet." There have been a lot of "famous people" sightings at Bridges. It gets so packed that people who have arranged to meet on the deck may not find each other and have to make new friends. But dogs are welcome and quite common in the summer, as long as they're tied to the perimeter of the deck, an 8' by 8' raised beam. Waitpersons cheerfully serve bowls of water for your canine friend. Seafood, exotic pizzas and pastas, and unique salads are the standard human fare on the deck, not to mention 30 different wines by the glass. Bridges is the big yellow building just west of the Public Market. 1696 Duranleau Street; (604) 687-4400.

Denman Street: One block from the dog-friendly Sylvia Hotel in Vancouver's West End, Denman Street demonstrates the ubiquitousness of outside dineries. About five blocks of Denman Street, between Pendrell and Robson Streets, is packed wall-to-wall with eateries that have sidewalk seating. You and yours could spend days trying the fare at the Pastameli Cappuccino Bar, Starbucks, Falafel King (chicken *shawarma,* beef *donair,* spinach pies), Viennese Coffee House, Le Veggie, The Bread Garden, Starbucks, Olympia Souvlaki Pizza & Pasta Restaurant. Wait wait, we're not three blocks from the Sylvia and there's another Starbucks. Then there's a Muffin Break (gourmet sandwiches), the Ukrainian Restaurant, Mum's Gelato Italiano, Vina Vietnamese Cuisine, and on and on.

Keep your dog leashed while you stroll the street trying to decide where to dine.

The Fish House in Stanley Park: The Fish House says yes to tying up dogs outside within sight of your inside dining table. They say lots of people do just that all year long and the waitstaff cheerfully serves water to Thirsty. Executive Chef Karen Barnaby creates wonderful dishes. She specializes in fresh, fresh seafood from around the world. Try the ouzo-flaming prawns, or calamari with smoked tomato sauce. In addition to a full-tilt dinner, the Fish House also has light lunches, brunches, and snacks—sort of a British "Tea." When you're there, call Chef Barnaby out from the kitchen to chat about the food, and ask her where she gets those fantastic rainbow-colored socks. The restaurant is a heritage building, formerly a house, with tall windows and a fireplace. It's open daily from 11:30 A.M. for lunch, and from 5 P.M. to 10 P.M. for dinner. Sunday brunch begins at 11 A.M. 8901 Stanley Park Drive; (604) 681-7275.

La Luna Cafe: Bring your four-legged friend to this Gastown dinery's outside area. The pizza is usually sold out by early afternoon, but the pasta salads are good, plus there's always a variety of soups and sandwiches. 117 Water Street; (604) 687-5862.

Milo Taverna: Downtown Milo Taverna's lunch and dinner menus linger in my mind. The menu's Greek to me, but it serves breakfast too. The chef specializes in roast lamb. Leashed dogs are allowed at the outside tables. Milo Taverna is open 9 A.M. to 10 P.M. in the summer and 9 A.M. to 9 P.M. in the winter. It's located under Robson Street between Hornby and Howe Streets. 800 Robson Street; (604) 688-6869.

Murchie's Coffee House: Murchie's has been to Canadian tea and coffee for a hundred years what Starbucks has been to Seattle coffee for about ten years. So why are there only eight in the Vancouver area, as opposed to Starbucks' 86 (and counting)? Hard to say, but their coffee has always been strong and tasty without giving it esoteric names. But judge for yourself. The one on Robson has outdoor stand-up-and-sip tables, so you can hang out with your leashed dog while you get your caffeine fix. 970 Robson Street; (604) 669-2649.

The Old Bailiff: In Robson Square, under Robson Street between Hornby and Howe Streets, you're welcome, in summer, to bring the pup to the patio area outside the main restaurant. The manager cautions that you must keep Igor on the perimeter of the seating area. Specialties include French onion soup, chicken cordon bleu, tuna salad sandwiches, and green-pepper asparagus quiche. In the winter, you can get your food to go and munch while you watch the ice-skating in Robson Square. 800 Robson Street; (604) 684-7448.

Picasso Cafe: On Broadway try the Picasso Cafe for above average vegetarian cuisine, Vietnamese spring rolls, curries, pastas, and pizzas. Not to lean on your liberal leanings and concern for the plight of humankind or anything, but it's worth knowing that the Picasso Cafe gets help from Vancouver's welfare department to employ and train kids whose families are on welfare. Sometimes, that's all it takes to make dining at the sidewalk tables all the more enjoyable. It's open for lunch Monday through Friday from 11:30 A.M.to 2 P.M. and Sunday from 10:30 A.M. to 2 P.M., near the corner of 1st Street on Broadway. 1626 West Broadway; (604) 732-3290.

Prospect Point Café: A city health inspector put the kibosh on dogs dining on the deck with you, but in front of the café is a takeout stand that uses the same kitchen. The salmonburgers are OK and so are the hot dogs, but don't write home about the cappuccino, which is more of a chocolate water drink than coffee. The classic Caesar salad is very good. In summer, Prospect Point Café's takeout stand is open daily 11:30 A.M. to 9:30 P.M. Winter weekdays it closes at 4:30 P.M. and on weekends at 8:30 P.M. While you're at Prospect Point, don't miss the overlook area. Just below you on the opposite side of the chain link fence is raccoon land. It looks like a rabbit warren in the bushes, but there's a plethora of raccoons living royally on human handouts. Emma and Quinn, of course, went starkers at the smell and sight. Luckily, they couldn't jump the fence, but they certainly tried. Quinn even broke free at the car, tore over a bench, and slid on his back trying to get back to the fence. A nice gentleman stepped on the end of Quinn's leash until I could retrieve him. 2099 Beach Avenue in Stanley Park; (604) 669-2737.

Seasons Coffee Shop: Dogs are welcome at this takeout-only coffee shop in Queen Elizabeth Park, but not next door in the very classy, and very good, Seasons in the Park Restaurant. You and Attencione can sit outside enjoying the good British takeout whilst watching the wedding parties come and go from next door. The coffee shop is open 9 A.M. to 5 P.M. weekdays and 9 A.M. to 5:30 P.M. weekends, May through September. Enter the park from Cambie Street and 33rd Avenue and follow the signs. The number for Seasons in the Park is (604) 874-8008; the coffee shop has no phone.

Sodas Diner: Sodas, a Gastown 1950s-style diner at the front of The Landing, has 12 varieties of burgers, and a few hot dogs too. Sodas is happy to serve people accompanied by dogs at the tables out front. The menu includes 8-ounce steaks, daily pasta specials, and that great Canadian snack: French fries with vinegar. This is Canada, eh, where restaurants sometimes offer fancy French fries as an hors d'oeuvre. You might as well be in Idaho, but the chicken wings are good too. 375 Water Street; (604) 683-7632.

Star Anise: Like the Wild Ginger in Seattle, the Star Anise excels as a Pacific Rim restaurant, melding Pacific Northwest and Asian foods. It's pricey, but worth it for the imaginative creations of one of Vancouver's most respected chefs. You have to hitch up your beast outside to the tree while you eat, but you won't be the first, and you can keep an eye out the front window. Let the maître d' influence your menu selections. It's open for dinner from 5:30 P.M. 1485 West 12th Avenue near Granville Street; (604) 737-1485.

Starbucks: Like everywhere else in Vancouver, Gastown has a Starbucks. And like everywhere else, this Starbucks has a whole sidewalk full of tables in an enclosed area. There are 86 Starbucks in Vancouver and environs, so trust that wherever you and Pedometer are in the city, there is a Starbucks to serve you. There are plenty on Robson Street, in particular. 199 Water Street; (604) 669-6297.

Vancouver's Best Coffee: This Kitsilano neighborhood coffeehouse is strong on cappuccinos and desserts, and sitting around in the morning sun. It's good on cloudy days too. Greet the morning with your pup (leashed, please), a newspaper, and a cup of Joe. 2959 West 4th Avenue; (604) 739-2136.

Water Street Café: In Gastown, this is a happy family restaurant specializing in Italian, and leaning toward Southern Italian, meals. The food is consistently very good, the prices are fair, and dogs are welcome outside when the weather allows outside service. 300 Water Street; (604) 689-2832.

PLACES TO STAY

Best Western Richmond Inn: Small dogs are welcome at this downtown Richmond hotel. Each of the 390 rooms has a balcony and the hotel has an outdoor pool. All rooms have coffeemakers. Room rates range from $99 to $265. Children 12 and under stay free, but pups are charged $10. People with dogs stay in ground-floor rooms with patio doors. 7551 Westminster Highway at Minoru Road; (604) 273-7878.

Bosman's Motor Hotel: Bosman's is a bargain-rate older hotel in downtown Vancouver. There are no special doggy policies, except that they prefer "small" ones, and there is no extra charge for pets. So it's dog friendly, comfortable, has a pool, and the rooms on the back side are quiet. Rates range from $69 to $125. 1060 Howe Street; (604) 682-3171.

Coast Plaza Suite Hotel: "Of course dogs are welcome here—they're some of our finest guests." This hotel, near Stanley Park, requires you to sign a statement of responsibility for any dog-induced damages. Coast Plaza has 267 large suites with city or ocean views; many of the rooms include kitchens and balconies. The hotel offers a health club, indoor pool, and two restaurants: the Brasserie and the Comox Long Bar & Grill. Business travelers can take advantage of the complimentary shuttle to the business district. Room rates range from $155 to $199. 1733 Comox Street; (604) 688-7711.

Delta Pacific Resort & Conference Centre: This dog-friendly resort (small dogs only) is on the main highway leading to Vancouver from the south. The Delta is also family-friendly, with its children's program, elaborate waterslide, tennis courts, playground, and three swimming pools. There is also a recreation program for everybody but the dog, a jogging trail, and bicycles for rent. Rates range from $135 to $155. To get there going north on B.C. Highway 99, take the Bridgeport exit (exit 39). 10251 St. Edwards Drive at B.C. Highway 99; (604) 278-9611 or (800) 268-1133.

Fairmont Hotel Vancouver: The Fairmont Hotel Vancouver is a City of Vancouver Heritage Building, and dogs are welcome to stay in your room, but they are not permitted in the restaurant or lobby lounge. The management asks that you call ahead of time if you plan to bring your pup and be prepared to supervise her at all times. Quinn didn't know what to make of the revolving door at the Fairmont Hotel Vancouver. He's mastered automatic sliding doors, which seem to open by means of his very presence. And elevator doors open for him if he waits long enough, just like car doors, house doors, and store doors. But the revolving door required him to be carried since no amount of his will power could prevent the approaching rear door from attacking his tail. Next trip we discovered a nearby sliding door for the luggage haulers. The nearest grassy area is on the grounds of the Vancouver Art Gallery, across from the hotel on Hornby Street. Rates range from $199 to $299; there's a doggy charge of $20. 900 West Georgia Street; (604) 684-3131 or (800) 441-1414.

Fairmont Waterfront Centre Hotel: This is a stunning Fairmont chain hotel with great views of the city, Stanley Park, and Vancouver Harbour. The Fairmont Waterfront Centre welcomes small dogs under 20 pounds and the extra doggy charge is $25 per night. Dogs must be supervised at all times. This is where we supervised Quinn and Emma's introduction to seagulls. The rooms each have a teeny window that opens for salt air off of Vancouver Harbour. It's guaranteed that if you open your window, a seagull will appear within ten seconds, day or night. People who live in seagull neighborhoods know that if you feed a seagull once, he's your guest forever. Put out a bit of muffin, and whoa, in they come for a landing. You guessed it. The dogs went berserk. They were basically in mid-air trying to claw through the glass, and doing a yapping performance like I've never heard. Their brain chemicals were broiling and it took a while to get them calm again, even after closing the curtains. The rest of the muffin was poor substitute for bird meat, but it helped. The nearest grass or dirt area to the hotel is a bit of a hoof, about a block northwest to the railroad yards. Rates for two range from an off-season low of $199 to a high-season high of $299. The Fairmont Waterfront Centre is directly across the street from Canada Place inside Burrard Inlet about a mile from Stanley Park. 900 Canada Place Way; (604) 691-1991 or (800) 441-1414.

Four Seasons Hotel: Simple elegance rules at the dog-friendly Four Seasons. It has both indoor and outdoor pools plus full fitness facilities. It's located smack in the middle of downtown and is linked to the underground shopping mall (which does not allow dogs). Rates range from $285 to $480. 791 West Georgia Street at Howe; (604) 689-9333.

Georgian Court Hotel: For sports fans, this Vancouver hotel is very close to B.C. Place Stadium and General Motors Place Stadium and walking distance to the theater district and downtown. Children 17 and under stay free, but there's a $20 charge for "small only please" dogs. Hmm. Room rates range from $115 to $260. 773 Beatty Street at Robson; (604) 682-5555.

Granville Island Hotel: Here's a chance to sleep under the bridge. It's a converted warehouse, just like almost everything else on Granville Island. The views of busy False Creek are great, and the island shops do a bustling business in arts, crafts, books, clothing, and of course groceries at the Public Market. Live theater performances go year-round. All rooms have coffeemakers and some have microwave ovens. Room rates range from $129 to $219. Small dogs are welcome, but you must call first. 1253 Johnston Street; (604) 683-7373.

Holiday Inn Hotel & Suites Vancouver Downtown: Uh-oh. This downtown Holiday Inn allows cats as well as dogs, so keep your eyes peeled for those feisty felines. It's so refreshing to hear from the deskperson, "Sure, the dog can stay in your room while you go out to eat. We like you to walk him once in awhile though." But what about the beds? "We know there's no way to keep a dog off the bed." Case closed. The Holiday is in the heart of downtown, and rates range from $129 to $199. The hotel also has a pool, exercise room, video games, and a jungle gym. 1110 Howe Street; (604) 684-2151.

Holiday Inn–Vancouver Centre: This Vancouver hotel on Broadway allows small dogs in the smoking rooms only. The indoor pool and exercise room are nice, and the phones have data ports for the computer-dependent. Room rates range from $109 to $199. 711 West Broadway; (604) 879-0511.

The London Guard Motel: Near Burnaby in East Vancouver, the London Guard welcomes dogs. Mind the garden flowers and landscaping though; the owners are proud of their work. Rates at the motel range from $50 to $80, and there is a deposit of $2 for dogs. 2227 Kingsway; (604) 430-4646.

Metropolitan Hotel: Small dogs are welcome at downtown Vancouver's "Met," which contains the highly rated Diva restaurant. The health club sports some courts and a pool. Rates at the Metropolitan range from $225 to $395. 645 Howe Street; (604) 687-1122.

Pacific Palisades Hotel: On Vancouver's "hot" Robson Street, the Pacific Palisades welcomes dogs for no extra charge and no deposit. The views are great and it's right in the middle of the action. But if the action is too much, the hotel has bicycles to rent so you can pedal to nearby Stanley Park and take comfort in the woods. There are grass strips right out front along Jarvis Street. Several rooms have kitchens. Rates range from $250 to $450. 1277 Robson Street at Jarvis; (604) 688-0461.

The Pan Pacific Fairmont Hotel Vancouver: At Canada Place right on the water of Vancouver Harbour, the Pan Pacific is a great place to watch the cruise ships come and go—not to mention the seaplane traffic. Small dogs are welcome and there is no extra fee. The Skytrain station (no dogs please) is right out front and the hotel is walking distance from Gastown and downtown shopping. Stanley Park is just over a mile to the west. Rates range from $370 to, yoiks, $525. 999 Canada Place; (604) 662-8111.

Quality Hotel Downtown at False Creek: At the north end of Vancouver's Granville Street Bridge, the Quality Hotel welcomes small dogs, entire families (some units have fully supplied kitchens), and busy executives. It's an extra $10 for the pup, half what you'd pay for an extra person. Rates range from $89 to $229. 1335 Howe Street; (604) 682-0229.

Radisson President Hotel & Suites: In downtown Richmond, the upscale Radisson welcomes small dogs no larger than a carrying kennel size. Expect to be accommodated in an executive suite (smoking) because management believes dogs require larger rooms. There is no extra charge and no pet deposit, but any damages must be paid for at checkout. The hotel has a fine Asian restaurant (try the dim-sum) and a Buddhist temple, and it's all connected to a terrific Asian shopping mall. Rates range from $215 to $290. 8181 Cambie Road at No. 3 Road; (604) 276-8181 or (800) 333-3333.

Renaissance Vancouver Hotel Harbourside: Located in Vancouver between Canada Place and Stanley Park, the Renaissance looks north over the harbor to the North Shore mountains. Small dogs are welcome at no extra charge, and the rooms are geared toward the business traveler. Renaissance rates range from $176 to $266. 1133 West Hastings Street at Thurlow; (604) 689-9211.

Residence Inn by Marriott, Vancouver: Full kitchens are available at this downtown Vancouver Residence Inn, and dogs are welcome. All rooms, even the ones without kitchens, have coffeemakers, microwave ovens, and refrigerators. Computer-dependent humans will appreciate the data ports in the rooms, plus the hotel has a coin laundry. Residence rates range from $130 to $235, including continental breakfast. The fee per stay for the pup is $75 plus a $15 deposit. 1234 Hornby Street at Davie; (604) 688-1234.

Sandman Hotel Downtown Vancouver: The Sandman Hotel welcomes trained dogs who "don't make a mess." There is a $5 per-night pet charge and dogs must weigh under 30 pounds. Room rates range from $139 to $194. It's conveniently located near Chinatown, Gastown, and all of the shops on Robson Street. A swimming pool is available, too. 180 West Georgia Street; (604) 681-2211 or (800) 726-3626.

Sutton Place Hotel and La Grande Residence: Emma and Quinn love trips to the big city. Vancouver is especially nice because 29 of its city parks have leash-free hours in the morning and evening. But overnights are the best. Pet-friendly lodgings like the Five-Diamond Sutton Place Hotel (and its adjacent La Grande Residence) pull out all the stops to treat the pups as well as they've always treated their human customers. The Sutton's V.I.P. (Very Important Pet) amenity program, costing $95, begins with check-in. The welcoming staff is mighty "peticular" about taking a Polaroid for the guest book and noting your pet's gourmet preferences. The room service meal choice is between grilled Alberta beef T-bone steak or seared fresh tuna fillet topped with caviar, served by a gallant waiter on porcelain dishes. A bottle of Evian accompanies the meal. Emma and Quinn favored the beef and wasted no time on manners when Gilbert arrived with the meal. They weren't rude, exactly, just hungry after running around a nearby park. Turndown service brought the bedtime reading—a personal copy of *Dog City Vancouver* with plenty of information and pictures of some pretty cute dogs. There were also some $5 gift certificates to Three Dog Bakery on West 4th Avenue and samples of the bakery's treats. Yum. Valet dog-walking is also available as part of the package.

The Sutton Place Hotel is in the heart of Vancouver, an easy walk to high-tone shopping on Robson Street and a longer walk to the live theater district.

The hotel has an excellent innovative continental French cuisine restaurant, Fleuri, that offers a Chocoholic Bar buffet three evenings a week. Le Spa is a complete European beauty and fitness center. It features La Stone therapy, an Arizona hot stone massage treatment. Hotel rates are $179 to $450 and Residence rates are $149 to $299. There is a one-time pet cleaning fee of $150. 845 Burrard Street; (800) 961-7555; www.suttonplace.com.

The Sylvia: One look at the vines crawling, almost leaping, up the side of the eight-story 1912 Sylvia will assure you that history is very much prized here. It has long been a favorite getaway hotel for Seattleites, and its proximity to English Bay and Stanley Park are just the excuse to justify the retro experience of staying in The Sylvia. Dogs are entirely welcome—no limit, no special rules, no extra charge. Well, they did say that a couple of St. Bernards would not be entirely welcome. A man who lives in the next block said this is a dog-intensive neighborhood. In his building of 20 apartments, 13 have dogs. Of The Sylvia's 119 rooms, 15 have kitchens. Cost for two people ranges from $65 to $125 year-round. Children 17 and under stay free. It's located right across Beach Avenue from the beach on English Bay, but the entrance is around the corner. 1154 Gilford Street; (604) 681-9321.

2400 Motel: The dog-friendly 2400 Motel is actually a collection of bungalows ranging in size up to three bedrooms, some with kitchens. It's located just over four miles from downtown Vancouver, east on Kingsway (B.C. Highway 99A) toward Burnaby. Although on the thrifty side, this place is really nice. Rates range from $71 to $175. Dogs (small please) must pay $4 per night. 2400 Kingsway; (604) 434-2464.

Vancouver Centre Travelodge: A downtown, economy-style hotel located near parks, shops, and theaters, this Travelodge has four rooms (in a separate building) for visiting canines and their humans. These rooms tend to fill up on weekends, so call ahead. No dogs are allowed in the main hotel. Rates for the doggy rooms range from $69 to $109. 1304 Howe Street; (604) 682-2767.

Westin Bayshore Hotel: Once the hoity-toity place to stay in Vancouver, the Bayshore still holds its own among the competition. The hotel overlooks Burrard Inlet just a few blocks from Stanley Park. Dogs are allowed as long as they're small (no more than 25 pounds) and well-behaved. Room rates range from $175 to $382. 1601 West Georgia Street; (604) 682-3377 or (800) 228-3000.

FESTIVALS

Basset Walk in Stanley Park: On the first Sunday in May, Vancouver's basset hounds meet for a 45-minute stroll in the park (unless you opt for the short route). Wiener races, a costume contest, a big raffle, and snacks follow the walk. The event is free, but proceeds from the raffle and T-shirt and muffin sales are donated to a basset rescue service. Everybody gathers before noon at the Prospect Point Picnic Area, a short drive past Prospect Point. Other dog breeds are invited, too. For more information, call Lynn Auton at (604) 438-2381 or Nancy Hardy at (604) 467-1162.

Granville Island: Granville Island is a 35-acre island under the south end of Granville Street Bridge. The island was reclaimed in 1973 from its declining industrial days. Granville Island is now both a tourist destination and a daily market for the people of Vancouver. The Public Market, just like Pike Place

Market in Seattle, is chock full of esoteric foodstuffs, craft tables, and snack stands. The island has 11 restaurants, 15 fast fooderies, three live theaters, two art schools, a dog-friendly hotel, and many, many stores and craft shops, for a total of 250 businesses. It's Vancouver's primo stroll for window-shopping and artist-watching. Throughout the year, the island hosts free art shows, a bluegrass festival, Shakespeare Under the Stars, a wooden boat festival, a garbage-can art contest, and much more. In the summer, buskers and other entertainers hold court every day on the street. Signage to the island is good from any direction. Approaching the Granville Island Bridge from either the south or the north, keep to the right and follow the little green and white signs that say Granville Island. Going west on Broadway, one block after Granville Street, there is a sign for Granville Island to the right on Fir Street. For 24-hour information, call the Talking Yellow Pages at (604) 299-9000, ext. 5784. The number for Granville Island information is (604) 666-5784.

When we were done for the day at Granville Island, we walked past rows of parked cars trying to find our own. Emma tried to pause at almost every car, hoping that it was the right one and she could climb into her mobile den for a richly deserved nap.

Vancouver International Jazz Festival: More than 1,000 jazz musicians gather from around the world to attend Vancouver's biggest music festival. The popular event typically runs for a week at the end of June, and is held at two-dozen venues around the city. Dog lovers should attend the concert at Granville Island's Market Stage, an outdoor stage framed by False Creek, where daily noontime performances are held (it's located behind the Granville Island Public Market). Musical events are free and open to appreciative dogs, who should honor the musicians by remaining quiet and leashed. (604) 872-5200.

DIVERSIONS

Scoot across the water: At the False Creek ferry dock on Granville Island, little jitney ferries, called aquabuses, left over from Expo 86, zip across to the Aquatic Center near Stanley Park and back across the mouth of False Creek to the maritime museum in Vanier Park. During the summer, they run every 10 minutes, less frequently in the winter, and dogs are welcome on board at no charge. Humans pay $2 to $3, depending on destination. It's a great way to see some of Vancouver from the water. The Granville Island dock of the **False Creek Ferries** is located a few yards north of Bridges, behind the Public Market, at 1804 Boatlift Lane; (604) 684-7781.

Go rockhoundin': **Rockwood Adventures,** which is based in West Vancouver, offers guided rain forest walks in Capilano River Regional Park and other recreation areas near Vancouver. Dogs are welcome if you give advance notice, and some hikes are specifically designed for dogs. Guide Manfred Scholermann, who has hiked the area hundreds of times, carries canine backpacks and umbrellas on doggy hiking trips. If you and Genghis are hard-core outdoor types, ask about the Ben Paul Trail from Lynn Canyon. (604) 926-7705.

Tough row to hoe: The **Avant Gardener** in busy Kitsilano has beyond-belief tools for the gardener, including Wilkinson Sword cultivators, Spear & Jackson chrome-plated pitchforks and shovels, and English hay racks. The store is "very dog friendly," but be careful—there's a very nice cat inside, and cat terriers won't be appreciated. 2235 West 4th Avenue; (604) 736-0404.

Bard on the Beach: Some of the best theater in Vancouver, and Vancouver is quite the theater town, is performed by the Bard on the Beach troupe in an open tent staked to the grass of Vanier Park. Two or three Shakespeare plays rotate in repertory from mid-June to mid-September. But are dogs welcome? We've seen a few as characters in the plays. We've heard many who voted "aye" to the question, "To bark, or not to bark" The actors joke about renaming the company Bark on the Beach. All in all, though, visiting dogs who won't bark will not be turned away. They may be staked outside the tent, yet inside the fence, during the evening performances. (604) 737-0625 (administration, off-season) or (604) 739-0559 (box office, on-season).

Old Yeller would have loved this place: The **Book Warehouse,** sort of like a Mr. Books, specializes in remaindered books, the most agonizing fact of life to writers who had loftier expectations of their work than was appreciated by readers. Sometimes they hand you a dollar-off coupon on your way in. Sure, dogs are fine, as long as they don't pee on the carpet. It's at 632 West Broadway; (604) 872-5711.

Have a gas: You can always have fun in **Gastown** on a fair weather evening. It's full of good restaurants and shops with neat and not so neat stuff, from fancy art stores to t-shirt shoppes. In fact, by the time you're reading this, some of the t-shirt stores will be restaurants and some restaurants will be t-shirt stores. One Gastown thing that will never change as time marches on is the Gastown Steam Clock on the corner of Cambie Street and Water Street. Make sure your dog finds a fire hydrant before you get to the clock. It's something of a totem for Gastown. It's the world's first steam-powered clock, dedicated to the citizens of Vancouver in 1977. The live steam from underground winds the weights and blows the whistles every 4.5 minutes. Each quarter-hour the clock sounds the Westminster chimes, and the large whistle sounds once on the hour.

The hound of music: Every Sunday afternoon, St. Andrew's-Wesley Church offers jazz vespers, and dogs who behave themselves can join the audience. This is a pleasant hour of live jazz interspersed with relevant Christian readings. The church passes the plate and the musicians get the proceeds. 1012 Nelson Street at Burrard Street; (604) 683-4574.

Ready for the dog wash?: **Launderdog** wants your body, but you must make a reservation first. No drop-ins please. This cleaning, grooming, and day care parlour is open weekdays from 6:30 A.M. to 6 P.M. and on Saturdays from 10 A.M. to 6 P.M. 1064 Davie Street; (604) 685-2306.

It's a dog's life: They know about skunking here, which usually happens in the dead of night when nothing's open, so **It's a Dog's Life** sells a skunking kit complete with the right enzyme. Or if you can wait till morning, they'll do the honors for you. "I could have retired on skunkings," says the owner. It's a Dog's Life is a dog wash, after all—$12 if you do it yourself, or $15 to $35 if they do it for you, depending on size of dog. This is also a consignment store, specializing in sterilized dog crates. It's located central to all the English Bay beaches and Pacific Spirit Park, at 3428 West Broadway; (604)739-3647.

A slice of the spicy life: For a new blend of sights, sounds, and smells, try strolling through South Vancouver's outdoor **Punjabi Market.** Leashed dogs are welcome. The Palika Bazaar is a Little India mini-mall full of clothing and accessories, and Singh Foods is a supermarket teeming with tinned mangoes, bulk specialty foods, and unusual kitchen utensils. The market is between the 6400 and 6600 blocks of Main Street, near 49th Street.

Scene around town: **Robson Street,** which runs from the West End east to downtown Vancouver, is where cruisers go to see and be seen. It can take an hour to drive three blocks, so it's a good thing you guys like walking. The forest of legs is a little dense for Emma, who looks longingly at parked cars, but Quinn's go-for-it attitude leads the way. There are plenty of fancy clothing shops and outside dining opportunities.

In the old days, like the 1970s, Robson Street was called Robsonstrasse. It's now more multiethnic, and it vies with Gastown and Granville Island for the best walking, browsing, and shopping in the city. I wager that if you take a Saturday evening stroll down Robson Street you'll see and hear musical instruments you've never seen nor heard before. If you do recognize every individual instrument, I've lost this bet and I'd like to hear from you. One man plays an amplified one-string affair with a bow, sounding like a one-string violin. There are magicians, buskers, street artists, palm readers, and people doing some activities I couldn't figure out. There was a guitar band on one side of the street trying to top the steel drum band on the other.

Suit yourself and bring your dog: **Straiths,** a specialty upscale clothing store in the Fairmont Hotel Vancouver, is one of only two Brioni suit outlets in Vancouver. It also carries Paul & Sharx yachting sweaters. Since the hotel allows dogs, so does Straiths, as long as they're small and well-behaved. 900 West Georgia Street; (604) 685-3301.

Woof for Waffles: **Woofles,** on Granville Island, is the new pet bakery in town. It's not a chain store, but Stuart the owner already has offers from people who want to franchise. The doggilicious deli treats are also human-consumable and free of all known harmful substances, including, according to Stuart, meat. Woofles is in the red caboose in front of the Kids Only Market at 1496 Cartwright Street; (604) 689-3647 or (877) 966-3537.

Let's you and I mosey on up to the bar, Rover: Dogs are welcome in the **Granville Island Brewing Company,** except in the "food preparation area." The shopkeeper who welcomes dogs opined that most dogs are better citizens than some people he knows. "We keep dog water out front and we always have dog treats on hand from Woofles across the street." Wine drinkers need not feel snooty about this beer place, because an excellent wine selection is served, too. Since a friend from Chile had invited us (and the pups!) to her Vancouver apartment for dinner, we chose a nice Chilean red to go with the bow tie pasta. Our hostess is actually descended from Corsican pirates, but that's a story for another time. The dinner was fine, all the animals enjoyed themselves, and, yes, we washed the dishes before we left. 1441 Cartwright Street; (604) 687-2739.

Listen up: Vancouver has **Talking Yellow Pages.** Simply dial the number, pick from the menu, and you may hear something like this: "You're probably embarrassed to admit it, but you lavish more attention on your pet than you do other people. And why not? Who else is a constant companion through good times and bad? With unconditional love and joy at the mere sight of you coming home? Spend as much time as possible with your dog, who thrives, just like you, on attention. Take the dog for an extra walk now and then." (604) 299-9000.

Chew on this: The **Classic Butcher Shop** in Tsawwassen, on the way to or from the ferry to Vancouver Island, has a doggy bar out front to keep Chowser busy while you go inside for takeout. The shop has ready-to-heat entrées for you and knuckle bones for the beast. They also make a custom dog food: 28-day aged beef, chicken, turkey, and lamb, plus five percent oats. It costs $3.75 per kilo, cooked and frozen into a four-chunk brick. 1212A 56 Street, Tsawwassen; (604) 948-0244.

Let's get outta town: The city of **Richmond**, just south of Vancouver on B.C. Highway 99, is actually an island in the mouth of the mighty Fraser River. It's called Lulu Island, and it sits below sea level between the river's North and South arms. There are 15 more islands to the "city," but the only other big one, Sea Island, contains Vancouver International Airport. Lulu Island is diked against high tides, and the dikes provide some of the best trails in the Northwest. Exercisers, dogs, horses, and bicyclists use the trails cooperatively. The trails look out to the horizon from the South Arm, Sturgeon Bank, and the Middle Arm of the Fraser. It's possible to cover the entire 50-kilometer perimeter, but most of the activity is on the South Dyke Trail, which leads through the historic, but still working, fishing village of Steveston. Steveston Landing, a boardwalk full of shops, marine supply stores, and eateries, is entirely open to leashed dogs. Dave's, a very good seafood restaurant, has outside dining with water bowls for dogs at the ready. The steamed mussels are excellent, and you can't beat the cappuccino pie for dessert. About one kilometer west along the trail from Steveston is Garry Point Park and Beach, with a huge grassy area perfect for flying kites and running dogs. Bring your own pup, but kites are available at Splash Toy Shop in the village. Garry Point is an intertidal salt marsh with terrific bird-watching opportunities. Keep Thor on the leash, though, when the birds are pecking about. Tourism Richmond: (604) 271-8280.

WHISTLER, BRITISH COLUMBIA

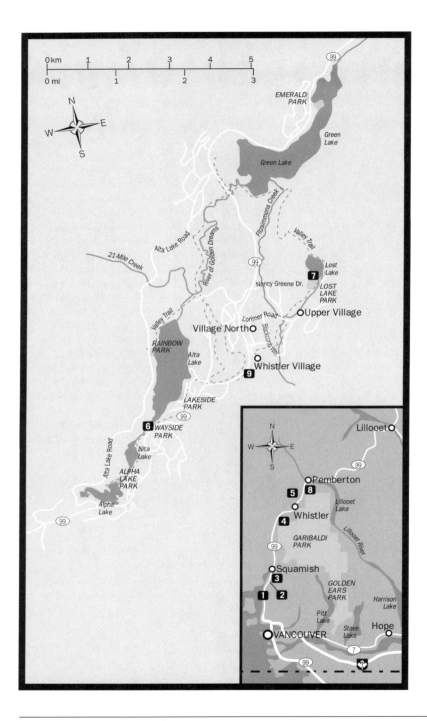

11
WHISTLER, BRITISH COLUMBIA

Very politically correct tourism drives the British Columbia tourism industry, and Whistler, 75 miles north of Vancouver, leads the way. There's even an underground drive-through McDonald's in Whistler, while the espresso cafés dot the walkways of the three, almost four now, Whistler villages.

Although universally recognized as the premier winter ski resort in North America, Whistler is just as much fun in the spring, summer, and fall. From street jugglers, mimes, musicians, and other buskers in the Village Square to the more formal Vancouver Symphony Orchestra playing "Night on Bald Mountain" in Whistler Mountain's Ego Bowl, Whistler is a celebration of the outdoor life. This area offers breathtaking vistas, alpine lakes, and lush meadows, which all became readily accessible when the Sea to Sky Highway (also called B.C. Highway 99 and Canadian Highway 1) was paved in 1966.

Whistler also celebrates the dog life, rivaling Victoria for Fido-friendliness. You will see plenty of dogs around, but very few leashes, so it may come as a surprise that there are no official off-leash areas as there are in Victoria.

The mountain biking here is unlimited. In fact, being in Whistler without a mountain bike is a lot like being in Dodge City without a horse. But don't worry, as several places rent them, and horses too, for that matter. Trail riding is popular in the summer, on horse or bike. And on Whistler Mountain you can take your bike (but not your horse or dog) up on the lift for a guided I-hope-these-brakes-work descent. You can even take a guided bear-sighting tour, but not with Bosco. Remember, no dogs on the ski hills, winter or summer.

ON THE WAY FROM VANCOUVER TO WHISTLER
PARKS, BEACHES, AND RECREATION AREAS
Note: this section is not listed alphabetically, but from south to north

On the way to Whistler, 75 miles north of Vancouver, there are some places you and your dog might especially enjoy. They are listed here in the order you'll pass them, not alphabetically. On our way, Quinn dug a burrow in the back of the station wagon by nosing clothes and towels around and into a hump, so he could crawl in for a nap.

• **Porteau Cove Provincial Marine Park** 🐾 See ❶ on page 174.
In addition to being a good pit stop between Vancouver and Whistler, Porteau Cove, about 24 miles north of Vancouver on Howe Sound, is the site of a renowned deep-sea diving area. There is a large public campground and

day-use area, plus parking and shower facilities just for divers. It has a nice wide boat launch, and a ferry dock is at the ready for those rare times that the road between here and Squamish is closed. The boat from here to Squamish used to be the only way to travel, and now that the highway is so well beefed up the ferry may never be needed again. But back in the old days. . . .

The camping area has walk-in sites for hikers and bikers, plus standard drive-in sites. There are 59 campsites in all, some to bike into and others to drive into. Firewood is supplied. Great tall cedar trees line the water's edge and screen the campsites from each other. The campsites are right on the edge of Howe Sound, so you can toss sticks into the water for your retriever's boundless delight. A blue and white highway sign will alert you two kilometers before Porteau Cove. (604) 898-3678.

•Shannon Falls Provincial Park 🐾 See **2** on page 174.

At 1,100 feet high, Shannon Falls is nearly 20 times the height of Niagara Falls (which only reaches a height of 158 feet). You can catch a glimpse of the falls from the highway, but a close-up view requires only a quarter-mile walk through the park. Shannon Falls is a day park and dogs must be leashed, but Quinn and Emma liked it anyway. They zipped around on the wet rocks, but wondered what the shower spray from the falls was all about. It was a trifle loud, too. Take heed of the prominent dog warning for all British Columbia provincial parks: "Sorry, Bowser, the parks are for people and the protection of our resources. Visitors come here to see wildlife and if you're romping free, you or your scent will frighten creatures away. People come to enjoy picnics and to play and lie on the beaches, and they don't like your deposits beside them. As long as you are in this provincial park, you'll have to stay on a leash, off the beach, and away from picnic areas. We know, it's a dog's life."

Drive 36 miles north from Vancouver on the Sea to Sky Highway, which is also called B.C. Highway 99 and Canadian Highway 1. Shannon Falls Provincial Park will be on your right; keep an eye out for signs. (604) 898-3678.

•The Stawamus Chief 🐾 🐾 See **3** on page 174.

More monolith than park, Stawamus Chief is the largest granite outcrop in the world, depending on whom you listen to. From the highway you can usually see rock climbers scattered midclimb on the face (bring binoculars for an even better view). The hike around and to the top of Stawamus Chief is a great place to take a dog—steep but short, taking less than two hours to complete. The 1,482 acres around Stawamus Chief and Shannon Falls, just one mile to the south, became a provincial park in 1995.

From Vancouver, drive 37 miles north on the Sea to Sky Highway (also called B.C. Highway 99 and Canadian Highway 1). The Stawamus Chief will be on your right. Signs will direct you to the park entrance. (604) 898-3678.

•Brandywine Falls Provincial Park 🐾 🐾 See **4** on page 174.

Reaching the waterfalls of Brandywine entails walking about one-third of a mile through the woods (well worth the stroll). When the beautiful falls are full (commonly the case), they plummet 300 feet into an immense pool surrounded by green lichens, moss, and ferns. The park has 15 campsites, a water pump, and outhouses. Dogs must be leashed.

From Vancouver, drive 63 miles north on the Sea to Sky Highway (also known as B.C. Highway 99 and Canadian Highway 1). Watch for signs to Brandywine Falls Provincial Park, which will be on your right. (604) 898-3678.

WHISTLER AREA

All of the Whistler Valley is an interconnecting network of trails. One way or another, all the parks, villages, golf courses, subdivisions, marketing centers, five lakes, and both Whistler and Blackcomb mountains are attached to each other by the well-marked trail system. Stay on the alert for bears. As one local said, "To see a deer is a rare treat; I see bears all the time." Remember that dogs must always be leashed in the Whistler villages and all parks. Scooping is required.

•Ancient Cedars 🐾🐾🐾 See 🕠 on page 174.

You may want to bike this one, or do it in stages. It's a hike/bike, or even drive part way, up Cougar Mountain to the trailhead for a cedar grove called Ancient Cedars. Being on top, in a cathedral-like forest grove, is worth anything it took to get there. You can turn the trek into a 20-mile mountain bike loop, which includes the Soo River Valley on your return to Highway 99 north of Whistler. Add another 19 miles if you bike the highway out and back from the village. The logging roads up Cougar Mountain vary from up to steep. At times it seems like you're bouldering, and if you're pushing a bike it's like acting out a Greek myth of pushing something uphill that only wants to roll down. But the Ancient Cedars forest at the summit is ample reward. It's a 1,000-year-old forest of cedars 10 feet in diameter and 30 feet around. Some people call it a cathedral bisected by a trail.

Drive north from Whistler on B.C. Highway 99. Turn left (north) at the first road past the second entrance to Emerald Estates and follow the rough logging road (take the right branch) up Cougar Mountain to the trailhead and parking lot. Take the trail past Showh Lakes. From the lakes, it's 2.5 miles round-trip to Ancient Cedars. (604) 938-7275.

•Lakeside Park 🐾🐾 See 🕕 on page 174.

A one-mile paved bike trail leads west from Whistler Village to Alta Lake and its Lakeside Park, where windsurfers and canoers congregate. Whistler Sailing operates at the south end of Alta Lake, just beyond the golf course adjacent to the village. For a really fun excursion, load Magellan into your rented canoe, paddle two miles to the other end of the lake, and coast down the River of Golden Dreams for a few miles to Meadow Park. Before you launch your boat, arrange for a pick-up by Whistler Sailing (open daily through the summer and on weekends in the fall).

From Whistler Village, drive south on B.C. Highway 99 and turn right (north) at the sign for Lakeside Park. Whistler Sailing: (604) 932-7245; Lakeside Park: (604) 938-7275 or (604) 938-3133.

•Lost Lake Park 🐾🐾🐾🐾 See 🕖 on page 174.

During the warmer months, hikers, bikers, and strollers frequent the cross-country trails used by skiers in the winter. Two and a half miles of the Lost

Lake trail system are lit at night year-round until 10:30 P.M. The lake is only six-tenths of a mile from the village, but there are 18 more miles to the looped trail system. At the lake, Rover can't go on the beach, but wait. This lake has definitely earned its four paws rating. It has a dog beach! When you reach the park from village, turn right for the dog beach. (Continue past the small dog beach to reach the unofficial clothing-optional human beach, but that's for another guidebook.) If you go the other way from the main park beach, north, just about 60 yards ahead there are two rivers. They're about 10 yards apart and they provide a brain teaser to the curious. One river flows into the lake, and the other flows out. This didn't concern Emma or Quinn a bit. They snarfed around the banks and bridges, but didn't find any salmon. A passing jogger stopped when she spotted a teeny frog hopping across the path. She scrunched into guard position and protected the frog with her hands from certain harm by our frog terriers until we passed. Hers was an apt act that symbolized how Whistler likes to think of itself. Lost Lake Park is open 24 hours.

Drive south from Whistler Village on Blackcomb Way, which passes the base of Blackcomb Mountain and the Upper Village. Blackcomb Way becomes Lost Lake Road, which leads directly into the parking area. To walk there from Whistler Village Square, head east on Skiers Approach past the Hard Rock Cafe on your left and Whistler Village Inns on your right. This leads to Blackcomb Way, which you cross and then continue straight through to the parking lot. Just before the footbridge over Fitzimmons Creek, take the left path option and follow the sign to Lost Lake. (604) 938-7275.

• **Nairn Falls Provincial Park** 🐾🐾 See **8** on page 174.
This is a very nice park and 88-site campground about 18 miles north of Whistler on B.C. Highway 99 and the Green River. There is one hand pump for water and the only toilets are the outhouse variety. At Nairn Falls itself, a little over a half-mile walk from the campground, the Green River appears to twist sideways to fall nearly 200 feet between the narrow cliffs. The forest here is composed of Douglas fir, cedar, and hemlock. The park is closed in the winter due to lack of snow plowing. Dogs must be on a leash at all times and they are not allowed on beach or picnic areas.

To get to Nairn Falls from Whistler Village, take B.C. Highway 99 north toward Pemberton. The park is 18 miles from Whistler, on the right side of the highway; watch for signs. (604) 898-3678.

• **Valley Trail** 🐾🐾🐾 See **9** on page 174.
Many walkers who don't feel the need for a gonzo hike into the mountains simply choose to stay on the valley floor, with its 20 scenic miles of paved, mostly flat trails for bicyclists, hikers, in-line skaters, and joggers (and with all of this activity, it makes sense that leashes are required). The Valley Trail winds by five lakes and a world-class golf course. It's legal for dogs to swim in areas accessed via the Valley Trail, except for the public beaches. The Valley Trail is open 24 hours.

From the Village Square in Whistler Village, walk toward the Whistler Conference Centre. Pass around it to the left, cross Whistler Way, and you will be on the trail. Take the trail to the right beneath the underpass and you can go around the Whistler Golf Course to connect with other trails. (604) 938-7275.

RESTAURANTS

As befits a first-rate year-round resort, many Whistler restaurants are destination dineries with very high-quality food and service. Overall, there are more than a hundred restaurants (70 with outdoor patios) among the three village areas and within the 37 hotels. Patio service is common in the spring and summer, and you'll see water dishes for dogs as a symbolic and real welcome to dogs. Whistler is a car-less village, so there is no problem dining "on the street." Delis, espresso shops, and other carryout restaurants increase the choices, so you and Appetitis need never be separated during those so-important victual bondings. A Whistler note: The entrances to most buildings have a snow grate upon which to stomp your boots. Emma and Quinn preferred to walk around the grates when there was enough room.

Auntie Em's Kitchen: No one believes that I had lunch with Toto at Auntie Em's one magical Saturday in Whistler. But what can I say? Dogs find me. I was going full tilt on a monster veggie sandwich at a window table and in walks Dorothy's buddy Toto. He was short and furry, with a bit of underbite like his jaw was too big for his face. He looked puzzled, thinking maybe this wasn't Kansas anymore. I called Auntie Em over, who explained that the dog could conceivably be Toto, and that he came in everyday for lunch with one of the construction workers from next door. Dogs weren't allowed, of course, but this particular one seemed to be an exception. Most dogs sit outside on the patio while sharing a sip of matzo ball soup or a bit of cranberry date bar. The sweets and sandwich breads are outstanding. There's usually a water bowl, too. Auntie Em's Kitchen is open from 6:30 A.M. to 6 P.M. seven days a week. It's located in the Village North Market Place at 129-4340 Lorimer Road; (604) 932-1163.

Bagel Street Café: The giant oven at this Whistler Village café produces an incredible variety of bagels, including a breakfast bagel with scrambled eggs. Skiers enjoy the "lunch to go:" a bagel, cream cheese, cookie, and a beverage. There are several outdoor tables for your human and canine convenience. 109-4295 Blackcomb Way; (604) 932-3131.

Bear Foot Bistro: The Listel Whistler Hotel's restaurant allows dogs on the patio, but if it's cold outside and you're staying at the hotel (which welcomes dogs, by the way) you could always order room service from the same menu and share an intimate meal with Fido. We opted to eat in the restaurant, without Emma and Quinn, and our table of 19 people polished off two jeroboams of an impeccable Italian red while feasting on crisp-baked Asian shrimp, crab cakes, and a hunter's pot of rabbit, duck, and Arctic musk ox. We topped that off with phyllo-crusted bananas with hot buttered rum and French vanilla ice cream. The 1,000 wines won an excellence award from *Wine Spectator* and the chef's creations won a North American Food Critics award. Other novelties at this bistro include working artists in the dining room (our night featured a painter and a potter) and live jazz every evening. 4121 Village Green; (604) 932-1133.

Evergreens: This restaurant in the Delta Whistler Resort opens onto one of the promenade hallways. Since the Delta welcomes dogs, so does Evergreens, but they must stay outside the railing and behave themselves. Buffet breakfast is served from 6:30 A.M. to 11 A.M. Evergreens is open for lunch from 11 A.M. to 2 P.M. and for dinner from 5:30 P.M. to 10 P.M. Right next door along the same promenade, the Cinnamon Bear Sports Bar, also with a railing, serves off the same menu from 11 A.M. until 11 P.M. 4050 Whistler Way; (604) 932-1982.

Hard Rock Cafe: Enough with the U.S. chain restaurants; this one's a Canadian chain, and Whistler's has guitars that were pre-owned by Pink Floyd, Randy Bachman, and many others. The main dining room is a bit like a Sistine Hard Rock Chapel with all the stars painted on the arched ceiling. But it is still very Whistler with the natural wood creations by Eric Scragg. His playground equipment, benches, and just plain smart art dot the entire Whistler Valley. But what's in the Hard Rock for Fido? Burger bites on the outdoor patio, perhaps? (Pups must remain outside the railing.) For humans with happy childhood memories there's the Elvis, a Graceland peanut butter and banana sandwich. The café is open 11 A.M. to 11 P.M. It's in Whistler Village. 4295 Blackcomb Way; (604) 938-9922.

Moguls Coffee Bean: Moguls has earned a strong reputation for its excellent espressos and pastries. You'll need to tie your dog outside while you order, but once you have your caffeine in hand, you can meander out to the Village Square and savor it on one of the dozens of benches. 202-4208 Village Square; (604) 932-4845.

Starbucks: Yes, even Whistler has a Starbucks. A few years ago the company turned down free real estate in the Fairmont Chateau Whistler, choosing instead to set up shop directly beneath the Hard Rock Cafe in Whistler Village. As with all Starbucks, there are plenty of outside tables where you and your dog can hang out. 11-4295 Blackcomb Way; (604) 938-0611.

Thai One On: At the street-side entrance to the Le Chamois building is a Thai restaurant that quickly became a favorite of the Whistler locals. There is no outside dining for you and Cuisinart, your canine food processor, but your stomachs will be very happy if you do takeout and find a nice place in the sun to eat. Try the *tod mun pla,* red curry fish cakes with a zingy cucumber sauce. The menu is big, so ask if you're not sure. *Pad Thai Jay* is a great-tasting vegetarian alternative. It's especially good washed down with Whistler Mother's Pale Ale, on tap. Open daily 5–11 P.M. Its entrance is through the Le Chamois Hotel, near the Fairmont Chateau Whistler. 108-4557 Blackcomb Way; (604)932-4822.

Wildflower: In the summer, this delightful café/restaurant sets up outdoor tables right at the base of Blackcomb Mountain on the back side of Fairmont Chateau Whistler Resort. Fairmont Chateau Whistler patrons and their dogs are welcome on the patio. Fresh seafood is the specialty, but chef Glenn Monk does wonders with northern Italian pasta dishes, too. The Wildflower entrance is in the lobby of the Fairmont Chateau Whistler Resort, itself worthy of a field trip. The Wildflower is open daily from 7 A.M. to 10 P.M. 4599 Chateau Boulevard; (604) 938-2033.

Zeuski's Taverna: This Mediterranean café with outdoor tables (your pup is welcome on the patio edge, and water bowls are served) is located in Town

Plaza. Emma preferred the tasty tomato sauce and feta on the mixed veggie casserole, whereas Quinn stuck with me for the *moussaka horta* (vegetables topped with béchamel). They both avoided my Greek salad. 4314 Main Street; (604) 932-6009.

PLACES TO STAY

Accommodations in Whistler range from dormitory bunks to European-style B&Bs to luxury hotels, but most visitors stay in the village condominiums. The range of choices and prices is wide, including, of course, tempting package prices that could include some golf, tennis, or skiing. There's even a weekend spa package at the Fairmont Chateau Whistler Resort. One toll-free call can take care of all your needs and answer any questions: 1-800-WHISTLER.

Brandywine Falls Provincial Park camping: See page 178.

Coast Whistler Hotel: Well-placed in Whistler, just off the hubbub of the central core, this 193-unit hotel offers views of the Whistler Golf Course. People with small, well-trained dogs can have their pick of the first-floor rooms, with rates ranging from a low of $139 in the summer to a high of $219 in the winter (ask about specials, too). The dog fee is $25. The Coast Whistler has an outdoor heated swimming pool, a sauna, a hot tub, and an exercise room. 4005 Whistler Way; (604) 932-2522 or (800) 663-5644.

Delta Whistler Resort: The Delta, very close to the Whistler Gondola, says yes (with enthusiasm!) to dogs. Small dogs (no more than 25 pounds) are the preferred size, of course. Room rates for two start at about $269 for units without kitchens; deluxe rooms with kitchens range from $299 to $379. 4050 Whistler Way; (604) 932-1982 or (800) 515-4050.

Fairmont Chateau Whistler Resort: The first new Canadian Pacific Hotel in 100 years, the 1989 Fairmont Chateau Whistler Resort in British Columbia welcomes travelers and their dogs in the grand European tradition. It's even become a favorite weekend getaway for Hollywood actors on break from moviemaking in Vancouver, 90 miles to the south. Hint: As dogs are a social lubricant everywhere, so too in the Chateau. Chatting up canine matters with William Baldwin in the Great Hall is much easier if your dogs have gotten acquainted first and then introduced you.

The Chateau recently expanded to 563 rooms and suites and added a bigger ballroom plus a rooftop garden terrace that doubles as an outdoor wedding chapel. The outdoor setting? Well, for starters, the Chateau sits at the base of Blackcomb Mountain with its vertical mile of skiing. No no, not a vertical mile of skiing: Blackcomb's alpine glacier ski bowls are only 7,280 feet above the valley floor, which itself is just 2,000 feet above sea level. So don't fear for Bowser's altitude problems. This is British Columbia's Coastal Mountains, not the high-altitude Rockies.

People commonly come to the Chateau with their dogs, particularly Europeans who are used to taking their dogs everywhere. The resort asks that dogs be accompanied at all times; in other words, not be left alone in the room. Dogsitters are available. There is a $20 per night charge for the dog and rates for two humans start at $349 in winter. But ask for the specials. 4599 Chateau Boulevard; (604) 938-8000 or (800) 606-8244.

Listel Whistler Hotel: The Listel welcomes dogs in first-floor rooms at no extra charge. It has 100 deluxe rooms and suites, plus an outdoor heated pool, hot tub, and sauna. Rates for two people (including a buffet breakfast) start at $199 in the spring, summer, and fall, and peak at $269 during the Christmas season. 4121 Village Green; (604) 932-1133 or (800) 663-5472.

Nairn Falls Provincial Park camping: See page 180.

Porteau Cove Provincial Marine Park camping: See page 177.

Residence Inn by Marriott-Whistler/Blackcomb: Dogs are welcome at the Residence. Both the manager and director of sales have dogs, and there are no room restrictions, that is, no particular set-aside rooms for dogs. Additional cost is $20 per night per dog. The units range from a summer low of $149 for a studio to a winter high of $569 for a two-bedroom suite. Its uniqueness in Whistler is that it's the only hotel on the hill itself, above the lower lift stations, that takes dogs, or people too for that matter. It's secluded, up at the end of Painted Cliff Road, away from the village hubbub. 4899 Painted Cliff Road; (604) 905-3400 or (888) 777-0185.

Tantalus Resort Condominium Lodge: Tantalus's 76 units all come with two bedrooms, two baths, fully equipped kitchens, a fireplace, and a balcony. Each unit easily sleeps six. The units range from a summer low of $119 to a winter high of $379. Other perks include outdoor tennis courts and a year-round outdoor pool, plus a sauna and whirlpool. There are no restrictions on dogs and no extra charge for their stay, although the staff would like to know ahead of time if you plan to bring your dog. The location, at the base of Whistler Mountain and a five-minute walk from the center of Whistler Village, is ideal. 4200 Whistler Way; (604) 932-4146 or (800) 268-1133.

FESTIVALS

Sure Whistler hosts special events all winter long, but the summertime brings many festivals to this neck of the woods. Be on the lookout for a children's art festival, mountain bike races, celebrity golf tournaments, daily street entertainment, country and blues music, jazz, a kite-flying challenge, special car club displays, and much more.

Whistler Classical Music Festival: The second week of every August brings classical music to Whistler in a series of indoor and outdoor events. You can bring your leashed dog to any of the outdoor shows; be sure to check out the Brass on a Raft Concert. (604) 932-2394.

Whistler Community Canada Day Parade: Everybody gets into this annual July 1st parade through Whistler. You and your leashed dog can enjoy both the parade and the post-parade fun in the Upper Village at the base of Blackcomb Mountain. (604) 932-5528.

Whistler Daily Street Entertainment: During July, August, and September, look for all manner of buskers, including musicians, jugglers, clowns, magicians, and comedians, on the ways and byways of Whistler. (604) 932-2394.

Whistler Fall for Jazz Festival: All varieties of jazz—from 1940s standards to gospel, brass, and bebop—can be heard the third weekend of September on the outdoor main stage and throughout Whistler's streets and clubs. Some shows are free. Leashed dogs can attend the outdoor events. (604) 932-2394.

Whistler First Night: This New Year's Eve party is an annual outdoor, nonalcoholic family event, with entertainment on two stages. Ring in the New Year with your four-legged friend; just be sure to keep the leash on. (604) 932-2394.

Whistler Roots Festival: This three-day fest, held the third week in July, features country rock, Delta blues, rockabilly, and Cajun music on the streets and stages of Whistler. Other free activities include line dancing, horseshoes, a root-beer garden, and a chili cook-off. If enough of us bring our dogs (which are welcome so long as they're leashed), maybe they'll establish some special events for canines. (604) 932-2394.

Whistler's Really Big Street Fest: In the United States it's spelled Labor Day and in Canada it's Labour Day, but they always occur on the same day. For the past decade on Labour Day weekend, Whistler's 20 best street acts have converged in the village for music, juggling, comedy, magic, and clowning. There are also cabaret evenings on Saturday and Sunday; leashed dogs are welcome to join the fun. (604) 932-2394.

World Ski & Snowboard Festival: This weeklong celebration beginning in early April features the Whistler Children's Festival, (604) 932-3928; the Air Canada Whistler Cup International Juvenile Ski Race, (604) 932-3434; and the KokaneeKicker Hot Air Contest, (604) 938-7351, among other popular events. Feel free to bring your leashed dog. (604) 932-3400.

DIVERSIONS

Expressions: OK, you and Domesticus are in Whistler, staying at one of the six hotels that allows dogs, it's pouring rain, and you need to GO somewhere and DO something. The solution is easy: head on over to Kona's place in Village North. Kona is a "Lab with pit bull from the animal shelter," says companion Sai Fon Woozley. Sai Fon operates Expressions, a "you-paint-it" ceramics studio where you can decorate cups, bowls, pitchers, whatever, to the limits of your imagination. The colors are wild, and there are stencils for the artistically impaired. Sai Fon says dogs are totally welcome "if they can chill and not knock the pottery with their tails." The studio is in the Stone Lodge in Village North. 125-4338 Main Street; (604) 932-2822.

Savage Beagle: This is sort of a bar/lounge/dance club with music that unleashes the savage beagle in you. More people watch than dance, but it's the dancers who have all the fun. Management is sorry that actual dogs are not allowed inside, but you could step in for a quick one and share the post-dance glow with Prancer later. The Savage is near the center of Whistler Village, 4222 Village Square, and it's open until 2 A.M. (604) 938-3337.

ADDITIONAL SERVICES

Coast Mountain Veterinary Services: Dr. David Lane operates a full-service vet clinic in Whistler and a hospital in Pemberton, about 22 miles north of Whistler on B.C. Highway 99. He offers 24-hour emergency service and he makes house calls. 201-2011 Innsbruck Drive; (604) 932-5391.

Whistler Pet Food & Dog Grooming: #1-1050 Millar Creek Road; (604) 932-3050.

Mountain FM Petfinders: If you've lost or found a dog, call the radio station at (604) 892-1047.

WAG: Whistler Animals Galore is a pets-friendly organization that puts out the *Pet Person's Guide to the Whistler Resort.* The one-page sheet gives local resource numbers for visitors with pets and lists where pets are welcome. It tells dog lovers, and dog haters for that matter, where dogs can be and where they cannot be, what is legal for dogs to do and what is not. The guide is not yet on the concierge desk of every hotel, but it ought to be; (604) 938-8642.

VICTORIA, BRITISH COLUMBIA

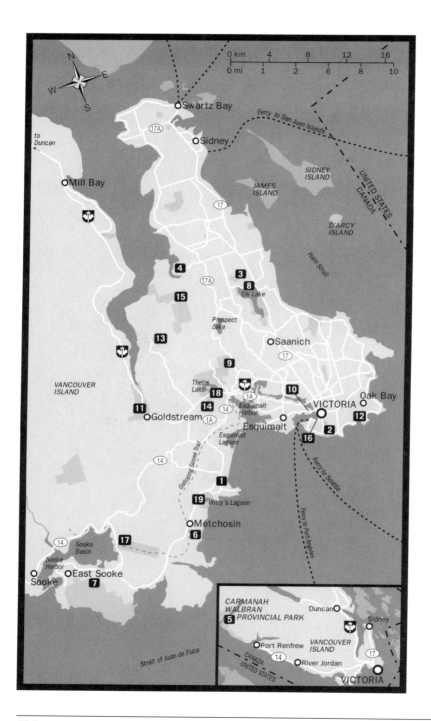

12
VICTORIA, BRITISH COLUMBIA

Vancouver Island has 7,000 miles of coastline, but it's about the size of Switzerland. The Trans-Canada Highway, the longest single paved road in the world, starts at the southern tip of the island in Victoria and runs for 4,860 miles to the east coast of Newfoundland.

People joke, half seriously, that Victoria, the provincial capital of British Columbia, is a place for the newly wed and the nearly dead. Honeymooners galore swarm to the swank Fairmont Empress Hotel, and retirees, who like the climate and the ambience, move here as soon as they call it quits at the office. Local residents, to prove they have the best weather in Canada, hold an annual "Flower Count" in February.

Victoria's government buildings, facing the Inner Harbour, are a big attraction in a city full of heritage architecture. Guided tours of the buildings, which were built in 1897, are in groups and without charge. The Royal British Columbia Museum is just across the street from the Fairmont Empress. It has more than 10 million artifacts in its anthropological, biological, and historical collections, only a fraction of which are on public display.

The city's public squares and small streets all have a history and atmosphere that make a walk in downtown Victoria pleasant and interesting. If you don't want an urban experience, Vancouver Island has more than 100 parks, and the largest is Strathcona, a half million acres right in the center of the island.

Consider a winter visit too. Even though Victoria gets half the rain of either Vancouver or Seattle, winter life there slows to a dull hubbub. That's the best reason to visit as a winter tourist.

Be sure to invest in a map of Victoria and Vancouver Island, or at least of Victoria and the Saanich Peninsula. One favorite is published in cooperation with the British Columbia Automobile Association. It has no particular tourism ax to grind, and therefore puts in ALL streets, ALL highways, ALL parks, and ALL bodies of water. The free maps you will see around town are sufficient only for walking through downtown Victoria (all six of the free maps we used on Vancouver Island were feeble attempts to direct us to what interested the mapmaker, or the map advertiser). Munro's Books on Government Street has a good map selection.

PARKS, BEACHES, AND RECREATION AREAS

In the 1850s, the indigenous Coast Salish people traded what is now Greater Victoria (also known as the Saanich Peninsula) for 386 wool blankets. That may not seem like such a bad deal after you see a 50-mile-per-hour headwind throwing waves over cars creeping along Dallas Road. Today, joggers and bikers commonly muscle their way into such extreme conditions, the same elements that keep Seattleites indoors. To Victorians, it's just another day in the park.

And speaking of parks, Victoria boasts a total of 48, all of which require dogs to be either leashed or under voice control. Within the city of Victoria, the Animal Control Bylaw requires dogs to be leashed either with a 7.9-foot-maximum standard leash or a 26-foot retractable leash held by "a person competent to restrain the dog." The exception is the two-mile leash-free stretch of grassy headland along Dallas Road that makes up the waterfront of Beacon Hill Park.

To learn about Victoria's park programs and to hear about recent wildlife sightings, call the 24-hour recording: (250) 474-7275.

•Albert Head Lagoon Regional Park 🐾🐾 See ❶ on page 186.

You can't beat this wildlife sanctuary, located about 10 miles west of Victoria on Royal Bay. A pleasant trail follows the great cobblestone beach for 1.5 miles. Dogs are welcome here, but must be kept leashed in the summer.

To get there from Victoria, take Douglas Street north and follow signs for B.C. Highway 1A (Gorge Street), which becomes the Old Island Highway. Continue on 1A until it turns right at the Colwood Shopping Centre. Drive straight on what is now B.C. Highway 14, which leads to Sooke Harbor, until you reach Metchosin Road, where you will turn left. Continue on Metchosin for about 2.6 miles to Delgada Road. Turn left and follow the signs. (250) 478-3344.

•Beacon Hill Park 🐾🐾🐾🐾 🐕 See ❷ on page 186.

This park is a big gem in the city of Victoria's crown. It was designed by John Blair, who won a 1889 competition for just that purpose. Around Fountain Lake he planted rhododendrons that still bloom every year. The park has 184 acres of exotic and Northwest native plants, with old carriage trails meandering through the gardens and wildflower meadows. There are jogging paths, broad expanses of lawn, hills, lakes, and lots of signs announcing that all dogs must be on a leash at all times.

That's true for the bulk of the park, which lies north of Dallas Road. But, as a bonus, about two miles of the stretch of Beacon Hill Park on the ocean side of Dallas Road is entirely leash-free. Under control, mind you, but leash-free. It's mostly a grassy bluff with a paved walkway and well-worn path. The waterfront includes three points: Holland, Finlayson, and Clover Points. Dallas Road is part of the annual Victoria Marathon route. Being right on the sea, the road has to be closed two or three times a year when ribald storms toss waves and logs over the roadway. You could ask around about why Ross Bay Cemetery needed a seawall built in front of it. We did some storm-watching and it was a good thing Emma and Quinn were leashed. They could have washed away.

Beacon Hill Park starts just two blocks southeast of the Inner Harbour. To drive to the leash-free area on Dallas Road, go south on Government Street from the Inner Harbour for just over a half-mile to Dallas Road. Turn left (east) onto Dallas Road, and the park begins in one-quarter mile. At the park's southwest corner, look for the Mile 0 marker for the Trans-Canada Highway. (250) 361-0600.

• Bear Hill Regional Park 🐾 🐾 🐾 🐕   See 3 on page 186.

Bear Hill is about nine miles north of Victoria, a great side trek on your way to or from the ferry. The trail to the summit of Bear Hill is about a half hour trek up less than a mile of gentle forest and steepish rocky trails. The hilltop has wildflowers in spring, and an all-the-time woodland mix of cedar, fir, oak, and arbutus, or madrona. The road to the park is about as British a road as you can find without going to Merry Old England. It's about one and a half cars wide, no line down the middle, winding through the countryside and up the hill. There are two signs for a frog crossing. Really, not kidding. They're standard red triangle yield signs with a nice silhouette of a frog. We drove careful, you bet. The parking "lot" is good for about three cars on the left. That's it. If you pass it, you will shortly come to a "Dead End Turn Here" sign. Do it.

The trail up Bear Hill is a bit rocky. Ferns grow everywhere, almost like fields of cultivated and mowed six-inch ferns. Emma and Quinn darted through and around, following scents only they could describe. We wondered just why this park is called Bear Hill, and speculated as to how the pups could serve as bear terriers. This trail must have been a gully wash during the big rains, but it's so rocky that there wasn't much dirt to wash away. Emma and Quinn forged ahead, securing the trail for us. They sprinted everywhere they went, uphill included. As we stopped for me to catch my breath, it was plain to see that Vancouver Island must be one giant rock.

Even before we reached the top, there were some great water views, not to mention the giant pumpkin field below. We summitted, and the dogs each pawed the ground three times. A three-paw park. It has no water to swim in, but the great chthonian woods and ferns have their dramatic appeal to the canine kingdom. We enjoyed the views of Mount Baker, the Saanich Peninsula, Gulf Islands, and San Juan Island.

At Bear Hill Park, there's no obvious reason for a leash. Other dog owners thought the same thing, and their beasts enjoyed cavorting with Quinn and Emma. But you at least ought to carry a leash, judging from the irregularly spaced horse droppings. These are bridle trails too, and there are a lot of horses on the farmettes in the Bear Hill neighborhood.

The park has no gates to close, but it's considered to be open from sunrise to sunset. No parking is allowed between 11 P.M. and 6 A.M. To get to Bear Hill Park from Highway 17, turn east on Sayward Road, which, as it quickly jogs left, becomes Hamsterley Road. In one block, the road turns right and becomes Brookleigh Road. Stay on it through Elk/Beaver Lake Park until it Ts at Oldfield Road. This is about a mile from Highway 17 and you should have passed a Bear Hill Road to the right. Good. You didn't take it. It's a dead end. Now turn right on Oldfield Road and go for about seven tenths of a mile until you reach another Bear Hill Road. Turn right for a quarter-mile and turn right on yet another Bear Hill Road. This is the real one. Follow it for one-half mile and park. (250) 478-3344.

• Butchart Gardens 🐾 🐾 🐕 See **4** on page 186.

Dogs yes! Finally, a beautifully cultivated garden, a great huge one that's privately owned, that embraces the logic of sharing life's peak experiences with the canine kingdom. They have to be leashed though, and stay on the paths. Technically speaking, the Butchart Gardens, 13 miles north of Victoria, are not botanical gardens. While open to the public, they are still the Butchart family gardens, and family gardens don't have signs to identify the plants. Appreciation of the beauty is what matters here, but if you really have to know what you're looking at, there is a Plant Identification Centre at the end of the walk.

Butchart Gardens cover 50 acres, set in the remnants of a wooded limestone quarry abandoned in the early part of the 20th century. Within the gardens are individual theme gardens—the English Rose Garden, Japanese and Italian Gardens, and the Sunken Garden with its dancing fountain. Tour buses bring visitors from downtown Victoria, and moorage is available for private yachts sailing in via Saanich Inlet.

The gardens are open every day of the year at 9 A.M. Until December 5, they close at 4 P.M., but visitors are welcome for another hour after closing. December 6 to 14, the gardens are open until 9 P.M., and from December 15 to January 6, they're open until 10 P.M. To get there either take a tour bus from Victoria's Inner Harbour or drive north from downtown on Blanshard Road, which becomes British Columbia Highway 17A. Stay on 17A (West Saanich Road) until you turn west on Bienvenuto Avenue. It ends at the gardens. (250) 652-4422.

• Carmanah Walbran Provincial Park 🐾 🐾 🐾 See **5** on page 186.

This newly dedicated 8,872-acre park on the west coast of Vancouver Island is a stunning old-growth temperate rain forest with perhaps the most dense biomass on Earth. It's about a three-hour drive from Victoria, but worth any effort it takes to get there. Carmanah Pacific Park (as it's locallly known) is an ancient rain forest that was saved from clear-cut logging a few years ago by a massive public outcry and protest. Canada's tallest trees are within the park, and there is a canopy research station 200 feet up.

Leashed dogs are welcome, and hikers are required to stay on marked trails. Some trails are more like boardwalks to avoid treading on the biomass floor, and some of the largest trees are roped off to prevent wear and tear on the root systems. The largest tree in Canada, the Carmanah Giant, is a Sitka spruce over 300 feet tall. At just 400 years, it's thought to be the tallest Sitka spruce in the world. Unfortunately for hikers, it's off-limits, near the end of a closed section of trail that used to connect with the famed West Coast Trail in Pacific Rim National Park. (Access to that trail is by Bamfield or Port Renfrew, both on the west coast, and requires a Canadian Parks Service permit and a hefty fee.)

Sitka spruce trees comprise only two percent of the biomass of Carmanah Pacific Park, so there is plenty more to see. The main hiking areas, with the most dramatic trees, fall within a three-mile range of Carmanah Creek, beginning one mile from the trailhead at park headquarters. A sign there says, "Weather, topography and trail conditions change quickly. Watch for flash floods and black bears."

The park is reached by a three- to four- hour drive from Victoria via Canadian Highway 1 to just north of Duncan; British Columbia Highway 18 west to the town of Lake Cowichan; and a local road paralleling the southern edge of Cowichan Lake to the town of Nitinat. The rest of the way, southwest to Nitinat Lake and beyond to the park, is on quite good dirt logging roads that do not require four-wheel-drive. But beware of monster non-highway logging trucks on weekdays. You may think you're alone in the universe here, but there are usually a few hundred windsurfers camping out on the southeast side of Nitinat Lake. (250) 391-2300.

• **Devonian Regional Park** 🐾🐾 See **6** on page 186.
Devonian has a walking trail that crisscrosses Sherwood Creek, past Sherwood Pond, and out to the beach on Parry Bay for a total of six-tenths of a mile. The bird-watching opportunities are great in this small nature sanctuary tucked between farmlands. From the cobblestone beach, you can see the Olympics, Race Rocks, and the Strait of Juan de Fuca. Dogs must be kept leashed.

To get there from Victoria, take Douglas Street north and follow the signs for B.C. Highway 1A (Gorge Street), which becomes the Old Island Highway. Continue on 1A until it turns right (west) at the Colwood Shopping Centre. Drive straight on what is now B.C. Highway 14, which leads to Sooke Harbor, until you reach Metchosin Road. Turn left (south) onto Metchosin, which becomes William Head Road just past Witty's Lagoon. Watch for the sign after you cross Taylor Road. (250) 478-3344.

• **East Sooke Regional Park** 🐾🐾🐾 🐕 See **7** on page 186.
The main attraction of this 3,500-acre park on Juan de Fuca Strait is one of the best day-hikes in Canada, the East Sooke Coast Trail. It's a heavy-duty hike that requires six hours even for experienced hikers (and yet only covers six-tenths of a mile). It is a rugged coastline trail ranging from moderate to difficult, with occasional beaches and rocky bays. The coast trail was once part of the Telegraph trail that ran from Bamfield to Victoria connecting the coast lighthouses. The forest meets the sea here as best it can, with trees clinging to windswept cliffs. There are 25 miles of other trails in this park as well, so go easy on the first day. You and Ruffs, who is welcome on a leash or under your control, may want to try this 2.5-mile round-trip from the Becher Bay Road parking lot: Aylard Farm heritage apple orchard to the Alldridge Point petroglyphs and back along the Becher Bay beach.

The park is open daily from sunrise to sunset. It's located off East Sooke Road in East Sooke. To drive there from Victoria, drive north from downtown on Douglas Street and follow the signs for British Columbia Highway 1A which you continue on. At the Colwood Shopping Centre, where 1A turns right, continue straight onto British Columbia Highway 14 (Sooke Road/West Coast Highway). Follow it until you turn left onto Gillespie Road. After crossing the Galloping Goose Trail and over the mouth of Roche Cove, in about a mile look for East Sooke Road. Take a right on it and follow the signs. (250) 478-3344.

• **Elk/Beaver Lake Regional Park** 🐾🐾🐾 🐕 See **8** on page 186.
Eight miles north of downtown Victoria, Elk Lake and its southern neighbor Beaver Lake combine to make a 1,015-acre park of dense biomass: lush

wetlands, forests, and rich water life, including water-skiers, rowers, and windsurfers.

There are trails for equestrians, joggers, birders, and walkers to many of the quieter areas. Bicycles are not permitted on park trails, and dogs must be under control or on a leash at all times. Got that? Leash-free is a good option, and the granddogs took full advantage of it. One caution though: Dogs are not permitted at the beach or in picnic areas from June 1 to September 15. But that leaves a lot of lake and trail to enjoy. So, control your Impulse, or keep her leashed. All plants and wildlife are protected by law here, so do not disturb or remove them.

On the notice board was this sign: "Lost: Cairn Terrier X, answers to Betty, gray neutered male, 2.5 years old. Last seen Tuesday at 7 P.M. at Elk Lake." Betty must not have been on the invisible leash system, or maybe the pull of an elk or a bear was stronger. As for Emma and Quinn, they chased the ducks back into Elk Lake where they belong. Good duckherds! We don't call them duck terriers for nothing. They secured the beachhead for us and we felt quite free to enjoy it.

A six-mile trail goes all around the lake, and it takes about 2.5 hours for a pleasant walk. The trail includes part of the old Victoria/Sidney railway line. The park is open daily from sunrise to sunset. It's located just off British Columbia Highway 17 (Patricia Bay Highway) in Saanich. To get to Elk Lake from Highway 17, turn east on Sayward Road, which, as it quickly jogs left, becomes Hamsterley Road. You are now in the park. (250) 478-3344.

• Francis/King Regional Park 🐾🐾🐾 See 🟑 on page 186.

The combined Thomas Francis and Freeman King Parks have 225 acres of forest, plus streams, marshes, rocky knolls, and flatlands. The park is attached on the west side to Thetis Lake Park, which is about four times the size of Francis/King. Attractions are the rare saprophytes (Indian Pipe), chocolate lilies, and coniferous forests rich in edible plants. There are nearly seven miles of gentle woodland trails, plus the Elsie King Trail, a cedar boardwalk for people with walking limitations. It loops out six-tenths of a mile from the park entrance through the forest. The trail widens in a dozen places allowing wheelchairs to pass. There is also a covered rest stop half way around.

Dogs must be leashed at all times in this park since it is a Capital Regional District Preserve, one of six nature appreciation parks in the region. There's even a sign saying "do not pick the mushrooms." This is one of two parks with a nature house open on weekends year-round. At 1710 Munns Road, the nature House is open noon to 4 P.M., Saturday, Sunday, Wednesday, and any holiday Monday. Munns Road is a third-gear sort of road, twisting and turning as it does in the British countryside fashion.

The park also has several archaeological sites, including three shell middens dating from the times of yore when ocean levels were much higher and the park was waterfront. The largest midden is mostly buried under the pavement of Munns Road, which divides the park. There is also a small Indian burial cave. The park is open April through September from 8 A.M. to 9 P.M. and October through March from 8 A.M. to 5 P.M. It's eight miles west of downtown Victoria.

From downtown Victoria, drive north on Douglas Street (B.C. Highway 1). Stay on 1 (also known as the Island Highway and the Trans-Canada Highway) until you reach Helmcken Road. Turn right (north) onto Helmcken, left (north) onto West Burnside Road, and then right (north) onto Prospect Lake Road. Follow Prospect Lake to Munns Road, which will take you into the park. (250) 478-3344.

• **Galloping Goose Regional Trail** 🐾🐾🐾 🐕 See **10** on page 186.
This old railroad trail requires Mighty Mutt to be either under voice control or on a leash. The Galloping Goose used to be a Canadian National motor train that ran from Victoria to Leechtown way up the Sooke River. Now open to the public as a 30-mile-plus trail, it passes near and through some incredible parks, and there are B&Bs along the way. Cyclists, hikers, and horseback riders share the trail through rolling farmland, into deep forest, and past rocky shoreline. Keep an eye out for deer, raccoons, herons, hawks, squirrels, and field mice.

To get to the trailhead from downtown Victoria, cross the Johnson Street Bridge. The trailhead will be to your immediate right. The trail is accessible at frequent intervals. While Galloping Goose Trail never actually closes, its open hours are considered to be sunrise to sunset. (250) 478-3344.

• **Goldstream Provincial Park** 🐾🐾🐾 See **11** on page 186.
Emma was ready to hop out as we pulled into Goldstream Park, where salmon sightings had been reported. The moss on the trees next to the river is absolutely uncannily bountiful. The green stuff goes all around the limbs and trunks, and hangs off about eight inches, dripping water. There is a huge log-jam in the river below. This is one wet park. Several hundred yards upriver, we spotted about a dozen salmon working their way upstream. They were in the shallows, taking turns in the shade of a downed log. A couple of giant red ones went back downstream, one floating on its side and the other zooming like he'd forgotten something. Maybe they'd laid their eggs and were moving on to their reward.

Bears, I thought. This is their open season on spawning salmon, and we're a mile upstream with no paddle, so to speak. Emma and Quinn, very unbear-like, displayed only perfunctory curiosity at the fish. They were more interested in the rich digs along the trail. Besides, you are requested to keep your dog out of the water during spawning season.

The Goldstream Provincial Park visitor center opens toward the end of September, gearing up for the salmon run program in October and November. And the park offers special "Nature of Winter" programming in December. Goldstream is really a park for all seasons. This is a designated Capital Heritage Tree Area, with giant Douglas firs, 300 feet high, that were protected by their thick bark from a fire that ravaged the area 130 years ago. Near the picnic area is an immense 700-year-old western red cedar, 70 meters high. On the floodplains of the lower Goldstream River, there are 80- to 100-year-old broadleaf maples, and farther downriver are 300-year-old black cottonwoods. They are among the most easily accessed old-growth trees found on southeastern Vancouver Island, a reminder of the great forests that once covered this entire area. If you don't bother the fish, you can pan for gold flakes in the gravel. This IS Goldstream Park, after all.

For camping at Goldstream, reservations are recommended in the summer because on weekdays it fills up late in the day, and even earlier on weekends. The reservations number is (800) 689-9025, good in all of North America, beginning March 15 of each year. There are 150 campsites in the campground, with nearby toilets, water, showers, and wood. There are no hookups, but RVs are welcome. Quiet hours in the campground are 10 P.M. to 7 A.M., and dogs must be kept on a leash and under control at all times. Some areas are signed as No Dogs Permitted. The park is 12 miles from downtown Victoria.

Take the Island Highway (Route 1) from downtown Victoria. Access to the campground from the highway at the southern boundary of the park is via Sooke Lake Road. The entrance to the day-use area, open sunrise to sunset, is near the junction of the highway and Finlayson Arm Road. (250) 391-2300.

•Gonzales Hill Regional Park 🐾🐾 See 🔟 on page 186.

This is a protected natural landscape at the southeastern corner of Victoria. It has great views of Victoria, Juan de Fuca Strait, the Olympics, and the Sooke Hills. It's a habitat for California quail, rare wildflowers, and a stand of Garry oak trees. It's also home to the Gonzales Observatory, a weather station for 75 years and now a heritage building. Located on a large rocky knoll on Denison Road in Victoria/Oak Bay, Gonzales Hill is open sunrise to sunset. Leashed dogs are welcome.

Take Dallas Road east from Beacon Hill Park (see page 188), continuing along the waterfront as the road changes names a few times. After it becomes Crescent Road and rounds Gonzales Bay (also called Foul Bay), turn left (north) onto Barkley Terrace. In one block, turn right (west) onto Glen Avenue. Go one block and turn right (south) onto Denison Road, which will take you into the park. (250) 478-3344.

•Lone Tree Hill Regional Park 🐾🐾 See 🔟 on page 186.

Getting out here is a bit of a stretch, but any park that honors its one tree is worth a look-see. The park's namesake is a bonsai-like Douglas fir that had been around for at least 200 years before it was struck down in a storm. Rare and beautiful plants nestle nearby in the steep dry rock faces, while bald eagles, red-tailed hawks, and turkey vultures soar overhead. Just one trail leads from the road, up through the delicate forest to the summit. You're welcome to take your dog for a walk on this trail, but a leash is mandatory.

The park is located on Millstream Road in the Highlands, and is open sunrise to sunset. To get there from Victoria, drive north on Douglas Street (also the Trans-Canada Highway or B.C. Highway 1) for about 10 miles. When you reach Millstream Road, turn right (north) and continue four and half miles to the park. (250) 478-3344.

•Mill Hill Regional Park 🐾🐾 See 🔟 on page 186.

The walk here is through cool woodland along Millstream Creek. If you climb to the summit, about a 30-minute trek, you'll likely see delicate wildflowers and arbutus, Douglas fir, and Garry oak. Capital Regional District Parks

---

offices in the park offer brochures and can answer any questions you may have. If you're wondering about dogs, they must be kept leashed.

From Victoria, drive north on Douglas Street (the Trans-Canada Highway or B.C. Highway 1) until you reach the 1A west exit, about seven miles. Take 1A west (but very briefly) to Atkins Road and turn right (west). Continue on Atkins for 1.8 miles to the park entrance on your right. (250) 478-3344.

• Mount Work Regional Park 🐾🐾🐾🐾 🐕 See 15 on page 186.

If you get to Mount Work, both you and Apollo will delight to the three freshwater lakes, seven miles of hiking trails through deep forest to the mountain's summit, and McKenzie Bight. Just keep that rascal under control, or on a leash. The Bight is where the scuba divers and tidepool explorers go. There is also an extensive shell midden at the Bight. Getting technical here, Mount Work is a monadnock (a residual hill) composed of hard rock that resisted the corrosive and erosive powers of the last glacier that went by. You can see glacial debris (clay and gravel) at the grotto on the McKenzie Bight trail. Durrance Lake is available for your swimming, fishing, and rowing pleasures (no swimming dogs in the summer, please). The park is open April through August from sunrise to 9 P.M. and September through March sunrise to sunset. It's located on Willis Point Road in the Highlands.

From Victoria, drive north on Blanshard Street (B.C. Highway 17). Turn left (northwest) onto B.C. Highway 17A, the West Saanich Road. Continue on 17A until you reach Wallace Drive, where you will turn left (northwest) and then left again (west) onto Willis Point Road. In about a mile you'll be in the park. (250) 478-3344.

• Reeson Regional Park 🐾 See 16 on page 186.

You can watch the hubbub on the Johnson Street Bridge and the seaplanes taking off and landing before your very eyes from this pretty patch of green at the foot of Yates Street in Old Town Victoria. It's tranquil and has a great view of the busy Inner Harbour. Leashed dogs are welcome here.

From the Visitor Information Centre on Victoria's Inner Harbour, walk five blocks north on Wharf Street to Yates Street. The park will be on your left. (250) 953-8800.

• Roche Cove Regional Park 🐾🐾🐾 🐕 See 17 on page 186.

Roche Cove is noted among sea kayakers and canoers, plus it has about 4.5 miles of trails through its 290-acre cedar forest and along the 30-mile Galloping Goose Trail. The Galloping Goose Trail (who can explain that name?) is the preferred way to get to all of the parks along the southern tip of Vancouver Island. Roche Cove does not welcome dogs on the beach or in picnic areas between June 1 and September 15, but in other park areas, they only have to be under voice control or leashed.

Drive north from downtown Victoria on Douglas Street and follow the signs to B.C. Highway 1A, which you will take. At the Colwood Shopping Centre, where 1A turns right (west), continue straight onto B.C. Highway 14 (Sooke Road/West Coast Highway). Turn left (south) onto Gillespie Road, and follow it for almost three miles to the park entrance. The parking lot is on your left as Gillespie crosses the Galloping Goose Trail. (250) 478-3344.

• **Thetis Lake Regional Park** 🐾🐾 See **18** on page 186.
Thetis Lake Regional Park does not allow dogs on the beach in the summer (June 1 to September 1), but you and your pup can enjoy plenty of trails into the deep dark shade of the forest canopy. Part of the 384-acre park is set aside as a nature sanctuary. Trails can be accessed from both sides of Thetis Lake Road (also called Highland Road). Leashes are the rule here.

From Victoria, drive north on Douglas Street (also known as the Trans-Canada Highway and B.C. Highway 1) for about 7.5 miles to the park entrance on your right. (250) 478-3344.

• **Witty's Lagoon Regional Park** 🐾🐾🐾🐾 🐕 See **19** on page 186.
This 138-acre park on Albert Head is on the Strait of Juan de Fuca, just across from the Olympic Peninsula in Washington. This is a great park to approach by sea kayak, and it has 3.5 miles of nature trails through lagoon woods and marsh. There are harbor seals that gravitate to the offshore islets. Witty's is a large lagoon known for its bird-watching opportunities. You can see nine kinds of gulls, five different woodpeckers, and even two kinds of humming-birds. Nearly 50 varieties in all. Also, there are five archaeological sites, two of them shell middens and two fortified sites. Get a park brochure at the Nature Information Centre, talk to the ranger, and maybe go on an interpretive hike on the three miles of trail through woodlands and around the lagoon and marsh. It has a sandy beach overlooking rocky headlands and offshore islets. Dogs are welcome, and the regulations say only to "keep dogs under control." Oh, and one more: don't pick the wildflowers. The park is located on Metchosin Road in Metchosin, and is open sunrise to sunset.

To get there from Victoria, take Douglas Street north and follow the signs for B.C. Highway 1A (Gorge Street), which becomes the Old Island Highway. Continue on 1A until it turns right at the Colwood Shopping Centre. Stay straight on what is now B.C. Highway 14, the road that goes to Sooke Harbor. Continue until you turn left (south) onto Metchosin Road, then follow the signs. The total distance from Victoria is only 11 miles, but allow a half-hour driving time. (250) 478-3344.

RESTAURANTS

Elephant and Castle: This trademark British pub, located on Government Street between View and Fort Streets, has plenty of outdoor seating. As at all sidewalk restaurants in Victoria, dogs must remain outside the railed food-service area. The Elephant and Castle is known for its fish-and-chips, steak and kidney pie, hearty soups, and, of course, pub-type beverages. 100 Eaton Victoria Centre; (250) 383-5858.

Green Cuisine Vegetarian Restaurant: On the ground floor of Market Square, this restaurant and bakery has a buffet and salad bar that lets you build your own plate. Go for the organic cappuccino, and there are plenty of fresh-squeezed juices. Green Cuisine is open 9 A.M. to 9 P.M. seven days a week. After 5 P.M. there is a 25 percent discount. 560 Johnson Street; (250) 385-1809.

Market Square: Market Square won a heritage Canada award for building preservation and imaginative marketing. Nine old buildings were connected around a pleasant courtyard circumnavigated by roofed walkways. But we're so sorry to say that dogs are supposed to be leashed to the back gate. No one stopped Emma and Quinn, who prowled around everywhere, but there is a sign we missed that says dogs are not allowed inside the gates. (See Market Square on page 201) Be that as it may, or being forewarned, there's some good take out chow to share and good shopping to be had in Market Square. There are several eateries, this one among them.

Sam's Deli: Outdoors at Sam's is the place to see and be seen. It's kitty-corner from the Visitors Information Centre at the Inner Harbour. It's always swarmed by citizens and tourists alike who scan the latest *Monday Magazine* and travel brochures for what to do and where to do it. Thin ladies order a spinach or Caesar salad, and robust men dig into the Ploughman's lunch. 805 Government Street; (250) 382-8424. There is room for your doggie companions on this cozy-sized patio, but their leashes must be attached to the outside of the patio fence.

Spinnakers Brewpub and Restaurant: Canada's first in-house brewpub has an impressive array of ales, lagers, and specialty beers brewed on the premises three or four times a week, depending on how much you and the other customers drink. If you prefer a private tasting, they will gladly bring you a round of six beers of your choice with a set of tasting notes. Friday evening specialties are cask-conditioned ales. Jazz and blues piano are performed live on Friday and Saturday from 5 P.M. to 7 P.M.

Spinnakers has affixed some eye bolts to a post outside to which you can affix Rotunda and Pluto, and there is also a long railing that serves the same purpose. The pub's two decks are both upstairs and thus off-limits to dogs. Spinnakers is open daily, serving breakfast from 7 A.M., lunch from 11 A.M., and dinner from 5 P.M. It's a 15-minute walk from downtown along the Songhees waterfront walkway. By car from town, drive over the Johnson Street Bridge and turn left at the second traffic light. It's located on the Inner Harbour waterfront at Lime Bay. 308 Catherine Street; (250) 386-BREW.

Steamers: This spirited fresh seafood, pasta, steak, and burger pub welcomes pups to the seating out front. The Tuscan flatbreads are great as a medium-weight snack or an appetizer for two. Lunch and dinner are served from 11 A.M. to 11 P.M., and tapas are served until 2 A.M. It's on the last block of Yates Street toward the Inner Harbour, across the street from the parkade. 571 Yates Street; (250) 381-4340.

Swans Hotel, Pub, Brewery, Fowl Fish Cafe & Oyster House, Wine & Beer Shoppe: This downtown dinery is a destination all by itself. Swans even has one of the best public displays of a private art collection in Victoria, although "Art Museum" is one category missing from its name. You're welcome to tie your dog up to the railing and chow down to your heart's content. Swans is located between Market Square and Chinatown, one block from the Johnson Street Bridge. 506 Pandora Avenue; (250) 361-3310 or (800) 668-7926.

Torrefazione Italia: We were on our way to find a Murchie's but stumbled instead over the outdoor tables at Torrefazione. I didn't know they'd expanded beyond Seattle's Pioneer Square, so it was a happy discovery. Their espressos are better than Starbucks' by a long shot. We enjoyed our drinks, bought a quarter-pound of Palermo Blend to brew in our kitchen unit at the Admiral Motel (see page 200), and the barrista even threw in a couple of paper filters. Torrefazione's decor is very classy, the barristas know their stuff, and dogs can join you at the tables out front. 1234 Government Street; (250) 920-7203 or (800) 827-2333.

PLACES TO STAY

Somebody ought to award Victoria an outstanding-achievement prize for dog friendliness. Believe it or not, there are so many hotels, motels, B&Bs, and inns that permit dogs in the Victoria area that only a partial list of favorites is featured here. When you call an 800 number, verify that the listing is current. I had a very nice chat with a woman who runs a backpackers' hostel, thinking the whole time she was in Victoria, British Columbia. Wrong. She was in Thunder Bay, Ontario, with the old Victoria phone number. But she was very nice, and perfectly willing to accept people with dogs in the single rooms, as long as the dogs are well behaved and are taken for walks at frequent intervals. That's good advice for any of the following pet-friendly lodgings.

Admiral Motel: Pets are welcome at the Admiral, just two blocks west of Victoria's Parliament buildings and less than a block from the Victoria Clipper terminal. Like most local hotels, there are no air-conditioned units, but then Victoria comes close to having an ideal, if somewhat wet, climate. Emma especially liked the Admiral, probably because the unit was more like a full apartment than a motel room—big, comfortable, and clean, with a comfy floor, a bedroom off the living room (its front window exactly at the 23-kilometer mark of the Victoria Marathon, held every May), and a grassy area just off the back parking lot. For travelers hoping to save a few bucks, most rooms come equipped with kitchens. Rooms range from $199 to $215. Local telephone calls are free. Yea! 257 Belleville Street; (250) 388-6267.

Best Western Emerald Isle Motor Inn: Sixteen miles north of Victoria in Sidney and about two miles from the ferry terminal, this suburban inn welcomes pets at the manager's discretion. The pet fee is an additional $20 per pet per stay. Summer rates are $129 to $169 for a standard double. Summer suites cost $225 to 275. This inn is near Butchart Gardens. 2306 Beacon Avenue; (250) 656-4441 or (800) 315-3377.

Dashwood Seaside Manor: In my opinion, you can't find better lodgings for pups (or people) than this historic inn. It bills itself as an Edwardian Inn by the Sea, and there couldn't be a more apt description. It's right across from the two-mile leash-free run on Dallas Road and the Strait of Juan de Fuca, and across Cook Street from Beacon Hill Park. We got to talking with the owner about the monster surf splashing across the road out front, and learned that a regular Victoria thrill is to drive Dallas Road through the crashing wave sprays. We checked it out for ourselves, and found the ride better than anything at Disneyland. The wave attack crashed all over the car and freaked the dogs, but we loved the high-impact seawater car wash. There are no telephones in the rooms, but each has a fridge stocked with breakfast.

The B&B only allows small dogs but doesn't have a set definition for "small," so you might want to call and describe your pooch before making a reservation. Summer rates for two range from $125 to $385. One Cook Street; (250) 385-5517 or (800) 667-5517.

Dutchman Inn Motel: For $10 per stay, small pets (less than 20 pounds) are welcome at the Dutchman, but they are not allowed to be left in the room alone. Rates for two range from $75 to $95 year-round. 2828 Rock Bay Avenue; (250) 386-7557.

Executive House Hotel: The centrally located Executive House, with nearly 200 rooms, welcomes your dog for $15 per day in assigned smoking rooms. Summer rates for two start at $175 and climb to $695. 777 Douglas Street; (250) 388-5111 or (800) 663-7001.

The Fairmont Empress Hotel: The Fairmont Empress, a Canadian Pacific hotel, is the big one in Victoria, with nearly 500 rooms just across the street from the Inner Harbour. The Fairmont Empress is a romance built on a strong foundation. The author of a book called *The Fairmont Empress of Victoria* dedicated it: "To my wife who graciously took second place during my affair with The Fairmont Empress." Named for Queen Victoria, the Empress of India, the hotel has been the standard for understated opulence and majesty since 1908. People today see it as a memorial to a grand era, but the grandness pulls you in and you can't help but feel elegant and romantic during your stay. Duchess at your side gets special treatment too. Dogs are welcome ($50 per visit) in several guestrooms set aside for the purpose. There is a doggie menu too. This is definitely the old world version of how to spend a vacation. First-timers are sometimes surprised, and grumpy, at the size of the rooms and the bathrooms. They're small by Holiday Inn standards, but the bonus square footage is in the common areas, libraries, lobbies, pool, exercise room, and other public areas where the guests can gather and enjoy all the comforts of travel. High Tea in the front lobby is an Fairmont Empress specialty, something you won't want to miss. Unfortunately, dogs may not attend High Tea. Summer rates for two range from $239 to $449. 721 Government Street; (250) 384-8111 or (800) 441-1414.

Goldstream Provincial Park camping: See page 195.

Harbour Towers Hotel: Pets can stay in the 185-room Harbour Towers, as long as they're small (15 pounds) and well-behaved. Summer rates for two range from $199 to $600, with no extra charge for pets. 345 Quebec Street; (250) 385-2405.

Hotel Douglas: Dogs are very welcome here for no extra charge if they're well-trained and kept on a leash. The hoteliers are very friendly and accommodating. Prices for two people start at $40 in winter and $85 in summer. 1450 Douglas Street; (250) 383-4157.

Mount Washington RV Park: If you drive to Mount Washington ski resort midway up Vancouver Island near Courtenay in January, you will find a fully serviced campground filled with RVs surrounded by 10-foot snowbanks. This is the economy route to great skiing, from your very own ski-in/ski-out lodging on the edge of paradise. The Mount Washington campground is privately operated (though on Crown-leased land). Since Vancouver Island has mild winters, provincial park campgrounds stay open year-round. (250) 334-5703.

Ocean Pointe Resort: The luxurious Ocean Pointe Resort doesn't object if you bring your small dog (20 pounds or less), and there is no longer an extra charge for the dog. The view over the Inner Harbour is stupendous, and the constant parade of walkers in front of the Ocean Pointe on Westsong Way could almost make you feel guilty for lounging around. The sea kayakers seem to have the most fun. The resort offers marine wildlife tours (such as whale-watching excursions), recreation programs, a full European spa, and a fitness center. Summer rates for two range from $159 to $309. 45 Songhees Road; (250) 360-2999 or (800) 667-4677.

Oxford Castle Inn: Small pets (weighing no more than 20 pounds) are welcome at this faux castle on motel row 1.5 miles northwest of the city on B.C. Highway 1A. Rooms are big here, and most have kitchens. Summer rates for two range between $118 and $138, and there is a $15 per night pet charge. 133 Gorge Road East; (250) 388-6431.

Quality Inn/Waddling Dog: John the basset hound, who rules the roost at the Waddling Dog, went bonkers when he spotted Emma and Quinn. And he got even more excited when we leashed up for the departure. We learned that guests take him for walks, and some even bring him presents on return visits (and we will, too). The Waddling Dog has a beer and wine shop, a restaurant, and a pub. You can't miss it from the highway. Two big, plastic basset hounds hang off the roof, and smaller ones serve as window decorations. Of course, dogs are welcome here, for $5 per night. Rooms for two people cost $99 to $139 in summer. 2476 Mount Newton Cross (X) Road; (250) 652-1146 or (800) 567-8466.

Rathtrevor Provincial Park camping: Wake up on Christmas morning, pull on your Cowichan wool knit sweater, and go combing for sand dollars on the broad beach at Rathtrevor Provincial Park near Parksville, 30 miles northwest of Victoria on the island's east coast. Dogs must be kept on a leash at all times. The campground has 174 sites. Winter is your best chance to get a campsite at this popular beach. Wander down to French Beach from the provincial park campground on any spring day and there's a good chance you will see migrating gray whales surfacing for air as they feed on their way to Alaska. A few of them usually linger here all summer. From the many hiking trails, you are likely to see bald eagles and osprey. (250) 954-4600.

Red Lion Motor Inn: Dogs are welcome at the Red Lion for $10 per night, and they must stay on the first floor. Summer rates for two start at $69. 3366 Douglas Street; (250) 475-7575.

Robin Hood Motel: Only small dogs (that's 25 pounds or less, please) are allowed here in suburbia, but the price is right and the landscaping is pretty. A room for two in the summer costs from $76 to $86. The surcharge for dogs is $5 each, per night. 136 Gorge Road East; (250) 388-4302.

Shamrock Motel: Dogs are the only pets allowed, and they have to weigh less than 20 pounds. The Shamrock sits at the entrance to Beacon Hill Park, away from the downtown hubbub, and all rooms have kitchens. Summer rates for two range from $99 to $119, with a $5-a-night surcharge for dogs. 675 Superior Street; (250) 385-8768.

Stay 'n Save Motor Inn: You're better off with a car if you choose to spend the night here, as the cab rides can get expensive (it's two miles north of downtown). But the rooms are large and the staff is very helpful. Small dogs (nothing bigger than a collie) can stay at no extra charge. Summer rates for two are $124. 3233 Maple Street; (250) 475-7500.

Tally Ho Motor Inn: The Tally Ho, which permits dogs at no extra charge, boasts a heated pool, a restaurant, and nearby shopping. Summer rates for two are $89 to $95. It's located 1.5 miles north of downtown Victoria on the Trans-Canada Highway (Highway 1). 3020 Douglas Street; (250) 386-6141.

Wintercott B&B: On two pastoral acres near Bear Hill, Elk Lake, and Butchart Gardens, this B&B resembles an English manor house with Laura Ashley fabrics, antiques, and collectibles. Breakfast is a full English affair. Dogs and kids are welcome at no extra charge. The rooms are light and airy and each has its own bath, TV, and VCR. Year-round rates range from $75 to $95.

From Victoria on Highway 17, turn left on Sayward Road between the Shell and PetroCan stations. It becomes Brookleigh. Stay on it until Oldfield. Turn right on Oldfield and drive to Nicholas Road, where there is a sign. 1950 Nicholas Road; (250) 652-2117.

FESTIVALS

Summer in the Square: Concerts given at various times of day and night in Centennial Square take place from mid-July through the end of August. Dogs, too, are welcome to enjoy the music, but they must be leashed. (250) 361-0388.

Symphony Splash: This free outdoor evening concert highlights the Victoria Symphony season. The orchestra plays from a barge in the Inner Harbour, and thousands of people fill the lawns and steps. Bring your lawn chair. It's always held on the Sunday of the B.C. Day Long Weekend, the first weekend of August. Leashed dogs are welcome. (250) 385-9771.

DIVERSIONS

Market Square and its animal fountain: No matter about the prohibition against dogs, there's a fountain in the courtyard you've got to see, and your Thirsty could probably claim that a grandfather clause allows him to lap from the fountain. The three-tiered fountain is over a hundred years old. It was erected by a guy with a brick-making business beyond the edge of town, so he could water his horses halfway through each trip to and from market. The horses drank from the top tier. What drank from the middle tier was pigs, and that was well into the 1930s. There must have been a big market in pigs in those days. And, you guessed it, the bottom tier was for dogs. So if dogs drank from the fountain for the last hundred years or so, it seems to me that any of their progeny have rights to do the same thing, no matter where the fountain was moved. So take a quick step in to the courtyard at 506 Johnson Street and pay homage to canine times of yore. Just don't say where you read about it; (250) 386-2441.

Coastal Connections of Victoria: Offering guided interpretive hikes through Carmanah and a number of other parks, Coastal Connections says dogs are too much for the overnight excursions to the Carmanah Valley, because of the Beaver flights, but they're more than welcome on the local half- or full-day hikes. Coastal Connections supplies binoculars, Pentax 8x, but often you cannot see into the woods far enough to make them useful. That is to say, you can't see the forest for the trees. (250) 480-9560 or (800) 840-HIKE.

Command Post of Military Collectables & Antiques: Dogs are quite welcome in this tiny military store. The collectibles (owner Brent Fletcher amasses them better than he spells) include uniforms stacked to the ceiling, medallions, pins, patches, badges, and hundreds of toy soldiers. Dogs come in all the time to the Command Post, but Quinn and Emma didn't seem too interested. 1306 Government Street; (250) 383-4421.

Munro's: Mr. Munro himself says, very politely, that dogs are not preferred to be allowed into the store. It sure is a fine bookstore though, so maybe you could hitch Literati to the parking meter and browse a bit. It's open 9 A.M. to 6 P.M. Monday, Tuesday, Wednesday, and Saturday, and 9 A.M. to 9 P.M. Thursday and Friday, and 11 A.M. to 5 P.M. Sunday. 1108 Government Street; (250) 382-2464.

Mucky Mutt Pet Emporium: Just what your Muddy needs after so much time on the road, a do-it-yourself wash and groom. Here's another instance where a small dog saves you money. If you want to wash and groom Peewee your Chihuahua, it's $5. For Gordota the St. Bernard, or Mongo the Newfy, it's more than double, up to $15. If you need a break from the chore, Mucky Mutt will wash and groom for you. Mucky Mutt's wellness products, such as chew toys and treats, are all natural, with no chemical additives or preservatives. They carry just four lines of dog food, for the same reason. 2950 Douglas Street; (250) 384-5224.

GETTING TO VICTORIA

Canine visitors to Canada are required to show evidence of rabies vaccination and a health certificate signed by a vet within 30 days prior to crossing the border. This is true for whatever form of transportation you use. We've never been asked to show the paperwork and tags, but we carry them everywhere just in case.

B.C. Ferry Corp.: Dogs may travel on B.C. Ferries if they're kept in the car. If you're traveling without a car, as a foot passenger, your dog still must stay on the car deck, tethered. Oddly, you are expected to go upstairs, but you can come down now and then to check on the dog. A lot of car people just stay in their cars and take naps, as we did. At the Tsawwassen lineup for the ferry, the ticket seller was so enthralled with my granddogs that she told us the wrong line for the ferry. She said 45, but the ticket said 43, a fact we discovered later when the line director said, "Hey, you're in the wrong line. Just pull over here and wait." We waited, and we waited, and we waited. We made the ferry eventually, but it was a stress. There is plenty of grass and a dike along the parking lineup for the dogs. The Tsawwassen ferry is the closest to the States. It's about an hour from Bellingham and is reached by driving north on I-5 and crossing the Canadian border at the Peace Arch Crossing. Continue north on what is now British Columbia Highway 99. Follow signs to the ferry, which will take you via B.C. 99 exit 20 onto B.C. Highway 10 (Ladner Trunk Road) and then B.C. Highway 17 (Tsawwassen Ferry Road), which ends at the ferry. (If you miss exit 20, exit 28, five miles farther, will take you to the same place.) Ferries go in each direction between Tsawwassen and Swartz Bay at least every two hours, departing on the odd hours; (888) 724-5223 within British Columbia.

Beacon Taxi: Carry your dog? You bet, not a problem, just call 'em up. The hitch is that it costs roughly $45 each way between the ferry landing at Swartz Bay and Victoria. (250) 656-5588.

Black Ball Transport: From mid-May to mid-September, Black Ball runs four car ferry sailings daily between Port Angeles, on the Olympic Peninsula, and Victoria's Inner Harbour. Three ferries per day run to mid-October, two during March, April, and October, and just one per day during November, December, and January. The sailing takes one hour and 35 minutes. Phone (360) 457-4491 in the United States or (250) 386-2202 in Canada. Office hours are 7 A.M. to 5:30 P.M. For a recorded schedule, call (206) 622-2222.

Clipper Navigation: The owners and operators of the *Victoria Clipper* and one *San Juan Express*, do not, as a rule, allow pet dogs on their passenger-only ferries from Seattle to Victoria, a 71-mile, 2.5-hour nautical trip. It's a corporate policy thing, so the rest of us wouldn't understand. But there is a loophole: "However, on rare occasions, permission is granted by the General Manager." You will have to seek permission in advance, and whether it's granted or not depends a lot on the weather and passenger load. And if Daisy's passage is approved, she must be caged, possibly sedated, and kept on the outside after-deck. Then there's the extra charge: $10 each way, and if you need a carrier, the company will rent you one for $10 each way. They have a large one and a small one on standby. From Seattle, the *Victoria Clipper* leaves daily (except Christmas Day) at 8 A.M., returning by 7:30 P.M. The Clipper also has overnight packages with many Victoria hotels. Pier 69, (206) 448-5000 or (800) 888-2535 (outside Seattle and B.C.). For recorded information, dial (800) 888-2535.

Washington State Ferries: Two daily car ferries travel between Anacortes (83 miles north of Seattle) and Sidney, B.C. (17 miles north of Victoria). Trips are usually three hours and departure times may vary from season to season. To get to the Washington State Ferry dock in Anacortes, take I-5 to Burlington/Exit 230, turn west onto State Highway 20, and follow it to Anacortes. From there, signs will direct you the last five miles to the ferry terminal. Call for departure times (800) 84-FERRY (recorded information) (360) 464-6400.

West Isle Air: West Isle Air, which flies small planes to the San Juan Islands, Vancouver, and Victoria from Boeing Field in Seattle and from Bellingham, will happily carry you and yours to, say, Victoria. But there's a catch. You have to charter the plane. There is no baggage storage area, so the dog gets a seat all to herself. The airline carries mostly businesspeople, and says it wouldn't be fair to make a guy in a business suit sit next to a hairy beast. In our case, the one-way charter for Quinn, Emma, and me, from Bellingham to Victoria, was $158; (360) 671-8463 or (800) 874-4434.

APPENDIX

PICK OF THE LITTER

There are hundreds of dog-friendly recreation areas and accommodations in *The Dog Lover's Companion to Seattle*, but those listed here (in order of preference) are exceptionally pleasing to pooches. For more unique parks and lodgings, see the individual chapters.

DOG DAY AFTERNOONS: THE TOP TEN FOUR-PAW PARKS

Genesee Park, Seattle, *pg. 37–38*
Schmitz Preserve, Seattle, *pg. 39–40*
Pacific Spirit Regional Park, Vancouver, B.C., *pg. 157–158*
Millersylvania State Park, Olympia, *pg. 90–100*
Boren Park/Interlaken Boulevard, Seattle, *pg. 27–28*
Quinault Loop Trail, Olympic Peninsula, *pg. 131*
Ambleside Park, Vancouver, B.C., *pg. 152–153*
Goldstream Provincial Park, Victoria, B.C., *pg. 193–194*
Titlow Park, Tacoma, *pg. 106–107*
Moran State Park, Orcas Island, *pg. 139*

DOGGY DIGS: THE TOP TEN DOG-FRIENDLY LODGINGS

The Alexis Hotel, Seattle, *pg. 25*
Resort Semiahmoo, Bellingham Area, *pg. 92*
Sheraton Tacoma Hotel, Tacoma, *pg. 107–108*
Four Seasons Olympic Hotel, Seattle, *pg. 25*
Fairmont Hotel Vancouver, Vancouver, B.C., *pg. 165*
Dashwood Seaside Manor, Victoria, B.C., *pg. 198*
Kalaloch Lodge, Forks, *pg. 132*
The Sylvia, Vancouver, *pg. 168*
Admiral Motel, Victoria, B.C., *pg. 198*
Hotel Monaco, Seattle, *pg. 26*

TRAVEL TIDBITS: ANIMAL CLINICS, SERVICES, AND MORE

To help you prepare for a fun-filled, safe journey with your four-legged friend, here's a list of resources—veterinarians, emergency animal clinics, visitor centers, chambers of commerce, departments of parks and recreation, transportation services, and other useful organizations—listed by state, county, and province.

WASHINGTON STATE RESOURCES

SEATTLE

USEFUL ADDRESSES AND PHONE NUMBERS

Capitol Hill Chamber of Commerce, Seattle: (206) 323-8035.

Central Area Chamber of Commerce Visitor Information Center: 2108 East Madison, Seattle; (206) 325-2864.

Chinatown Chamber of Commerce: 409 Maynard Avenue, Seattle; (206) 323-2700, (206) 382-1197 (fax).

Greater Seattle Chamber of Commerce: 1301 5th Avenue, Suite 2400; (206) 389-7200; www.seattlechamber.com.

Greater University Chamber of Commerce: 4519 1/2 University Way Northeast; (206) 547-4417.

Rainier Chamber of Commerce: 5504 Rainier Avenue South, Seattle; (206) 725-2010.

Sea Tac International Airport Visitor Information Center: Sea Tac Airport, Seattle; (206) 433-5218.

Seattle Animal Control: (206) 386-4254; 2061 15th Avenue West. Adoptions, redemptions of lost pets, stray animal drop-offs, pet licensing, (206) 386-4262. Spay-neuter clinic, call (206) 386-4260; www.ci.seattle.wa.us/rca/animal.

Seattle Department of Parks and Recreation: 100 Dexter Avenue North; (206) 684-8021.

Seattle/King County Convention and Visitors Bureau: 520 Pike Street, Suite 1300, Seattle, WA 98101; (206) 461-5800; www.seeseattle.org.

Seattle Parks & Recreation Off-Leash Hotline: (206) 386-4004.

Seattle Purebred Dog Rescue: (206) 654-1117, a nonprofit organization, accepts purebred dogs, generally ages six months to five years, from private homes and area shelters for placement in adoptive homes. Also can give advice on dog problems, and on suitable breeds for specific situations. Requests donations; www.goodwin.org/spdr.

Shoreline Chamber of Commerce: 18560 1st Avenue Northeast, Seattle; (206) 361-2260, (206) 361-2268 (fax).

Southwest King County Chamber of Commerce Visitor Information Center: (800) 638-8613, (206) 575-2007 (fax); www.swkcc.org.

University of Washington Visitors Information Center: 4014 University Way Northeast, Seattle; (206) 543-9198.

West Seattle Chamber of Commerce Visitor Information Center: 4750 California Avenue Southwest, Seattle; (206) 932-5685.

TRANSPORTATION

Kenmore Air (float planes to the San Juan Islands and Vancouver Island): (425) 486-1257 or(800) 543-9595; www.kenmoreair.com.

Victoria Clipper (foot ferry service between Seattle, the San Juan Islands, and Victoria): 2701 Alaskan Way, Pier 69, Seattle; (206) 448-5000 or (800) 668-1167 (recorded information); www.victoriaclipper.com.

Washington State Ferries (car ferries to the Olympic Peninsula, San Juan Islands, and Sidney on Vancouver Island): 801 Alaskan Way, Pier 52, Seattle; (206) 464-6400 or (800) 84-FERRY; www.wsdot.wa.gov/ferries.

CLALLAM COUNTY

VETERINARY SERVICES

Angeles Clinic for Animals: 1134 East Front Street, Port Angeles; (360) 452-7686.

Olympic Veterinary Clinic: 1417 East Front Street, Port Angeles; (360) 452-8978.

USEFUL ADDRESSES AND PHONE NUMBERS

Clallam Bay-Sekiu Chamber of Commerce: Post Office Box 355, Clallam Bay; (360) 963-2339; www.clallambay.com or www.sekiu.com.

Clallam Bay-Sekiu Visitor Information Center: Post Office Box 66, Clallam Bay, WA 98326.

Clallam County Humane Society: 2105 West Highway 101, Port Angeles; (360) 457-8206.

Forks Chamber of Commerce Visitor Information Center: (360) 374-2531 or (800) 443-6757, (360) 374-9253 (fax); www.forkswa.com.

North Olympic Peninsula Visitor and Convention Bureau: Post Office Box 670, Port Angeles, WA 98362; (360) 452-8552 or (800) 942-4042, (360) 452-7363 (fax); www.olympicpeninsula.org.

Olympic National Park Visitors Center: 3002 Mount Angeles Road, Port Angeles, WA 98362; (360) 452-0330.

Port Angeles Chamber of Commerce Visitor Information Center: 121 East Railroad Street; (360) 452-2363, (360) 457-5380 (fax); www.cityofpa.com.

Sequim Visitors Information Center: Sequim Chamber of Commerce; (360) 683-6197, (800) 737-8462, (360) 683-6349 (fax); www.cityofsequim.com.

GRAYS HARBOR COUNTY

USEFUL ADDRESSES AND PHONE NUMBERS

Cranberry Coast Chamber of Commerce, Grayland Beach Visitor Information Center: (360) 267-2003 or (800) 473-6018, (360) 267-2003 (fax).

Elma Chamber of Commerce Visitor Information Center: (360) 482-3055,(360) 482-2068 (fax).

Grays Harbor Chamber of Commerce: 506 Duffy Street, Aberdeen; (360) 532-1924, (360) 533-7945 (fax); www.graysharbor.org.

Grays Harbor Historical Seaport Authority: Aberdeen; (360) 532-8611 or (800) 200-5239, (360) 533-9384 (fax); www.ladywashington.org.

McCleary Community Chamber of Commerce: (360) 495-4147.

Montesano Chamber of Commerce Visitor Information Center: (360) 249-5522; www.montesano-wa.com.

Ocean Shores Chamber of Commerce: (360) 289-2451 or (800) 762-3224, (360) 289-0226 (fax); www.oceanshores.org.

Port of Grays Harbor, Aberdeen: (360) 533-9528, (360) 533-9505 (fax); www.portofgraysharbor.com.

Washington Coast Chamber of Commerce Visitor Information Center: Ocean City; (360) 289-4552 or (800) 286-4552.

Westport-Grayland Chamber of Commerce Visitor Information Center: Westport; (360) 268-9422 or (800) 345-6223, (360) 268-1990 (fax); www.westportgrayland-chamber.org.

ISLAND COUNTY

VETERINARY SERVICES

Northwest Veterinary Clinic of Stanwood: 8500 Cedarhome Drive, Stanwood; (360) 629-4571.

The Vets Animal Hospital: 61 Southeast 11th Avenue, Oak Harbor; (360) 675-4425.

USEFUL ADDRESSES AND PHONE NUMBERS

Camano Island Chamber of Commerce Visitor Information Center: (360) 629-9193; www.whidbey.net/camano.

Central Whidbey Chamber of Commerce, Visitor Information Center, Coupeville: (360) 678-5434; www.whidbey.net/coup.

Oak Harbor Chamber of Commerce Visitor Information Center: 32630 Highway 20; (360) 675-3535, (360) 679-1264 (fax); www.oakharborchamber.org.

South Whidbey Information and Accommodation Referral Service, Langley (keeps a daily list of vacancies): (360) 221-6765; www.whidbey.com/langley.

JEFFERSON COUNTY

VETERINARY SERVICES

Oak Bay Animal Hospital: 975 Oak Bay Road, Port Hadlock; (360) 385-7297.

USEFUL ADDRESSES AND PHONE NUMBERS

Greater Quilcene/Brinnon Chamber of Commerce, Quilcene: (360) 765-4999.

Olympic National Forest: 1835 Black Lake Boulevard Southwest, Olympia; (360) 956-2400.

Olympic National Park Visitors Center: 600 East Park Avenue, Port Angeles; (360) 565-3130.

Olympic Peninsula Gateway Visitor Center, Port Ludlow: (360) 437-0120, (360) 437-0120 (fax); www.portludlowchamber.org.

Port Hadlock Chamber of Commerce: (360) 379-5380; www.porthadlock.org.

Port Townsend Chamber of Commerce Visitor Information Center: 2437 East Sims Way; (360) 385-2722; www.ptguide.com.

KING COUNTY

VETERINARY SERVICES

Northeast Veterinary Hospital: 9505 35th Avenue Northeast; (206) 523-1900.

Northgate Veterinary Clinic: 12345 15th Avenue Northeast; (206) 363-8421.

USEFUL ADDRESSES AND PHONE NUMBERS

Bellevue Chamber of Commerce: 10500 Northeast 8th Street, Suite 212; (425) 454-2464, (425) 462-4660 (fax); www.bellevuechamber.org.

Bellevue Humane Society: 13212 Southeast Eastgate Way; (425) 641-0080.

Bellevue Parks and Recreation Department: 11511 Main Street; (425) 452-6881.

Greater Issaquah Chamber of Commerce: 155 Northwest Gilman Boulevard; (425) 392-7024, (425) 392-8101 (fax); www.issaquah.org.

Greater Kirkland Chamber of Commerce: 401 Parkplace Center, Suite 1023; (425) 822-7066, (425) 827-4878 (fax); www.kirklandchamber.org.

Greater Redmond Chamber of Commerce Visitor Information Center: (425) 885-4014, (425) 882-0996 (fax); www.redmondchamber.org.

Greater Renton Chamber of Commerce Visitor Information Center: 300 Rainier Avenue North; (425) 226-4560, (425) 226-4287 (fax).

Humane Society of Seattle and King County: 13212 Southeast Eastgate Way, Bellevue; (425) 641-0080. Adoptions, a spay-neuter clinic, pet licenses for King County, Seattle, and Renton; pet cremations. Also offers boarding facilities, (425) 643-5960; www.seattlehumane.org.

Issaquah Parks and Recreation: 301 Rainier Boulevard South; (425) 837-3300.

King County Animal Services: Information Line: (206) 296-PETS. Takes complaints, handles strays, adoptions, licenses, and spay-neuter services. Adoptions: (206) 296-3946; licensing: (206) 296-2712; shelters: 821 164th Avenue Northeast, Bellevue, (206) 296-3940; 21615 64th Avenue South, Kent, (206) 296-7387; www.metrokc.gov/services.

King County Parks: 2040 84th Avenue Southeast, Mercer Island; (206) 684-4075.

Main Street Issaquah: 17 Northwest Alder Place, Suite 203; (425) 391-1112; www.issaquah.org.

Mercer Island Chamber of Commerce: (206) 232-3404, (206) 232-3404 (fax).

Vashon-Maury Island Chamber of Commerce, Vashon: (206) 463-6217; www.vashonisland.com/chamber.

KITSAP COUNTY

VETERINARY SERVICES
Animal Hospital of Central Kitsap: 10310 Central Valley Road Northeast, Poulsbo; (360) 692-6162.

USEFUL ADDRESSES AND PHONE NUMBERS
Bainbridge Island Chamber of Commerce: 590 Winslow Way East, Bainbridge Island; (206) 842-3700, (206) 842-3713 (fax); www.bainbridgechamber.com.

Bremerton Area Chamber of Commerce: (360) 479-3579, (360) 479-1033 (fax); www.bremertonchamber.org.

Bremerton Parks and Recreation: 680 Lebo Boulevard; (360) 478-5305.

Greater Poulsbo Chamber of Commerce Visitor Information Center: (360) 779-4848 or (877) 768-5726, (360) 779-3115 (fax); www.poulsbo.net.

Kingston Area Chamber of Commerce: (360) 297-3813, (360) 779-8018 (fax); www.kingstonwa.net.

Kitsap County Animal Control: 9167 Dickey Road Northwest, Silverdale; (360) 698-9654.

Kitsap County Health District: 109 Austin Drive, Bremerton; (360) 337-5285 or (360) 692-7137 (lost-pet hot line).

Kitsap Fairs and Parks: 1200 Northwest Fairgrounds Road, Bremerton; (360) 692-3655.

Kitsap Humane Society: 9167 Dickey Road Northwest, Silverdale; (360) 692-6977.

Kitsap Peninsula Visitor and Convention Bureau: Port Gamble; (360) 297-8200 or (800) 416-5615, (360) 297-8208 (fax); www.visitkitsap.com.

Port Orchard Chamber of Commerce Visitor Information Center: 1014 Bay Street; (360) 876-3505 or (800) 982-8139, (360) 895-1920 (fax); www.portorchard.com.

Silverdale Chamber of Commerce: (360) 692-6800, (360) 692-1379 (fax); www.silverdalechamber.com.

MASON COUNTY

USEFUL ADDRESSES AND PHONE NUMBERS
Shelton-Mason County Chamber of Commerce Visitor Information Center: Shelton; (360) 426-2021 or (800) 576-2021.

PACIFIC COUNTY

USEFUL ADDRESSES AND PHONE NUMBERS
City of Long Beach: (360) 642-4421; www.willapabay.org/~lngbeach/index.

Long Beach Peninsula Visitor's Bureau: (360) 642-2400 or (800) 451-2542, (360) 642-3900 (fax); www.funbeach.com.

Megler Visitor Information Center: 116 Spruce, Ilwaco; (360) 777-8388.

Naselle Chamber of Commerce Visitor Information Center: (360) 484-7700.

Ocean Park Area Chamber of Commerce Visitor Information Center: Ocean Park; (360) 665-4448.

Pacific County Museum Visitors Information Center: South Bend; (360) 875-5224.

PIERCE COUNTY

VETERINARY SERVICES
Parkway Veterinary Clinic: 14107 Pacific Avenue, Tacoma; (253) 531-0454.

USEFUL ADDRESSES AND PHONE NUMBERS
Fife Area Chamber of Commerce: 5303 Pacific Highway East, Post Office Box 272, Fife; (253) 922-9320 or (800) 577-0773; www.fifechamber.org.

Gig Harbor Peninsula Chamber of Commerce Visitor Information Center: 3302 Harborview Drive; (253) 851-6865; www.gigharborchamber.com.

The Humane Society for Tacoma and Pierce County: 2608 Center Street, Tacoma; (253) 383-2733.

Tacoma-Pierce County Visitor and Convention Bureau: 1001 Pacific Avenue, Suite 400, Tacoma; (253) 627-2836, extension 13 or (800) 272-2662, (253) 627-8783 (fax); www.tpctourism.org.

SAN JUAN COUNTY

VETERINARY SERVICES
Islands Veterinary Clinic: 700 Mullis Street, Friday Harbor; (360) 378-2333.

USEFUL ADDRESSES AND PHONE NUMBERS
Animal Inn (boarding kennel): 25 Boyce Road, Friday Harbor; (360) 378-4735.

Animal Protection Society: One Shelter Road, Friday Harbor; (360) 378-2158.

Inter-Island Medical Center (human medical services): 550 Spring Street, Friday Harbor; (360) 378-2141.

Lopez Island Chamber of Commerce: (360) 468-4664 (recording checked once per week), (360) 468-4000 (fax); www.lopezisland.com.

Orcas Island Chamber of Commerce: Eastsound; (360) 376-2273; www.orcasisland.org.

San Juan Island Chamber of Commerce: Friday Harbor; (360) 378-5240; www.sanjuanisland.org.

San Juan Islands Visitor Information Services: (360) 468-3663 or (888) 468-3701; www.guidetosanjuans.com.

TRANSPORTATION
Paraclete Charters (inter-island transportation): Skyline Marina, Anacortes; (360) 293-5920 or (800) 808-2999; www.paracletecharters.com.

Washington State Ferries: Pier 52, 801 Alaskan Way, Seattle; (206) 464-6400 or (800) 84-FERRY.

West Isle Air: See page 84, 205.

SKAGIT COUNTY

VETERINARY SERVICES

Anacortes Animal Hospital: 2504 Commercial Avenue, Anacortes; (360) 293-3431.

Fidalgo Animal Medical Center: 3303 Commercial Avenue, Anacortes; (360) 293-2186.

Highland Animal Clinic: 110 North 15th Street, Mount Vernon; (360) 424-7965, (360) 424-7966 (emergency).

USEFUL ADDRESSES AND PHONE NUMBERS

Anacortes Chamber of Commerce Visitor Information Center: 819 Commercial Avenue, Suite G; (360) 293-3832; www.anacortes-chamber.com.

Burlington Chamber of Commerce Visitor and Information Center: 600 East Victoria Avenue, Burlington; (360) 757-0994, (360) 757-0821 (fax).

Humane Society of Skagit County: 18911 Kelleher Road, Burlington; (360) 757-0445.

La Conner Chamber of Commerce: (360) 466-4778; www.laconnerchamber.com.

Mount Vernon Chamber of Commerce: (360) 428-8547, (360) 424-6237 (fax); www.mvcofc.org.

TRANSPORTATION

Black Ball Transport (ferry between Victoria and Anacortes): See page 202.

West Isle Air: 4000 Airport Road, Suite A, Anacortes; (360) 671-8463 or (800) 874-4434.

SNOHOMISH COUNTY

VETERINARY SERVICES

Animal Emergency Clinic of Everett: 3625 Rucker Avenue; (425) 258-4466.

Animal Emergency Service North: 19511 24th Avenue West; Lynnwood; (425) 745-6745.

Animal Hospital of Lynnwood: 6501 196th Street Southwest, Suite F; (425) 771-6300.

USEFUL ADDRESSES AND PHONE NUMBERS

Edmonds Chamber of Commerce Visitor Information Center: 121 5th Avenue North, Edmonds; (425) 776-6711, (425) 712-1808 (fax).

Everett Area Chamber of Commerce: 11400 Airport Road, Everett; (425) 438-1487, (425) 252-3105 (fax); www.everettchamber.com.

Marysville/Tulalip Visitor Information Center: I-5 exit 199, Marysville; (360) 653-2634.

Progressive Animal Welfare Society (PAWS): 15305 44th Avenue West, Lynnwood; (425) 787-2500. Accepts animals from Seattle by appointment only; places them in suitable homes. No appointment necessary for Snohomish residents to drop off animals and accepts strays.

Snohomish Chamber of Commerce Visitor Information Center: Snohomish; (360) 568-2526, (360) 568-3869 (fax); www.cityofsnohomish.com.

Snohomish County Parks and Recreation: 9623 32nd Street Northeast, Everett; (425) 388-6600.

Snohomish County Tourism Bureau: 909 Southeast Everett Mall Way C300, Everett; (425) 348-5802, extension 10 or (888) 338-0976, (425) 348-5701 (fax); www.snohomish.org.

Snohomish County Visitor Information Center: 101 128th Street Southeast, Suite 5000, Everett; (425) 338-4437.

South Snohomish County Chamber of Commerce: 3500 188th Street Southwest, Suite 490, Lynnwood; (425) 774-0507, (425) 774-4636 (fax); www .sscchamber.org.

THURSTON COUNTY

VETERINARY SERVICES

Animal Emergency Clinic: 5608 South Durango Street, Tacoma; (253) 474-0791.

Critter Calls (veterinary house calls): 7602 Steilacoom Road Southeast, Olympia; (360) 456-5684.

USEFUL ADDRESSES AND PHONE NUMBERS

Animal Services: 3120 Martin Way, Olympia; (360) 352-2510.

Olympia/Thurston County Chamber of Commerce Visitor Information Center: Olympia; (360) 357-3362, (360) 357-3376 (fax).

Olympic National Forest: 1835 Black Lake Boulevard Southwest, Olympia; (360) 956-2400.

Thurston County Parks and Recreation Department: 2617-A 12th Court Southwest, Olympia; (360) 786-5595.

Tumwater Area Chamber of Commerce: 488 Tyee Drive; (360) 357-5153, (360) 786-1685 (fax).

Washington State Capitol Visitor Services: Olympia; (360) 586-3460, (360) 586-4636 (fax).

WHATCOM COUNTY

VETERINARY SERVICES

Animal Medical Center (24-hour emergency care): 720 Virginia Street, Bellingham; (360) 734-0720.

Fairhaven Veterinary Hospital: 2330 Old Fairhaven Parkway, Bellingham; (360) 671-3903.

Village Veterinary Hospital: Sehome Village Shopping Center, 236 36th Street, Bellingham; (360) 647-1980.

Whatcom Veterinary Hospital: 5610 Barrett Avenue, Ferndale; (360) 384-0212.

USEFUL ADDRESSES AND PHONE NUMBERS

Bellingham/Whatcom County Convention and Visitors Bureau: 904 Potter Street, Bellingham; (360) 671-3990 or (800) 487-2032, (360) 647-7873 (fax); www.bellingham.org.

Northwest Kennels: 4796 Northwest Road, Bellingham, WA 98226-9019; (360) 384-6578.

Whatcom County Humane Society and SPCA: 3710 Williamson Way, Bellingham; (360) 733-2080 (24-hour lost/found pet recording).

TRANSPORTATION

Alaska Marine Highway (ferry service to Alaska): 355 Harris Avenue, Bellingham, WA 98225; (360) 676-8445 or (800) 642-0066.

Whatcom Transit Authority (bus service within Whatcom County): 2011 Young Street, Bellingham, WA 98225; (360) 676-RIDE.

CANADA RESOURCES

Canadian Customs: 28-176th Street, Surrey, B.C., Canada V4P 1M7; (604) 535-9754.

PROVINCE OF BRITISH COLUMBIA

Tourism British Columbia: (800) 663-6000.

VANCOUVER

VETERINARY SERVICES

Adored Beast (first licensed holistic clinic in Canada): 101-1956 West Broadway; (604) 738-4664.

Cambie Animal Clinic and Pacific Dental Service: 7555 Cambie Street; (604) 321-6600.

Granville Island Veterinary Hospital: 1635 West 4th Avenue; (604) 734-7744.

Kitsilano Animal Clinic: 2645 West 4th Avenue; (604) 736-8648.

Vancouver Animal Emergency Clinic: 1590 West 4th Avenue; (604) 734-5104.

USEFUL ADDRESSES AND PHONE NUMBERS

City of Vancouver Animal Control Services: 1280 Raymur Avenue; (604) 251-1325.

Vancouver Regional Society for the Prevention of Cruelty to Animals: 1205 East 7th Avenue; (604) 879-7721.

Vancouver Tourist Info Centre: 200 Burrard Street, Suite 210; (604) 682-2000.

TRANSPORTATION

False Creek Ferries: 1804 Boatlift Lane; (604) 684-7781.

VICTORIA

VETERINARY SERVICES
Central Victoria Veterinary Hospital: 760 Roderick Street; (250) 475-2495.

USEFUL ADDRESSES AND PHONE NUMBERS
British Columbia Society for the Prevention of Cruelty to Animals: 3150 Napier Lane; (250) 388-7722.

Tourism Victoria: 812 Wharf Street, Suite 710; (250) 953-2033.

TRANSPORTATION
B.C. Ferries: 1112 Fort Street; (250) 669-1211 or (888) 724-5223 within British Columbia.

Black Ball Transport (ferry service between Victoria and Anacortes): 101 East Railroad, Port Angeles, WA 98362; (360) 457-4491 (in the United States) or (250) 386-2202 (in Canada).

Victoria Star (ferry service between Victoria and the Bellingham area): See page 84.

Washington State Ferries: See page 144, 203.

West Isle Air: See page 84, 205.

WHISTLER

VETERINARY SERVICES
Coast Mountain Veterinary Services: 201-2011 Innsbruck Drive; (604) 932-5391.

USEFUL ADDRESSES AND PHONE NUMBERS
Tourism Whistler: 4010 Whistler Way; (604) 932-3928.

Whistler Parks and Recreation Department: 4325 Blackcomb Way; (604) 938-7275.

Whistler Pet Food and Supply: 1-1050 Millar Creek Road; (604) 932-3050.

INDEX

ACCOMMODATIONS INDEX

RESTAURANT INDEX

MAIN INDEX

ABOUT THE AUTHOR

Steve Giordano is the Northwest correspondent for *DogGone* magazine. He writes a monthly "On the Road" column for *RV Life Magazine,* and contributes to the guidebooks *Ski America and Canada* and *Ski Europe.* His magazine articles are carried in *The Meeting Professional* and *Alaska Airlines Magazine,* and he does Internet writing for the Great Outdoor Recreation Pages, ESPN.com, and SkiMaps.com.

His other books include: *Now Hiring! Ski Resort Jobs, Scenic Driving Washington,* and *Camping Washington.*

His CD-ROM writings include *Mt. Everest, Quest for the Summit of Dreams* and *Leonardo,* for *Corbis.*

Steve is a member of the Society of American Travel Writers and the North American Snowsports Journalists Association.

His favorite meal is an alligator steak at Seattle's Perché No—his way of getting even for all the little dogs who have disappeared from the shores of Florida's lakes.

ABOUT THE DOGS

Emma (ears up) and Quinn (ears down) are distant cousin fox terriers who have no patience for hanging around the house. If a car door opens, they hop in, hoping that the next stops will be a leash-free park and a hotel with room service, in that order. They've been booted out of several places in Washington and British Columbia in the pursuit of honesty in travel writing.

THE DOG LOVER'S COMPANION ANIMAL PARTNERSHIP PROGRAM

The Dog Lover's Companion series is pleased to promote animal rescue and adoption organizations nationwide. In an effort to create an awareness of these worthy causes, we ask you to support your local non profit animal rescue and adoption organization, Humane Society, or SPCA, such as:

THE HUMANE SOCIETY
FOR SEATTLE/KING COUNTY

The Humane Society for Seattle/King County protects and provides loving homes for abandoned and abused animals. For over a century, people have entrusted The Humane Society with their pets when they can no longer care for them. This non-profit agency operates independently of any national humane organization, is not government funded and does not provide animal-control services. The agency relies on fundraisers and donations from the community to operate, as well as the tireless efforts of a dedicated staff and more than 700 volunteers. The Humane Society's programs include:

- **ADOPTION:** Every year over 4,000 animals find new homes through The Humane Society. Staff veterinarians conduct health and temperament evaluations on all animals, vaccinate, spay/neuter and microchip all dogs and cats before they are placed for adoption.

- **PUBLIC LOW-COST SPAY/NEUTER CLINIC:** The agency offers a low-cost spay/neuter clinic to the public.

- **COMMUNITY OUTREACH PROGRAMS:** Educational programs include teacher curriculums, shelter tours, workshops, pet parenting classes for new pet owners, dog training classes, and pet-loss support.

- **PET FOOD BANK & PET PROJECT:** In order to help those in need keep their beloved companions, The Humane Society operates a Pet Food Bank. Humane Society volunteers deliver more than five tons of pet food monthly to low-income seniors and people disabled with HIV/AIDS. The Pet Food Bank relies heavily on its annual Holiday Pet Food Drive and donations throughout the year to operate. In addition to supplying supplemental pet food, The Pet Project also offers free preventative veterinary services and grooming to the pets of people with HIV/AIDS.

For more information on The Humane Society for Seattle/King County, call (425) 641-0080 or visit us at 13212 SE Eastgate Way, Bellevue, WA 98005. Information on our agency as well as animals available for adoption can be seen online at www.seattlehumane.org.

AVALON
TRAVEL
publishing

How far will our travel guides take you? As far as you want.

Discover a rhumba-fueled nightspot in Old Havana, explore prehistoric tombs in Ireland, hike beneath California's centuries-old redwoods, or embark on a classic road trip along Route 66. Our guidebooks deliver solidly researched, trip-tested information—minus any generic froth—to help globetrotters or weekend warriors create an adventure uniquely their own.

And we're not just about the printed page. Public television viewers are tuning in to Rick Steves' new travel series, *Rick Steves' Europe*. On the Web, readers can cruise the virtual black top with *Road Trip USA* author Jamie Jensen and learn travel industry secrets from Edward Hasbrouck of *The Practical Nomad*. With Foghorn AnyWare eBooks, users of handheld devices can place themselves "inside" the content of the guidebooks.

In print. On TV. On the Internet. In the palm of your hand.
We supply the information. The rest is up to you.

Avalon Travel Publishing
Something for everyone

www.travelmatters.com

Avalon Travel Publishing guides are available at your favorite book or travel store.

 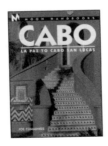 

MOON HANDBOOKS
provide comprehensive coverage of a region's arts, history, land, people, and social issues in addition to detailed practical listings for accommodations, food, outdoor recreation, and entertainment. Moon Handbooks allow complete immersion in a region's culture—ideal for travelers who want to combine sightseeing with insight for an extraordinary travel experience in destinations throughout North America, Hawaii, Latin America, the Caribbean, Asia, and the Pacific.

WWW.MOON.COM

Rick Steves shows you where to travel and how to travel—all while getting the most value for your dollar. His Back Door travel philosophy is about making friends, having fun, and avoiding tourist rip-offs.

Rick's been traveling to Europe for more than 25 years and is the author of 22 guidebooks, which have sold more than a million copies. He also hosts the award-winning public television series *Rick Steves' Europe*.

WWW.RICKSTEVES.COM

ROAD TRIP USA

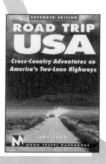

Getting there is half the fun, and Road Trip USA guides are your ticket to driving adventure. Taking you off the interstates and onto less-traveled, two-lane highways, each guide is filled with fascinating trivia, historical information, photographs, facts about regional writers, and details on where to sleep and eat—all contributing to your exploration of the American road.

"[Books] so full of the pleasures of the American road, you can smell the upholstery."
~BBC radio

WWW.ROADTRIPUSA.COM